Building a PC For Dummies,®
3rd Edition

Cheat

‖‖‖‖‖‖‖‖‖‖‖‖‖‖‖‖
W9-CEW-608

Mark's Common-Sense Assembly (CSA) Rules

Keep the following CSA rules in mind when you're handling and connecting parts:

- Give yourself plenty of elbow room and adequate lighting.
- Don't start without all the parts and components. If you don't have everything you need to follow a chapter from beginning to end, don't stop halfway through. It's too easy to miss a step or forget something.
- Treat your components carefully. Don't drop a part on the floor or toss it to a friend. Never bend any circuit board or adapter card. If something doesn't seem to fit, take the component out, check the instructions again, and try it a different way.
- Read all documentation that comes with each device.
- Keep the manuals for all your parts together for easy reference.
- Save your boxes and receipts. Although it's really rare, you may find yourself stuck with a brand-new defective item, and you'll need the original packaging to return it.
- Use bowls to hold small parts. Or, if you're a true technogeek, get thyself to a hardware store and buy one of those wall racks with all the little compartments.
- Keep a magnetic screwdriver handy. I recommend using a magnetic screwdriver to pick up wayward screws just by touching them.
- Check *all* connections after you install a part.
- Leave the computer cover off. Test your new device first, if possible — as long as you don't touch any circuit boards inside the case, you'll be fine.

Requirements for a Top-of-the-Line Pentium-Class Computer

Computer Component	What to Look For
Case	Full-tower model, dual fan
CPU/motherboard	The fastest doggone Pentium III or Athlon processor available, AGP and PCI slots
System RAM	128MB (megabytes) to 256MB
Hard drive	One EIDE drive with at least 30GB (gigabytes) of storage capacity
Floppy drive	One 3 ½-inch, 1.44MB disk drive
Video card	Windows-accelerated AGP 3-D SVGA adapter with at least 16MB of video memory, 3DFX or TNT graphics chipset
Modem	56 Kbps v.90 internal data/fax
CD-ROM	DVD drive (with AC-3 decoder if you watch DVD movies)
Sound card	PCI Sound Blaster wavetable card (64 voices, 3-D positional sound, hardware MP3 encoding)
Monitor	19-inch SVGA or 17-inch LCD "flatscreen" display
Ports	Two USB, one FireWire, two serial, and one parallel
Input	Ergonomic keyboard with extra Windows keys, trackball
Optional	Scanner, inkjet or laser printer, Orb or Jaz drive, SCSI adapter, network adapter, 21-inch monitor, cable modem, videoconferencing camera

For Dummies®: Bestselling Book Series for Beginners

Building a PC For Dummies,® 3rd Edition

Cheat Sheet

Requirements for a Middle-Range Pentium-Class Computer

Computer Component	What to Look For
Case	ATX minitower model, single fan
CPU/motherboard	450 MHz Pentium III or 650 MHz Athlon, AGP and PCI slots
System RAM	64MB (megabytes)
Hard drive	One EIDE drive with at least 6GB (gigabytes) of storage capacity
Floppy drive	One 3 ½-inch, 1.44MB disk drive
Video card	Standard 8MB AGP 3-D video adapter, 3DFX, or TNT graphics chipset
Modem	56 Kbps v.90 internal data/fax
CD-ROM	24x internal drive
Sound card	PCI Sound Blaster-compatible with wavetable
Monitor	17-inch SVGA
Ports	Two USB, two serial, and one parallel
Input	Standard 101-keyboard and mouse
Optional	Inkjet printer, scanner, 19-inch monitor, internal DVD drive

Requirements for a Bare-Bones Pentium-Class Computer

Computer Component	What to Look For
Case	Standard "pizza box," ATX minitower, or desktop model, single fan
CPU/motherboard	300 MHz Celeron, ISA and PCI slots, 256K cache
System RAM	32MB (megabytes)
Hard drive	One EIDE drive with at least 3GB (gigabytes) of storage capacity
Floppy drive	One 3 ½-inch, 1.44MB disk drive
CD-ROM	16x internal drive
Video card	Standard 2MB PCI SVGA adapter
Monitor	14-inch SVGA
Ports	Two serial and one parallel
Input	Standard 101-keyboard and mouse
Optional	A modem for connecting to the Internet

IDG BOOKS WORLDWIDE

For Dummies®: Bestselling Book Series for Beginners

TM

References for the Rest of Us!®

BESTSELLING BOOK SERIES

Are you intimidated and confused by computers? Do you find that traditional manuals are overloaded with technical details you'll never use? Do your friends and family always call you to fix simple problems on their PCs? Then the ...*For Dummies®* computer book series from IDG Books Worldwide is for you.

...*For Dummies* books are written for those frustrated computer users who know they aren't really dumb but find that PC hardware, software, and indeed the unique vocabulary of computing make them feel helpless. ...*For Dummies* books use a lighthearted approach, a down-to-earth style, and even cartoons and humorous icons to dispel computer novices' fears and build their confidence. Lighthearted but not lightweight, these books are a perfect survival guide for anyone forced to use a computer.

> "I like my copy so much I told friends; now they bought copies."
>
> — Irene C., Orwell, Ohio

> "Quick, concise, nontechnical, and humorous."
>
> — Jay A., Elburn, Illinois

> "Thanks, I needed this book. Now I can sleep at night."
>
> — Robin F., British Columbia, Canada

Already, millions of satisfied readers agree. They have made ...*For Dummies* books the #1 introductory level computer book series and have written asking for more. So, if you're looking for the most fun and easy way to learn about computers, look to ...*For Dummies* books to give you a helping hand.

IDG BOOKS WORLDWIDE

1/99

Building a PC

FOR

DUMMIES®

3RD EDITION

Building a PC

FOR

DUMMIES®

3RD EDITION

by Mark L. Chambers

IDG Books Worldwide, Inc.
An International Data Group Company

Foster City, CA ◆ Chicago, IL ◆ Indianapolis, IN ◆ New York, NY

Building A PC For Dummies, **3rd Edition**

Published by
IDG Books Worldwide, Inc.
An International Data Group Company
919 E. Hillsdale Blvd.
Suite 400
Foster City, CA 94404
www.idgbooks.com (IDG Books Worldwide Web Site)
www.dummies.com (Dummies Press Web Site)

Library of Congress Control Number: 00-106299

ISBN: 0-7654-0782-6

Printed in the United States of America

10 9 8 7 6 5 4 3 2

3B/ST/RQ/QQ/IN

Distributed in the United States by IDG Books Worldwide, Inc.

Distributed by CDG Books Canada Inc. for Canada; by Transworld Publishers Limited in the United Kingdom; by IDG Norge Books for Norway; by IDG Sweden Books for Sweden; by IDG Books Australia Publishing Corporation Pty. Ltd. for Australia and New Zealand; by TransQuest Publishers Pte Ltd. for Singapore, Malaysia, Thailand, Indonesia, and Hong Kong; by Gotop Information Inc. for Taiwan; by ICG Muse, Inc. for Japan; by Intersoft for South Africa; by Eyrolles for France; by International Thomson Publishing for Germany, Austria and Switzerland; by Distribuidora Cuspide for Argentina; by LR International for Brazil; by Galileo Libros for Chile; by Ediciones ZETA S.C.R. Ltda. for Peru; by WS Computer Publishing Corporation, Inc., for the Philippines; by Contemporanea de Ediciones for Venezuela; by Express Computer Distributors for the Caribbean and West Indies; by Micronesia Media Distributor, Inc. for Micronesia; by Chips Computadoras S.A. de C.V. for Mexico; by Editorial Norma de Panama S.A. for Panama; by American Bookshops for Finland.

For general information on IDG Books Worldwide's books in the U.S., please call our Consumer Customer Service department at 800-762-2974. For reseller information, including discounts and premium sales, please call our Reseller Customer Service department at 800-434-3422.

For information on where to purchase IDG Books Worldwide's books outside the U.S., please contact our International Sales department at 317-572-3993 or fax 317-572-4002.

For consumer information on foreign language translations, please contact our Customer Service department at 1-800-434-3422, fax 317-572-4002, or e-mail rights@idgbooks.com.

For information on licensing foreign or domestic rights, please phone +1-650-653-7098.

For sales inquiries and special prices for bulk quantities, please contact our Order Services department at 800-434-3422 or write to the address above.

For information on using IDG Books Worldwide's books in the classroom or for ordering examination copies, please contact our Educational Sales department at 800-434-2086 or fax 317-572-4005.

For press review copies, author interviews, or other publicity information, please contact our Public Relations department at 650-653-7000 or fax 650-653-7500.

For authorization to photocopy items for corporate, personal, or educational use, please contact Copyright Clearance Center, 222 Rosewood Drive, Danvers, MA 01923, or fax 978-750-4470.

is a registered trademark under exclusive license to IDG Books Worldwide, Inc., from International Data Group, Inc.

About the Author

Mark L. Chambers has been an author, computer consultant, BBS sysop, programmer, and hardware technician for more than 15 years. His first love affair with a computer peripheral blossomed in 1984, when he bought his high-tech 300 bps modem — now he spends entirely too much time on the Internet. His favorite pastimes include watching LSU football, collecting gargoyles, playing his three pinball machines, fixing and upgrading computers, playing the latest computer games, and rendering 3D flights of fancy — and during all that, he listens to just about every type of music imaginable.

With degrees in journalism and creative writing from Louisiana State University, Mark took the logical career choice and started programming computers. . . . However, after five years as a COBOL programmer for a hospital system, he decided that there must be a better way to earn a living, and he became the documentation manager for a well-known communications software developer. Somewhere in between organizing and writing software manuals, Mark began writing computer books; his first book, *Running a Perfect BBS,* was published in 1994. He now writes several books a year and edits whatever his publishers throw at him. You can leave him mail by visiting his Web page, at `www.geocities.com/SiliconValley/Bay/4373/ index.html`.

Mark is also the author of *Hewlett-Packard Official Printer Handbook, Hewlett-Packard Official Recordable CD Handbook, Recordable CD Bible, Teach Yourself the iMac Visually* (all for IDG Books Worldwide, Inc.), *Official Netscape Navigator Guide to Web Animation, Windows 98 Optimizing and Troubleshooting Little Black Book,* and *Running a Perfect BBS.*

ABOUT IDG BOOKS WORLDWIDE

Welcome to the world of IDG Books Worldwide.

IDG Books Worldwide, Inc., is a subsidiary of International Data Group, the world's largest publisher of computer-related information and the leading global provider of information services on information technology. IDG was founded more than 30 years ago by Patrick J. McGovern and now employs more than 9,000 people worldwide. IDG publishes more than 290 computer publications in over 75 countries. More than 90 million people read one or more IDG publications each month.

Launched in 1990, IDG Books Worldwide is today the #1 publisher of best-selling computer books in the United States. We are proud to have received eight awards from the Computer Press Association in recognition of editorial excellence and three from Computer Currents' First Annual Readers' Choice Awards. Our best-selling ...For Dummies® series has more than 50 million copies in print with translations in 31 languages. IDG Books Worldwide, through a joint venture with IDG's Hi-Tech Beijing, became the first U.S. publisher to publish a computer book in the People's Republic of China. In record time, IDG Books Worldwide has become the first choice for millions of readers around the world who want to learn how to better manage their businesses.

Our mission is simple: Every one of our books is designed to bring extra value and skill-building instructions to the reader. Our books are written by experts who understand and care about our readers. The knowledge base of our editorial staff comes from years of experience in publishing, education, and journalism — experience we use to produce books to carry us into the new millennium. In short, we care about books, so we attract the best people. We devote special attention to details such as audience, interior design, use of icons, and illustrations. And because we use an efficient process of authoring, editing, and desktop publishing our books electronically, we can spend more time ensuring superior content and less time on the technicalities of making books.

You can count on our commitment to deliver high-quality books at competitive prices on topics you want to read about. At IDG Books Worldwide, we continue in the IDG tradition of delivering quality for more than 30 years. You'll find no better book on a subject than one from IDG Books Worldwide.

John J. Kilcullen
John Kilcullen
Chairman and CEO
IDG Books Worldwide, Inc.

WINNER
Eighth Annual Computer Press Awards ≥1992

WINNER
Ninth Annual Computer Press Awards ≥1993

WINNER
Tenth Annual Computer Press Awards ≥1994

WINNER
Eleventh Annual Computer Press Awards ≥1995

Dedication

This book is respectfully dedicated to my friend and teacher, retired LSU journalism professor Jim Featherston. Jim, you taught me everything I need to know — now I can put ideas to paper.

Author's Acknowledgments

I find that writing the acknowledgments is always the easiest part of any book, for there's never a shortage of material. I always have a big group to praise.

First, a well-earned round of thanks to my technical editor, Jeff Wiedenfeld, who checked every word for accuracy (while enduring every bad joke and pun).

I'd like to thank Jody Cooper, for his knowledge of the latest in hardware; Bryan Chilcutt, for his continuing technical assistance; and my two favorite fellow PC salespeople — the *good* guys — Mike McGuirk and Andy Lewis, for their help in documenting what I like to call The Thomas Effect.

As with every book I've written, I'd like to thank my wife, Anne, and my children, Erin, Chelsea, and Rose, for their support and love — and for letting me follow my dream!

Finally, I'll send my heartfelt appreciation to the two hard-working editors at IDG Books Worldwide, Inc., who were responsible for the launch and completion of this epic third revision: my project editor, Rebecca Whitney, and my acquisitions editor, Ed Adams. They're talented, dedicated people, and I count myself very lucky that I had their assistance for this project — and many to come, I hope!

Publisher's Acknowledgments

We're proud of this book; please register your comments through our IDG Books Worldwide Online Registration Form located at http://my2cents.dummies.com.

Some of the people who helped bring this book to market include the following:

Acquisitions, Editorial, and Media Development

Project Editor: Rebecca Whitney

Acquisitions Editor: Ed Adams

Proof Editor: Teresa Artman, Dwight Ramsey

Technical Editor: Jeff Wiedenfeld

Editorial Manager: Mary C. Corder

Editorial Assistant: Sarah Shupert

Production

Project Coordinator: Dale White

Layout and Graphics: Karl Brandt, Jill Piscitelli, Erin Zeltner

Proofreaders: Susan Moritz, Carl Pierce, Marianne Santy, Charles Spencer, York Production Services, Inc.

Indexer: York Production Services, Inc.

Special Help
Constance Carlisle

General and Administrative

IDG Books Worldwide, Inc.: John Kilcullen, CEO; Bill Barry, President and COO; John Ball, Executive VP, Operations & Administration; John Harris, CFO

IDG Books Technology Publishing Group: Richard Swadley, Senior Vice President and Publisher; Mary Bednarek, Vice President and Publisher; Walter R. Bruce III, Vice President and Publisher; Joseph Wikert, Vice President and Publisher; Mary C. Corder, Editorial Director; Andy Cummings, Publishing Director, General User Group; Barry Pruett, Publishing Director

IDG Books Manufacturing: Ivor Parker, Vice President, Manufacturing

IDG Books Marketing: John Helmus, Assistant Vice President, Director of Marketing

IDG Books Online Management: Brenda McLaughlin, Executive Vice President, Chief Internet Officer; Gary Millrood, Executive Vice President of Business Development, Sales and Marketing

IDG Books Packaging: Marc J. Mikulich, Vice President, Brand Strategy and Research

IDG Books Production for Branded Press: Debbie Stailey, Production Director

IDG Books Sales: Roland Elgey, Senior Vice President, Sales and Marketing; Michael Violano, Vice President, International Sales and Sub Rights

◆

The publisher would like to give special thanks to Patrick J. McGovern, without whom this book would not have been possible.

◆

Contents at a Glance

Table of Contents

Introduction

You've decided to build your own computer. Congratulations! That statement may seem a little like "You've decided to fly a 747" or "You've decided to teach yourself accounting" — but I'm here to tell you that this book was especially written to make it both *easy* and (believe it or not) *fun* to build your own Pentium III or Athlon multimedia computer.

To sum it all up, this book explains the mysterious parts in the box in honest-to-goodness English, with a little humor and without the jargon — and then helps you build the PC that's perfect for you!

Foolish Assumptions

Here's a friendly warning: You may run across one or two doubting Thomases when you announce that you're building your own PC. Those folks probably make lots of foolish assumptions about what's involved in building a PC, and you may want to burst their bubble by telling them the following truths:

- You *don't* have to be a computer technician with years of training, and you don't need a workshop full of expensive tools. In this book, no assumptions are made about your previous knowledge of computers, the Internet, programming your VCR, or long division.

- No experience? Don't let that stop you! I introduce you to each of the systems in your computer, what they do, and how you install them, including advanced technology that would make a technoid green with envy.

- Some people still think that you don't save a dime by building your own PC. If that's the case, why is it such a booming business? By assembling your own computer, you can save *hundreds* of dollars (and take advantage of used parts from an older computer).

- Finally, some people may ask you what you plan to learn by building your own PC — and that's an easy one! By the time you're done, you'll be ready to add and repair parts yourself so that you'll save money in the future as well — and computer-repair techs will growl when you meet them.

Now that I've put those myths to rest, it's time for the good stuff!

About This Book

You'll find that each chapter in this book acts as a reference for one type of computer hardware you can add to your computer; some are required components, and others are optional devices that add extra functionality to your PC. You can start at any point — each chapter is self contained — although the chapters are arranged in a somewhat linear order that you can follow. The book also includes a glossary of computer terms and an appendix with information about the various operating systems available for the PC, which comes in handy if you haven't decided on an operating system to run.

Each chapter also provides the general information you need in order to make a buying decision between different flavors of the same component; for example, Chapter 9 discusses both bare-bones and advanced sound cards (without resorting to technical mumbojumbo).

Conventions Used in This Book

If you're interested in buying and installing a particular component, such as a CD-ROM drive or a video adapter card, you can jump directly to that chapter and start reading. Each chapter ends with general installation instructions that familiarize you with the installation process. (They don't replace the specific documentation that accompanies each component, although the steps I provide give you an idea of what's involved.)

On the other hand, if you're interested in building a computer from scratch, start with Chapter 1 and follow the chapters in order; you can also skip to other chapters whenever necessary for information you may need.

Stuff you type

From time to time, I may ask you to type a command within DOS (or whatever operating system you're using). That text often appears like this:

```
Type me
```

Press the Enter key to process the command.

Menu commands

I list menu commands using this format:

File⇨Open

For example, this shorthand indicates that you should click the File menu and then choose the Open menu item.

Display messages

From time to time, I mention messages you should see displayed on-screen by an application or the operating system. Those messages look like this:
`This is a message displayed by an application.`

Extra credit

Although you don't really need to know a great deal of technical information to build a computer, you may be curious about the technical details that surround computers and the components you're using. This technical information is usually formatted as a sidebar (in a separate box) to separate it from the stuff you really *have* to know.

How This Book Is Organized

I've divided this book into six major parts, each made up of a number of chapters, and each chapter is further divided into sections. You'll find all the nasty acronyms, part names, and relevant items in the index; important topics and information that appear elsewhere in the book are cross referenced to make them easier to find. The book has six parts.

Part I: "Can I Really Do This?"

This part introduces you to the tool of the PC assembly trade (a screwdriver, which tells you how complex the hardware *really* is), what components make up a PC, and how they work together within your computer. You also determine what type of computer you should build by examining your current and future needs.

Part II: Building Your PC

In this part, you assemble the required components to build a bare-bones PC — it won't play the latest multimedia golf game, but it will have all the basic features you need. You'll be able to run DOS programs, and you can load your choice of operating system after you've finished this part.

Part III: Adding the Fun Stuff

This part of the book covers the addition of hardware that really makes a multimedia PC fun to use — like a stereo sound card, a CD-ROM or DVD drive, and a modem. After you've completed this part, you can use your new PC to access the Internet or listen to an audio CD while you work — or play that latest multimedia golf game.

Part IV: Adding the Advanced Stuff

In this part, I introduce you to advanced hardware that pumps up the performance of your PC, including simple networking, ISDN, cable and DSL Internet connections, digital scanners, and SCSI devices. Not every computer owner needs the technology found in this part, but after you've read these chapters, you'll be familiar with the enhancements you can add to create a power user's PC.

Part V: The Part of Tens

These five chapters are a quick reference of tips and advice on several topics relating to the assembly of PCs. Each list has ten tips. The Part of Tens includes a chapter devoted to potential problems and a chapter to help you speed up your new computer.

Part VI: Appendixes

The appendixes feature a comparison between the different operating systems typically used on Pentium- and Athlon-class PCs — if you haven't considered what type of operating system you'll use, this information can be very helpful to you. You'll find a glossary of computer components, terms, and acronyms.

Icons Used in This Book

Some things you encounter while building your PC are just too important to miss. To make sure that you see certain paragraphs, they're marked with one of these icons:

The Tip icon makes it easy to spot information that will save you time and trouble (and sometimes even money).

Are you thinking of adding used hardware from an older computer or used hardware you've bought or been given? If so, stay on the lookout for the Scavenger icon; it highlights information and recommendations on using older hardware.

If you're like me and you're curious about what's happening behind the scenes, this icon is for you. The Technical Stuff icon highlights information that you don't really need for assembling your PC — but you may find interesting. This information can also be blissfully ignored.

As you can imagine, the Warning icon steers you clear of potential disaster. *Always* read the information under this icon first!

Consider this information as the printed equivalent of those sticky notes that decorate the front of some PCs. You may already know this stuff, but a reminder never hurts.

Where to Go from Here

Before you turn the page, grab yourself a pencil and some scratch paper for taking notes — or throw caution utterly to the wind and write directly in the book. (After all, this isn't an e-book — in electronic format that you display on your computer screen — so you're reading real pages made of paper!) If you need specific help on a particular component, jump to the right chapter; if you need to start from the beginning, start with Part I.

Enjoy yourself and take your time — remember that you're *not* running a race! Although the process of building your own PC may seem a little daunting now, it *really is* easy to learn. Plus, nothing is more satisfying than using a computer you built yourself or answering PC questions from friends and relatives because "you're the computer expert!"

Part I
"Can I Really Do This?"

The 5th Wave   By Rich Tennant

"That reminds me - I have to figure out how to install our CD-ROM and external hard drive."

In this part . . .

I introduce you to the various components used to build a computer, and you find out what task each of these parts performs. I also cover some of the basic rules of computer assembly, and I explain how you can use scavenged parts from an older computer to help cut the cost of your new PC. Finally, you'll act as your own consultant and determine which type of custom computer you should build to fit your needs.

Chapter 1

What's in a Computer, Anyway?

• •

In This Chapter

▶ Discovering how simple PCs really are

▶ Using CSA (Common Sense Assembly)

▶ Understanding the standard PC components

▶ Connecting components

• •

Ask most people what they know about computers, and they'll tell you that a PC is a complex, sealed box full of confusing parts you need an engineering degree to understand — something like a cross between an unopened Egyptian pyramid and a rocket engine. Ask those same people whether they want to try their hand at actually *building* a computer, and they'll probably laugh out loud. Even if you did buy all the mysterious electronic parts (which technotypes affectionately refer to as computer *components*), where would you start? Where do you buy everything? How do you fit the components together? Nobody but an honest-to-goodness computer nerd could possibly put a computer together!

Well, ladies and gentlemen, I've got great news: If you can handle the tool shown in Figure 1-1, you can safely assemble your own computer — and even enjoy doing it! After you discover how to build your own computer and start to use it, you'll probably agree with me: Building a computer is actually easier than figuring out how to use some of the complicated software the computer can run. The idea that building a computer is as difficult as building or repairing a car is just a myth (probably encouraged by computer salespeople).

This chapter introduces you to the standard electronics and peripherals you can use to build your computer and shows you how they fit together.

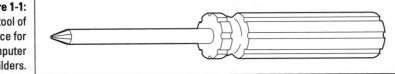

Figure 1-1:
The tool of
choice for
computer
builders.

Anyone Can Assemble a PC

You may have heard a horror story or two about someone who tried to upgrade a PC and ended up being sucked through a black hole into another dimension. When you announce to the world that you're going to build your own computer, you're likely to face a number of common myths:

- ✔ **"Why, you have to be practically psychic about how machinery works to stick your hands inside a computer!"** Wrong — in fact, you really don't have to know how any of the components work, so you don't have to be an expert in laser optics, magnetism, or electronic theory. You just need to connect them correctly and attach them to the computer case.

- ✔ **"You can't build a computer on a card table, you know. You're going to need an airstrip, a complete toolkit, and a warehouse full of parts."** Nope. Not only can you assemble a computer on your dining room table, but also no special tools are required. Find your favorite screwdriver, and you're a lean, mean, computer-assembling machine.

- ✔ **"It's going to take you years to put together a computer. Heck, by the time you're finished, your computer will already be out of date."** Depends on how long it takes. No, no — just kidding! This myth is definitely false. If you have all your components ready to go, assembling a PC is a first-time project you can easily finish on a long weekend.

- ✔ **"Something's not going to work with something else. You'll see."** Wrong again. (Geez, who is this person? He probably still thinks that airplanes will never get off the ground.) Today's computer components are designed to work with each other. Regardless of what brand name you buy or how much you spend, if you buy a standard computer device, it should join in that big cooperative team effort that makes a working computer.

What's the secret to building a PC? There really isn't one. That's why many people have started their own home businesses building custom computers in their spare time. Building a computer is actually fun — after you conquer that initial fear. Plus, you get a big ego boost after people find out that you built your own computer. Suddenly, you're a genuine PC guru to your family and friends, so be prepared to handle those technical support questions at your next party.

Building a better mousetrap (or computer)

Over the past few years, I've developed a simple rule for myself, which applies perfectly to building anything, from a mousetrap to a computer. I call this rule *CSA* — or, for those who can't stand acronyms, *Common Sense Assembly*. The idea is a simple one: You can prevent most mistakes while assembling a PC by using a little common sense.

Keep the following CSA rules in mind when handling and connecting computer components:

- ✔ **Give yourself plenty of empty space and adequate lighting.** If you're building a computer on the dining table, make sure that your work area is covered with a heavy cloth to avoid scratches. If you have an adjustable desk lamp handy, use it to shine light where you need it.

- ✔ **Don't start without all the necessary components.** If you don't have everything you need to follow a project from beginning to end, don't stop halfway through. It's too easy to miss a step or forget something if you leave your computer's bedside and come back the next day.

- ✔ **Treat your components carefully.** This common-sense rule doesn't mean that you need to wear gloves when handling the cables, nor that you need to refrigerate your adapter cards — just don't drop a part on the floor or toss it to a friend. Keep components in their antistatic packaging until you're ready to install them.

Never bend any circuit board or adapter card, and make sure the cables that connect your parts aren't pinched. If something doesn't seem to fit, don't try to *make* it fit. Take the component out, check the instructions again, and try it a different way.

Installing adapter cards on your motherboard can sometimes take a little longer or require a little more force than, for example, plugging a game cartridge into a video game. But determining whether a card is aligned correctly with the slot is usually pretty easy.

- ✔ **Read any documentation that comes with each computer component.** Although I provide step-by-step assembly instructions throughout this book, there's always a chance that one of your components may require some sort of special switch settings or some other unique treatment.

- ✔ **Keep all your parts manuals together for easy reference.** After your computer is running, you can refer to your manuals quickly if you need to change any settings. If you decide to upgrade in the future and you want to sell the old device, it's considered good manners to provide the original manual with the component.

✔ **Save your boxes and receipts.** Although it's really rare, you may find yourself stuck with a brand-new defective item, and you'll need the original packaging to return it.

✔ **Use bowls to hold small parts.** Loose screws, jumpers, and wires have a habit of wandering off if left on their own. If you end up with extra screws or doodads after successfully assembling a PC, put these parts in a bowl and start your own "spare parts warehouse" — they'll come in handy in the future. If you're a true technogeek, get thee hence to a hardware store and buy one of those wall racks with all the little compartments — they're perfect for organizing everything from screws to wires and jumpers.

✔ **Keep a magnetic screwdriver handy.** It never fails — sooner or later, you end up dropping a screw inside your computer case. If no loose components are in the case, feel free to pick up the case, turn it upside down, and let gravity do its thing. If you've installed a component that's not screwed down yet, I recommend using a magnetic screwdriver to pick up wayward screws just by touching them.

✔ **Check *all* connections after you install a component.** I can't explain this phenomenon (other than to invoke Murphy's Law), but you'll often connect a new component firmly, only to discover later that you somehow disconnected some other connector accidentally.

✔ **Leave the computer cover off during assembly.** There's no reason to replace the case's cover immediately after installing a part — you may end up having to reconnect a component if the cable is connected upside down, for example. Instead, test your newly installed device first, if possible — as long as you don't touch any of the circuit boards inside the case, you'll be fine.

By the way, nothing inside your machine will explode or spew nasty radiation, so you don't have to step behind a lead screen when you fire it up. Simply make sure that you don't touch any of the circuit boards inside while it's running. Personally, I replace the case's cover on a work in progress only at the end of the day (to keep dust and small fingers off).

The primary, A-number-one, all-important, absolutely necessary, required rule

Do not panic!

There's very little chance that you can destroy a component simply by connecting it the wrong way. Take your time as you build your computer and move at your own pace — you can avoid mistakes that way. ***Remember:*** *Building a computer is not a contest, and there is no time limit.*

After you've gained experience and built a few machines, you can work on speed records. For example, I know several supertechs who can assemble a complete PC in a single hour. Of course, people often laugh at them at dinner parties — being a technonerd does have its dark side, I guess.

The other primary, A-number-one, all-important, absolutely necessary, required rule

Liquids are taboo!

If you even so much as think of parking your soda or mineral water next to your computer (even "just for a second"), you may remind yourself of Chernobyl or Three Mile Island. If you spill beverages or other liquids on your computer components, that liquid will ruin everything it touches — period.

PCs Are Built with Standard Parts

When the first personal computers appeared way back in the late 1970s, you had to be good with electronics — and with a soldering iron — to build one. Everything was soldered by hand to circuit boards, and you even had to build the computer's case yourself. If you've ever heard of the term *hacker,* this is where the term originated: A hacker was a person who "hacked together" a computer from bits and pieces of hardware.

Computers have advanced a couple light years since then; they're more like appliances now, in that one computer is put together pretty much like another. Ever since IBM introduced the IBM PC, computers have been built using standard components with the same connectors and dimensions, so you no longer need the experience of an electronics engineer to assemble one. These parts are self-contained, so you don't need to worry about soldering (or gears and springs, either). Everyone uses the same building blocks, and they fit together in the same way.

In fact, assembling standardized computer components is how popular mail-order and direct-sale computer manufacturers now build their machines. Like you, they order standard computer components and peripherals and then follow a procedure (much like the ones described in this book) to assemble the computer according to your specifications.

The process you follow to build your own computer is much like following a recipe. Like baking a cake, you add certain parts to your mixture in a certain order, and before you know it you're taking a big bite — or, in this case, surfing the Internet, writing the great American novel, or blasting your favorite aliens from the planet Quark.

Understanding Your Computer's Components

Before you find out more about where to buy the parts that make up a computer (or, if you're lucky, where to scavenge them), allow me to introduce you to each of the major components of your computer. A computer needs at least one of each of the following components in order for everything to work. In this section, I describe each component in general, although you can find out all the details on each computer part in the other chapters.

By the way, *scavenging* parts is more wholesome than it sounds; I use the term to refer to components you've removed from an older computer, used components you've bought, or used parts that someone has given you. Chapter 2 gives you some good tips and hints on where to scavenge computer components.

The metal mansion

Your computer's *case* is its home, complete with a power supply, the various buttons and lights on the front, and the all-important fan that keeps the inside of your computer cool. Some high-power machines even have more than one fan, depending on how many devices inside are generating heat.

You may notice several large, rectangular holes (called *drive bays*) in the front of your case. Don't worry — your computer case is not defective; it's supposed to have them. These holes enable you to add new components, such as a removable-media drive or a CD-ROM. If they aren't being used, they're usually covered by a plastic insert. The front of your case may have a door that swings open for access to the bays.

You can get computer cases in various sizes. The size you choose depends on how many additional computer toys (usually called *peripherals*) you want to add to your computer. Chapter 3 discusses your computer's case in more detail.

The big kahuna

A number of different circuit boards are inside a computer — but only one is big enough, complicated enough, and important enough to be called your computer's *motherboard.* Your computer motherboard holds the *CPU chip,* which acts as the brain of your PC, and the *RAM chips,* which act as your computer's memory while it's turned on. In fact, the motherboard holds just about everything, as you can see in Figure 1-2.

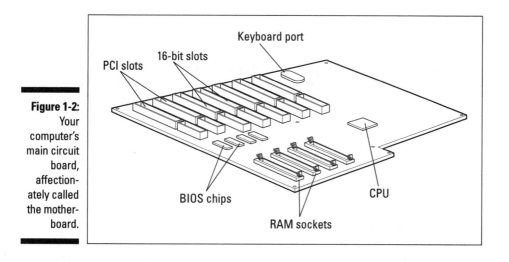

Figure 1-2:
Your computer's main circuit board, affection-ately called the mother-board.

If you really enjoy acronyms, CPU stands for *central processing unit,* and RAM stands for *random access memory.* Feel free to ignore the longer names com-pletely — most people know what they are, although they have no idea what the letters mean.

Computer CPUs come in different speeds. CPU speeds are measured in mega-hertz (MHz), such as "350 MHz." Sometimes, the CPU speed is just mentioned after the processor name, like "Pentium III 500." The faster the CPU speed, the faster your computer.

The most popular brand of CPU these days is the Intel Pentium series, which includes the Pentium II and Pentium III (as well as the Intel Celeron), but you can find a number of other brands, like AMD and Cyrix. Usually, these alterna-tive CPUs are somewhat less expensive, and they often run faster and more efficiently than the Pentium. I discuss the most popular processors and their advantages later in this book.

Your motherboard is probably one of the most expensive parts you need to buy. If you can find a used motherboard in good shape with a Pentium II- or III-class CPU, you should buy it if the price is right. What price is right? Motherboard prices fluctuate every month (usually downward), so check the price on a new motherboard that has a similar Pentium-series chip to determine whether you're getting a good deal on the used board.

For all the details on your motherboard, see Chapter 3. I discuss CPU chips and RAM chips in Chapter 4.

The eye candy

Next on your list are the *monitor* and *video card* — together, these two parts display everything from your e-mail to your latest financial figures to all those killer Web pages (and don't forget those flashy enemy Quarkians you need to disintegrate).

All video cards have their own, special, onboard RAM chips; the more RAM, the more colors and detail the card can display. Today's state-of-the-art video cards also help speed up your computer as it displays 3D graphics or digital video. The video card performs most of the display work itself, giving your CPU a well-deserved rest.

Monitors have screen areas that typically range from 14 inches to 21 inches in diameter (measured diagonally across the screen). You can go even larger if you crave that much space. Naturally, the larger the monitor, the more expensive it is.

Chapter 6 contains just about everything you ever (or never) wanted to know about video cards and PC monitors.

The places for plugs

Your power cord isn't the only connection you need on the outside of your computer. For example, you also need to attach a keyboard and mouse, and you may also want to add an external modem, a joystick, a CD recorder, and a printer. Some of the connectors used by these devices are built into the motherboard, and others are installed separately.

Remember the old-fashioned mouse? You can still find one these days, but you can also use other things to point and click, like a trackball, touchpad, or drawing tablet. A mouse is practically a requirement for Windows (although you can still navigate strictly from the keyboard if necessary).

Even the traditional keyboard has changed. You can find new ergonomically shaped keyboards designed to make typing easier on your hands and fore-arms. Windows 98 recognizes two or three new keys to activate the Start button and display menus within an application. (Thank goodness Bill Gates can't add new letters to the alphabet.) However, if you can scavenge a stan-dard PC keyboard, it should still work just fine.

Your computer also needs at least one serial and one parallel port in order to use many external devices. For example, most modems are connected with serial ports, and your printer uses a parallel port. Other proprietary, specialized ports may eventually end up sticking out of the back of your new computer, depending on what components you add. (Need the complete run-down on ports? Jump to Chapter 5.)

The data warehouse

Earlier in this chapter, I mention that your RAM chips act as your computer's memory while the computer is running. However, when you switch off your computer, it forgets the data in RAM, so you still need a permanent place to store Uncle Milton's Web page address or your latest report. This permanent storage comes in three forms: hard drives, removable storage drives (such as CD recorders and cartridge units, like the Zip and Jaz drives), and floppy disk drives (with their accompanying floppy disks).

Your computer needs at least one hard drive and one floppy drive; the stan-dard PC floppy drive still uses the traditional 3½-inch disk that holds 1.44MB. Hard drives, on the other hand, have much greater storage capacities. Older drives can store hundreds of megabytes. Newer hard drives hold gigabytes (or GB) of data (that's a thousand megabytes). A typical hard drive now ranges in capacity from 6GB to 30GB.

Newer hard drives are typically faster than old drives, too; the new ones can deliver more data to your computer in less time than drives made as little as two or three years ago can.

If you're buying a new hard drive, buy as much data territory as possible. On the other hand, if you plan to use a scavenged hard drive with a smaller capacity, you may have to remove programs later if you add new programs and data. Chapter 7 is your guide to both hard drives and floppy drives.

The bells and whistles

Today's multimedia PCs have almost more extras, add-ons, and fun doodads than any mere mortal can afford — well, except for Bill Gates, that is. If you want to be able to run a multimedia game or educational title, though, you need at least a CD-ROM drive and a sound card, along with a set of speakers. Chapter 8 tells you more about CD-ROM drives and the new DVD drives, and Chapter 9 discusses PC sound cards.

Another common addition to a PC is a printer. I guarantee that you'll retire your old typewriter after you've used a word processor. If you need the low-down on today's printer technology, jump to Chapter 14. And don't forget a modem for connecting your computer to other computers across telephone lines, especially if you're an Internet junkie. (I cover modems in Chapter 10.)

Even if you don't run multimedia programs or play audio CDs on your computer, you may want to consider adding a CD-ROM drive anyway. Why? For a purely practical reason: The vast majority of programs available these days are distributed on CD-ROM. Finding floppy disk versions of anything is becoming harder and harder, so a CD-ROM drive is rapidly becoming a required part of every computer.

In later chapters, I also discuss advanced stuff for "power users," like network hardware, scanners, and ISDN. You don't have to read those chapters, and you won't be tested on them, but they're there in case you feel adventurous (or you really need them).

Connecting Your Computer Components

You may be wondering how to connect all the various components that make up a computer. "What happens if I connect something wrong? Am I going to light up like a Christmas tree? Will I burn up an expensive part?"

I admit, when I built my first computer, I was more than a little worried by these same concerns. To reassure you, consider these facts:

- ✔ Most connectors for computer components are marked to help you plug them in correctly. In fact, some connectors are designed so that you can install them in only one direction.

- ✔ Ruining a computer component simply by plugging it in the wrong way is almost impossible. At the worst, the device simply won't work. Just connect the component properly, and it should work just fine.

🖝 Although you connect your computer to a wall socket, unless you disassemble the power supply or monitor (which you are *not* going to do), you won't be exposed to anything close to a dangerous voltage. Of course, it pays to take basic precautions — if you follow the assembly procedures step-by-step, you'll be perfectly safe.

Most components within a computer are connected with cables. For example, Figures 1-3 and 1-4 show a floppy drive cable and a power cable. As you add these parts to your computer, I give you instructions on how to make sure that you're connecting cables properly.

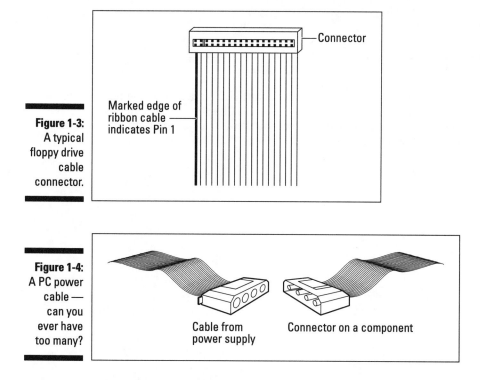

Connector

Marked edge of ribbon cable indicates Pin 1

Figure 1-3: A typical floppy drive cable connector.

Figure 1-4: A PC power cable — can you ever have too many?

Cable from power supply

Connector on a component

You'll also be adding parts called *adapter cards*. These circuit boards "plug in" to your computer, much like a game cartridge plugs into a video game console. Adapter cards provide your computer with additional capabilities, such as sound cards (Chapter 9) and internal modems (Chapter 10). Adapter cards are arranged in rows at one end of a computer, as shown in Figure 1-5.

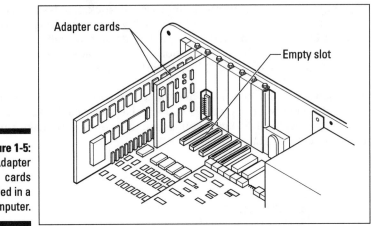

Adapter cards

Empty slot

Figure 1-5:
Adapter
cards
installed in a
computer.

Depending on the type of motherboard you install, you'll be using either
16-bit ISA, PCI, or AGP adapter cards (in Chapter 3, I explain how to select the
right type of adapter card). Make sure that you get the right kind of adapter
card — the wrong type of card won't fit.

Chapter 2

"What Type of PC Should I Build?"

. . . .

. . . .

*W*hen you walk into a megahuge retail electronics store these days to buy a computer, the salesperson is supposed to help you pick out the right one for your needs. If you build your own computer, however, you need to figure out *for yourself* what type of computer is best for you. Take it from me — you're likely to come up with the answers far better than many so-called experts who sell computers. Remember that they're interested primarily in making money for themselves, so it's in the salesperson's best interest to talk you into a more expensive model than you really need.

In this chapter, I show you how to figure out what type of computer fits your needs, and I suggest three basic configurations. I tell you what parts you need to buy — including the special stuff. I also fill you in on the different sources for buying computer parts — especially used parts, which can cut the cost of building your new machine even further.

Interrogating Yourself on Your Computer Needs

If every computer owner had the same needs, only a single model would be available. But because today's computers are used at home *and* at the office, for business *and* for pleasure, what works well for one person usually doesn't quite fit for another. Although most computers sold today are Pentium III computers, they're about as different from each other as the 30-some-odd flavors at your local ice cream parlor — or, at least they *should* be.

To custom-build the computer you need, you have to design it around who you are and what you plan to do — and the easiest way to determine what type of computer you need is to ask yourself a series of questions. If you really enjoy TV shows about lawyers, here's a chance to cross-examine yourself — grab a pen and a notebook and write down your answers to the questions on this checklist:

✔ **Primary Application:** What will be the main function of your computer — in other words, what will you be doing with it about 75 percent of the time you're using it? For example, do you plan to use the computer for word processing, drafting, or Internet surfing? Are you a big-time game player who likes to play the latest and hottest 3D game releases? Jot down the main function of your computer under the heading Primary Application.

If you're not quite sure what your Primary Application will be, just write down a general term like Office Work, Home Use, or Very Expensive Paperweight.

✔ **Secondary Application:** What will be the secondary function of your computer — in other words, what will you typically use it for if you're not performing the main function? Do you play games during the evening, or does your family use the computer for education or Internet surfing? Write down the secondary use for your computer under this heading.

✔ **Family Computer:** Will children be using your computer for education or games? If so, write down that use under this heading.

✔ **Hi-Resolution Video:** Will you be staring at your computer screen for more than three or four hours a day? For example, do you run a home business or write novels on your computer? Will you be using your computer for heavy-duty graphics, such as the latest cutting-edge 3D games, professional desktop publishing, or image editing with a program such as Photoshop? If so, write down *Hi-Res Video Required* under this heading.

✔ **Power User:** Are you going to run an entire suite of computer programs, like Microsoft Office 2000? Will you be running sophisticated, expensive applications, like Adobe Photoshop or AutoCAD? If you're planning on using complex programs, write down *Power User.*

Some people want the fastest possible computer — they hate waiting, and they're willing to pay the extra green to get the Cadillac of computers that's ready for anything. If you fit this description and you don't mind paying extra for many of your computer components, go ahead and write down *Power User.* You'll spend more money than the typical person because you're buying more-powerful and expensive parts, but you'll probably end up with the nicest computer on your block.

> ✔ **Network User:** Will you connect your computer to other computers over a LAN? (That's technobabble gibberish for Local Area Network — or, if you have a life, just "the network.") If the answer to this question is Yes, write down *I'm a Network User* (and prepare yourself for an extra headache or two later, in Chapter 12, where I discuss networks).
>
> ✔ **One last question:** Where were you on the night of the 15th? (Too bad Perry Mason didn't have a computer to keep track of all those details!)

See, that didn't hurt too badly! You've now eliminated the salesperson and built a list of your computer tasks and activities. From this list, you can build your own description of your computer needs. Pat yourself on the back and pour yourself another cup of coffee or grab another soda. In the following section, you use this list to determine what type of components you need to build into your computer.

Answering Your Computer-Needs Questions

If you were buying a computer through a retail store, the salesperson's next move after inquiring into your computer needs would be to saunter over to one particular model and say something reassuring, like "Based on what you've told me, I'd recommend this as the perfect computer for you. Will that be cash, check, or charge?"

Whoa, Nellie! Chances are that the salesperson's pick *may* meet your needs, but when you're building your own computer, *you* get to decide which parts are more important than others. Are you looking for speed? Storage space? The best sound or the best color?

In this section, you use the description of your computer needs (which you create in the preceding section) to choose between three standard computer designs. I've created each of these basic designs to fit a particular type of computer owner. Later in this chapter, you find out whether you need to add special stuff to your base model. (You may recognize this method — it's the same one used by savvy car buyers to get exactly the car they want at the lowest possible price.)

Look through the descriptions of each of the three designs that follow and then select one that can best serve as the base model for your computer. Of course, you can add or subtract parts, select more expensive parts for any of these designs, or just jot down extra parts you want to add after your computer is up and running. The following computer designs aren't hard-and-fast specifications, just suggestions.

I include in each of the following designs a final entry (the *Optional* field) that names one or more "extras" that most people find very useful for one reason or another. They're not absolutely required in order to run programs, but they make life a heck of a lot easier! Some optional items I suggest may be upgrades to an existing part in that design. For example, if you're willing to spend extra for a faster processor, I recommend the type of processor you should look for.

Design 1: The bare-bones economy class

Of course, one of the reasons you may want to build a computer yourself is to save money — my first design is specifically tailored for those who want to build a basic, no-frills computer for the least amount of money. You won't be piloting the latest flight simulator on this computer — but then again, life doesn't begin and end with games. However, you can only skip certain pieces of hardware; for example, avoid the question "Do I really need a keyboard?"

This type of computer is suitable if the checklist description you compiled in the preceding section fits this profile:

✔ Both your Primary and Secondary Applications are word processing, home finance, keeping track of household records, or similar simple applications that don't require the fastest computer.

✔ Your checklist description does *not* include Family Computer, Hi-Res Video Required, or Power User.

In Table 2-1, I list the appropriate details about the computer components you need for building this bare-bones, basic computer design. Although it has no bells and only a few whistles, it still qualifies as a Celeron-based PC — and it's also representative of what you can build from used parts.

Table 2-1	Requirements for a Bare-Bones Pentium-Class Computer
Computer Component	*What to Look For*
Case	Standard "pizza box," ATX minitower, or desktop model, single fan
CPU/motherboard	300 MHz Celeron, ISA and PCI slots, 256K cache
System RAM	32MB (megabytes)

Computer Component	What to Look For
Hard drive	One EIDE drive with at least 3GB (gigabytes) of storage capacity
Floppy drive	One 3½-inch, 1.44MB disk drive
CD-ROM	16x internal drive
Video card	Standard 2MB PCI SVGA adapter
Monitor	14-inch SVGA
Ports	Two serial and one parallel
Input	Standard 101-keyboard and mouse
Optional	A modem for connecting to the Internet

Design 2: The Cunningham standard edition

Remember Richie Cunningham and his family from *Happy Days?* If home computers had been around in the 1950s, Richie and crew would have used this standard edition design. It's typical in every way, including the moderate amount of money you'll spend in building it. This computer has basic multimedia capabilities, and it can handle the Internet without blinking.

This type of computer is suitable if your checklist description fits this profile:

- ✔ Your Primary Application involves browsing the Web, using Internet e-mail and newsgroups, working with more advanced office programs (such as spreadsheets and scheduling applications), using simple desktop publishing software, or creating computer artwork.

- ✔ Your Secondary Application involves computer games, multimedia, or educational software on CD-ROM.

- ✔ Your description does *not* include Hi-Res Video Required or Power User.

Table 2-2 lists the requirements on the most important parts you need for building this midrange design.

Table 2-2	Requirements for a Middle-Range Pentium-Class Computer
Computer Component	*What to Look For*
Case	ATX minitower model, single fan
CPU/motherboard	450 MHz Pentium III or 650 MHz Athlon, AGP, and PCI slots
System RAM	64MB
Hard drive	One EIDE drive with at least 6GB of storage capacity
Floppy drive	One 3½-inch, 1.44MB disk drive
Video card	Standard 8MB AGP 3D video adapter, 3DFX, or TNT graphics chipset
Modem	56 Kbps v.90 internal data/fax
CD-ROM	24x internal drive
Sound card	PCI Sound Blaster-compatible with wavetable
Monitor	17-inch SVGA
Ports	Two USB, two serial, and one parallel
Input	Standard 101-keyboard and mouse
Optional	Inkjet printer, scanner, 19-inch monitor, internal DVD drive

Design 3: The Wayne Manor Batcomputer

"Holy microchips, Batman!" Design 3 is the power user's dream — everything is first class. This system can handle even the toughest jobs, such as creating 3D artwork, processing the largest Excel spreadsheets, and editing images with Adobe Photoshop. The Batcomputer you build can be as good as any top-of-the-line computer you may buy at That Big Store That Sells PCs — except, of course, that you'll spend hundreds of dollars less.

This type of computer is suitable if your checklist description fits this profile:

✔ Your Primary Application involves advanced or heavy computational work, like computer-aided drafting, multimedia video editing, or 3D animation. If your Primary Application is playing the latest and greatest computer games in all their glory, you should consider the Batcomputer too.

✓ Your checklist includes Hi-Res Video Required and Power User.

✓ You simply want the best possible computer, which will last the longest
  time before it requires upgrading. (Speaking of upgrading, in the sidebar
  titled "Finding bargains in so-called obsolete computers," later in this
  chapter, I show you how to take advantage of *other people* upgrading
  their computers.)

Table 2-3 lists the requirements for the most important components you need
for this design.

Table 2-3	Requirements for a Top-of-the-Line Pentium-Class Computer
Computer Component	*What to Look For*
Case	Full-tower model, dual fan
CPU/motherboard	The fastest doggone Pentium III or Athlon processor available, AGP and PCI slots
System RAM	128 to 256MB
Hard drive	One EIDE drive with at least 30GB of storage capacity
Floppy drive	One 3½-inch, 1.44MB disk drive
Video card	Windows-accelerated AGP 3D SVGA adapter with at least 16MB of video memory, 3DFX or TNT graphics chipset
Modem	56 Kbps v.90 internal data/fax
CD-ROM	DVD drive (with AC-3 decoder if you watch DVD movies)
Sound card	PCI Sound Blaster wavetable card (64 voices, 3D positional sound, hardware MP3 encoding)
Monitor	Nineteen-inch SVGA or 17-inch LCD flat-screen display
Ports	Two USB, one FireWire, two serial, one parallel
Input	Ergonomic keyboard with extra Windows keys, trackball
Optional	Scanner, inkjet or laser printer, Orb or Jaz drive, SCSI adapter, network adapter, 21-inch monitor, cable modem, videoconferencing camera

After you select the best base-model computer that meets your needs, you're ready to identify any special add-ons (or, in the language of the technowizards, *peripherals*) you need in order to use your applications.

Getting Your Hands on the Special Stuff

If you plan to use your new computer almost exclusively for a particular purpose (composing music or drafting, for example), you may already know what special stuff you need. In case you're a complete newcomer to your particular application, however, the following sections outline some of the special stuff you may need.

Drafting, graphics, and pretty pictures

If you're an artist or you're interested in computer graphics, you may want to get your hands on some of the equipment in this list. The first two are peripherals, and the second two are upgrades to standard components of your computer:

✔ **Drawing tablet:** This computer peripheral is something like an electronic piece of paper — now there's a real technological advancement, right? You can draw on the surface of the tablet, as shown in Figure 2-1, which in turn sends your drawing directly to the screen. Many freehand artists and drafting gurus prefer drawing with natural movements of the hand rather than trying to draw a line by using a mouse cursor. (For more information on the drawing tablet, jump to Chapter 5.)

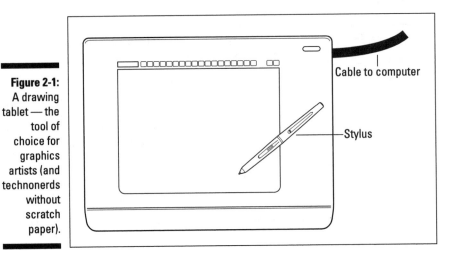

Figure 2-1:
A drawing tablet — the tool of choice for graphics artists (and technonerds without scratch paper).

Cable to computer

Stylus

✔ **Digital scanner:** A scanner (shown in Figure 2-2) enables you to "read in" pictures from printed material directly into a graphics program. You can also use a scanner to read (or *acquire*) text from a magazine article or book directly into your word processing program. Some scanners use a feature named OCR — an acronym that's actually easier to use than the full phrase, *optical character recognition.* (For all the details on scanner technology, head to Chapter 14.)

✔ If you wrote down Hi-Res Video Required on your description, you need a faster, more expensive video card with these features:

- **3D accelerator chip:** This accelerator chip takes care of the video processing that would normally be handled by your CPU, so your Windows games and programs with high-resolution graphics run faster.

- **Additional video RAM:** Extra video RAM enables your monitor to display more colors with higher resolutions within Windows (which is easier on your eyes). With extra RAM, your computer can display higher resolutions (for example, a professional desktop publishing application can easily create layouts that require a minimum resolution of 1152 x 864). And you can display larger pictures with more accurate colors.

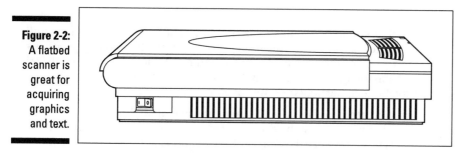

Figure 2-2:
A flatbed scanner is great for acquiring graphics and text.

Home-office and small-business stuff

Are you going to get all businesslike on me? No problem — a computer can help you organize a home office so that you can find the right information when you need it. (Imagine that!) Consider these extras as company money well spent:

✔ Most home office computers need either an *inkjet* or a *laser printer.* Both these printers have distinct advantages, and I explain the differences in detail in Chapter 14.

✔ If you plan to add a data/fax modem to your computer, you may consider adding a digital scanner. Besides the advantages I mention in the preceding section, a scanner provides the "missing link" for your modem's fax capabilities. Without a scanner, you can fax only electronic documents you create on your computer — you're stuck if you want to fax something from a paper copy. With a scanner, you can scan in the pages from your hard copy and then fax the images.

✔ Speaking of modems, how would you like your computer to answer the phone for you? If you pick up a data/fax/voice modem, you can set up separate voice mailboxes for you and your business. I talk more about voice modems in Chapter 10.

Mozart's musical computer

Too bad that Wolfgang Amadeus never got to jam using a computer. If you're a musician, you may already know some of the cool stuff you can do with a computer. Whether you're a musician or not, the following computer components can turn your PC into a miniature recording studio. Check out these toys:

✔ No self-respecting computer musician would be without a sound card with *MIDI* support. Using the MIDI standard, you can "play" music directly into the computer from your instrument and then edit the music. Or your computer can actually take control of your instrument and play it automatically. (For the complete description of MIDI, visit Chapter 9.)

✔ Another sound card enhancement you've got to have for a home studio computer is *wavetable sound support.* Wavetable technology produces more lifelike, accurate notes that sound much more like a real musical instrument. (For more information on sound cards in general — and wavetable in particular — surf over to Chapter 9.)

✔ Are you interested in riding the recent wave of MP3 popularity? These digital music files can be downloaded from the Internet and stored on your computer's hard drive, yet they sound exactly like you're listening to an audio CD. You can also transfer these files to one of the new generation of handheld MP3 personal players and listen while you're walking or working. A sound card with MP3 hardware support can create superb MP3 files or allow a slower computer to play MP3 files without distortion. (I serve up the MP3 details in Chapter 9.)

✔ One of my favorite extras enables you to record your own audio CDs. Musicians and audiophiles can take advantage of the big drop in *CD recorder* prices. For around $200, you can pick up a complete CD recorder kit, complete with software (and blank recordable CDs cost about $1 each, when you buy them in bulk). Your "home-brewed" CDs can sound as good as the commercial music CDs you can buy in a store. Figure 2-3 illustrates a typical CD recorder. (For all the details on CD recorders, skip to Chapter 8.)

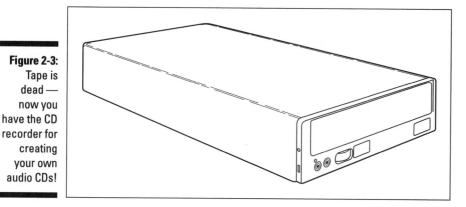

Figure 2-3:
Tape is dead — now you have the CD recorder for creating your own audio CDs!

The ultimate bad-guy blasting box

Now, you may have to pretend with your friends and family, but you can relax around here: I know the *real* reason that you need a computer. If you haven't played some of today's best action, strategy, and simulation computer games, you're missing out on the chance to fly an Apache helicopter, play 18 holes with Arnold Palmer, or take over the entire galaxy planet-by-planet! Here's the special stuff you need to create your ultimate game machine:

✔ When you mention that you're ready to play games, most people think of a computer *joystick* first. Joysticks, the traditional favorite for flight games, come in a wide range of styles. Some have 2 buttons and sell for less than $10, and others have 20 buttons that are completely programmable for every game and sell for more than $100. Joysticks aren't the only controller choice, though — you can find steering wheels and pedals for car racing, video-game-style gamepads, and even 3D controllers for games like Halo and Quake.

If you're willing to spend the extra cash, you can even get a *force feedback* joystick (as shown in Figure 2-4) that shakes and rumbles when your F-16 or your Spitfire gets hit. Thank goodness no one's developed a missile you can launch from your computer! (Set your sights on Chapter 15 to find out more about this hot joystick.)

✔ If you prefer 3D games like Mechwarrior, Quake, or Unreal Tournament, you need an advanced *3D video card* that can help speed up the action. This type of card takes care of the complex math necessary for realistic 3D effects, leaving your computer free to concentrate on running the program. In fact, a 3D video card also fits the bill if you're looking for extra video RAM. Most 3D video cards use the special AGP slot on today's motherboards. (Chapter 6 includes more info about AGP and 3D video cards.)

Figure 2-4:
An
advanced
programma-
ble force-
feedback
joystick
for those
Top Gun
wanna-bes.

✔ A great game machine needs the same *wavetable sound card* demanded by computer musicians. Most games released these days have spectacular soundtracks, and the wavetable sound really enhances the sound quality. Some games even use a technique called *stereo positioning* (which the more expensive sound cards can take advantage of). If a race car passes you on the right, you hear the sound of its engine through your right speaker. (If you're interested in sound cards, check out Chapter 9.)

✔ Speaking of speakers, if you really want to feel like you're inside your game, consider a more expensive PC speaker system that includes a subwoofer. Audiophiles know that a *subwoofer* speaker provides the richest, deepest bass (even down to subsonics you can't actually hear), and game players enjoy the rumble it adds to special effects, like laser blasts, machine guns, and afterburners. (Chapter 9 has more details on speaker systems and subwoofers.)

By the way, for complete information on today's hottest game technology and expert advice on playing everything from the sims to those old arcade favorites, I heartily recommend the book *Computer Gamer's Bible,* written by yours truly and Robert Smith and published by IDG Books Worldwide, Inc.

Picking Up the Parts

"Okay, Mark, now I know what parts I need, but where am I going to find them?" As little as five years ago, you would have had a hard time locating all the individual components for a computer. But now that a personal computer is becoming a household necessity (and more people are building their own computers), you have several sources for the parts you need.

In general, I recommend that you buy brand-new components for your computer. Why? Some components in a computer (for example, the hard drives, which are complex and have a large number of moving parts) may fail after a few years of use. In addition, prices for the fastest and most powerful components are constantly dropping. Consider the example of a used hard drive: Why install an older, slower, used hard drive that holds only 1GB when you can add a newer, faster drive that holds a whopping 30GB (for less than $300)?

In this section, I compare new versus used parts and tell you several likely sources for each.

Everybody's a critic

From time to time during your computer shopping, you may feel as though you're alone and there's no one to help you decide between brands or make decisions on features. Not so! If you feel that you need more information before deciding on parts to buy or scavenge, consider these sources:

✔ **Computer magazines:** You need look no further than your local newsstand to find a half-dozen excellent magazines that specialize in product reviews, tips and tricks for the novice computer owner, and coverage of the newest and hottest computer technology.

Some magazines hand out awards for the hardware and software they rate most highly. If the computer component you're considering carries two or three of these awards on its box, you probably have a winner. For example, I personally rate the *PC* magazine Editor's Choice Award as a real indicator of a high-quality product.

✔ **The Web:** Most publishers of computer magazines also offer online versions of their printed material, and you can search through an entire site for product information, reviews, and product comparisons. Some good examples are IDG.net (at www.idg.net), ZDNet (at www.zdnet.com), and other sites, like CINET (at www.cnet.com).

✔ **Internet newsgroups:** Although you need an Internet connection and a newsgroup reader program to read messages, newsgroups such as `alt.comp.hardware.homebuilt` and `comp.hardware` are chock-full of interesting reviews, hints, and tips. If you need to ask something specific, you can simply post a message to the newsgroup and receive an answer by e-mail or in a reply posting on the newsgroup.

✔ **Computer user groups:** Computer user groups come in handy! You'll likely find someone who has already traveled down the same road and bought a similar computer component. You can learn from that person's mistakes or success without spending a dollar out of your own wallet.

I live for mail order

What's that you say, Bunkie? You say that you need to buy some new parts, like your motherboard, hard drive, and video card? You say that you still want to save money and you don't want to pay the inflated prices at your Maze O' Wires computer store? Or perhaps you live in a smaller town without a local computer store? Never fear — use mail order, and let the U.S. Postal Service (or, more likely, FedEx or UPS) leap to the rescue.

When you order parts from a reputable mail-order company, you can choose from a huge selection of computer parts, and you always save money over buying them from a retail computer store. Depending on where you live, you may also save money by avoiding a local sales tax on your purchase.

If you've never ordered parts through the mail and you're not sure whether you're working with a reputable company, keep these guidelines in mind:

✔ Ask the salesperson for a complete description of the part before you complete the order, just to make certain that you're buying the right item. Feel free to ask questions — for example, "Is that a 16-bit ISA adapter card or a PCI adapter card?" If you like things in writing, you can also ask the salesperson to mail or fax you the specifications and the price.

✔ Make sure that the company allows you to return a part for a full refund if it turns out not to be what you need. If you return a component, some companies charge you a *restocking fee,* which is basically a charge you pay the company for the hard work involved in sticking a box back on a shelf. (I wish I had a piece of *that* action!)

✔ Some people are wary of using a credit card over the phone — if you prefer, ask for COD shipment instead. Ordering COD will cost you extra, but it's better than mailing a personal check and then waiting for it to clear. Personally, I always use a credit card, which provides me with additional leverage if there's a problem.

✔ If you can't get exactly the part you need at one company, you can *always* get it elsewhere. Beware of salespeople who tell you that they're out of the particular part you're looking for but can sell you a better model of the same part for a higher price.

✔ Some companies tack on an additional shipment charge, or they automatically charge you for "next day" shipment unless you request regular shipment. Unless you really *do* need that part tomorrow, you can probably save ten dollars or more by choosing regular ground shipment.

After you build your first computer, you'll develop a good relationship with at least one or two mail-order companies, and you can continue to order from them in the future. I have several favorite companies, each of which is my first stop for a particular type of part. (It's always a good idea to find a monitor locally, though, because you can evaluate it with your own eyes and you won't pay a fortune on shipping.)

Ordering parts online

If you have access to the Internet at work, at school, or at a neighbor's house, you can also travel through the limitless world of cyberspace looking for computer parts.

If you need a start in online shopping, visit one of my two favorite online computer stores: the Computer Shopper site, at www.computershopper.com, and Price Watch, at www.pricewatch.com.

Both these Web sites enable you to search for computer goodies from many different manufacturers, and both offer specials on overstocked parts. You can display side-by-side comparison charts of different parts so that you can compare features and performance online and then check for the site with the current lowest price without ever leaving the comfort of that swivel chair you bought for the computer room.

If the computer you're using has a printer, you can use your browser to print full descriptions of the parts you're researching. These descriptions can come in handy later when you have to make that final decision on which brand to buy.

Most of these Web sites accept only credit cards, although they offer secure connections if you're using Netscape Navigator or Microsoft Internet Explorer. The guidelines I mention for mail-order purchases apply to online ordering too.

Finding bargains in so-called obsolete computers

Most computers now being replaced or scrapped actually work just fine. For most of us, a computer generally doesn't become obsolete until it no longer runs the programs you want to use. I have several friends who are still quite pleased with their 486-based computers — they're not technical wizards and they don't use their computers very often. Besides, if they can still run WordPerfect for DOS and PrintMaster, their older computers suit them just fine.

You won't find any single answer to why a computer is deemed obsolete, but the answer doesn't matter all that much. The important point is that lots of people are upgrading their computers, which gives you a great opportunity to scavenge this perfectly functional, used equipment for your own computer.

Here are some reasons that people replace their "outdated" computer equipment:

✔ For some technowizards, a computer becomes outdated the moment a faster CPU hits the scene. Because these people are always on the leading edge of technology, they upgrade continually — and continually get rid of older, yet functional, equipment. It's a great opportunity to get your hands on some good used gear.

✔ Although you may not believe it at first, it's not network computers or office PCs that wear out their welcome the quickest — that dubious honor goes to the PCs used by the computer gaming crowd. Computer games now demand much more horsepower and advanced hardware than the average office suite of programs is likely to need. Computer games are a good source of used equipment.

✔ The Internet is also a major reason that people are replacing their older computers — connecting to the Web by using Windows 98 is easier, and the plug-ins and mulltimedia animation offered by the Web don't run well on older hardware. Some people think "New Web technology? Time to upgrade!" (and time for you to scam on their "older" equipment).

Look in the classified ads in your local newspaper (or check some of the resources mentioned in the section "Picking Up the Parts," earlier in this chapter). You're likely to find hundreds of people looking to unload their computer equipment — often at bargain-basement prices.

Scavenging can be fun!

For a computer technonerd, nothing is more exciting than rooting around in an older computer and looking for spare parts — there's no telling what treasures you may uncover! RAM chips, a tape backup unit, or perhaps just a hard drive cable: All these components can go into your parts box for that next project or for a quick repair if a component fails on your new computer.

For your scavenging pleasure, here are a number of possible sources for used parts:

- **Computer stores:** Each time I visit my favorite local computer store and repair shop — hi, guys! — I always ask whether they have any "new" (recently removed) used parts. Because these techies are always upgrading computers, they often hang on to the older parts, which they may be more than happy to sell to you at a reduced price. This technique won't work with the MegaMultiMillion Computer Mall — they don't sell used parts. In fact, you may get stuck with that "used-car" computer salesperson again.

- **Computer user groups:** If you're a member of a local computer user group, ask around at the next meeting to see whether anyone has a spare video card or CD-ROM they'd be willing to sell. If you're lucky, you may even get an offer of help with installing it. Some user groups can get special pricing on hardware and software through special arrangements with manufacturers, too.

- **The Web:** A number of online companies specialize in selling used computer hardware on the Web. Many of these sites let you buy your components with a credit card over a secure Web connection, too. Try eBay, at www.ebay.com, or the ONSALE Online Auction Supersite, at www.onsale.com; both sites offer new and used components online, through a real-time auction. Or try Web sites like Computer Discount Warehouse, at www.cdw.com; TechShopper, at www.techweb.com/shopper; or The Used Computer Mall, at www.usedcomputer.com, for super deals.

- **Computer bulletin board systems:** Do you or someone else in your family have access to a modem? Why not call a *BBS?* In the Grand Old Days before the arrival of the Internet, these computer *bulletin board systems* were the kings of cyberspace. Even today, tens of thousands of bulletin boards are still operating online throughout the country. If you live in just about any middle- to large-size town, at least one or two bulletin board systems is likely to carry advertisements to sell used computer equipment.

- **Friends and family:** Is Uncle Milton using that old original Pentium to hold up the garage wall? After you're known in your family as a computer guru, you'll likely be presented with all sorts of older equipment. Friends will approach you for your opinion on how much they can get for their older computer (which is the perfect opportunity to make an offer of your own).

- **Garage sales:** I've found hundreds of dollars worth of good parts at local garage sales and bought them for pennies! Typically, you have to buy the entire computer, but as long as everything is working, you can get a really great deal. Make sure that you plug the computer in and check it out before handing over the cash.

✔ **Classified ads:** Here's another source for used parts — unfortunately, though, most owners who advertise in the classifieds think that their computers are worth far more than they actually are, so it may take some haggling to get a good price.

What's the deal with used parts?

Why do I continue to jabber away about used parts — after all, you're building a new computer, so why the heck should you add old parts to it? One reason is pretty obvious: A used part can cost half as much as a new part — an important consideration if you're trying to save money. You may even find someone willing to give you an older computer, from which you can scavenge components for your new computer.

If you're building your first computer, you may be surprised to discover that most computer parts can last for many years — for example, keyboards, and mice can operate just as well on your new Pentium III computer as they did on that older 486 computer. Circuit boards and solid-state electrical components are surprisingly strong and hardy, and they have a long operational life.

You can find an increasing number of older computers out there, which you can buy for peanuts — it's their *CPUs* that just can't keep up with today's software. However, all the *other* parts within that older computer work fine, and they can continue to work fine in your new computer for many years. The modular design of today's computers enables you to yank a circuit board easily from an older computer, and you can be pretty safe in assuming that it can work on your new machine. For example, you can easily remove a Sound Blaster AWE-32 sound card from a 486 computer and plug it right into your new computer.

If you decide to add used parts to your computer, you need to make sure of two things beforehand: You must make sure that the used parts are working fine and that they are not too old for your computer. As I discuss each computer component in other chapters, I provide a description of which types of used items are suitable for an Athlon or Pentium III computer.

In general, you can scavenge used parts from a 486 computer to build Design 1 (which I discuss in the section "Answering Your Computer-Needs Questions," earlier in this chapter). You can even scavenge some components (such as a floppy drive, computer case, or keyboard) from an older 386 computer. Design 2 can also benefit from a used floppy drive, computer case, mouse, and keyboard. However, if you're a power user and you're building a computer based on Design 3, I suggest that you buy only the latest new parts — older technology that wasn't designed for Pentium III and Athlon speeds will just slow down your supercomputer.

Part II
Building Your PC

The 5th Wave   By Rich Tennant

"RIGHT NOW I'M KEEPING A LOW PROFILE. LAST NIGHT I CRANKED IT ALL UP AND BLEW OUT THREE BLOCKS OF STREETLIGHTS."

In this part . . .

The real fun commences as you build a "bare-bones" PC from the ground up. You install the required stuff that every computer needs, such as RAM modules, a CPU, circuit boards, a hard drive, and a video card. If that sounds a little frightening, don't worry; I explain each part in detail, and each chapter ends with a general set of step-by-step installation instructions that give you a good idea of what you can expect. After you're done with this part, you'll be able to boot your new computer. *Remember:* All you need is a screwdriver!

Chapter 3

Building the Foundation: Your Case and Motherboard

● ●

In This Chapter

▶ Getting acquainted with your computer case

▶ Choosing a case

▶ Selecting a motherboard

▶ Guarding against static

▶ Installing your motherboard

▶ Connecting the power supply

▶ Hooking up the lights and buttons

● ●

*Y*ou don't have to be an architect or a construction foreman to know that a building is only as good as its foundation. Build a skyscraper on sand and it doesn't matter how well you wallpaper the bathrooms or how fast the elevators run. Eventually, a building with a weak foundation will fall, and it's certain to take everything with it.

In this chapter, you discover the various components that are common to all computer cases. I show you how to construct a sturdy foundation for your computer by selecting the right size and type of computer case, which provides the framework that houses all your other computer components. I introduce you to the geography of your motherboard; then you find out how to install the motherboard and connect it to the computer's power supply.

After you put together your computer's chassis, you find out how to add new components, such as a hard drive and a CD-ROM, to this chassis and continue your construction project in later chapters.

A Case Is Not Just a Box

Why is selecting the proper case for your computer so important?

- If you're a *power user* (someone with considerable computer experience or someone who needs a powerful computer for advanced applications), you need room to expand. Adding devices and other toys can easily lead you to outgrow a standard desktop case. Believe me, it's a royal pain to upgrade to a larger one — you basically have to disassemble your entire computer, remove the motherboard and other components, and move them all to a larger case. Keep this upgrade possibility in mind when you select your case, and think about your future needs.

- If your desktop space is limited, you can save yourself some of that valuable real estate by selecting a tower case and placing it underneath your desk.

- Today's cases even come in designer colors and shapes, so you can pick up an aerodynamic case in black or olive green, if you like (but keep in mind that you'll probably find it difficult to find other parts in such exotic colors later on). Most computer components with external faceplates — like CD-ROMs and floppy drives — come only in almond or white, which tend to stand out like a sore thumb in a black case. That's why the primary colors for computer cases are still off white and almond, and I recommend that you stick with them — unless you want a computer that looks like you assembled it at the junkyard.

New hard drives, CD-ROM or DVD drives, and tape backup components can be added inside the case in what are called *drive bays*. Most cases have at least one or two rectangular cutouts in the front of these empty drive bays. You can use these open bays to hold parts that need access to the outside world (after all, it's a little hard to load a CD-ROM or a floppy disk into a drive if it's buried inside the case). When an open bay is empty, it's covered with a rectangular plastic piece that blends in with the outside of the case. Other drive bays remain hidden; these bays are usually reserved for additional hard drives, which don't need to be handled during routine use.

Most new cases come with the mounting hardware necessary to attach your motherboard, although it never hurts to ask. You need screws and plastic spacers, and they should be included with either the case or the motherboard.

You can choose from three standard types of cases, each of which gives you a certain amount of elbow room for upgrading.

Pizza-box case

Figure 3-1 illustrates the *pizza-box case,* which is very thin — and before you ask, it's not made of cardboard. This case doesn't offer much in the way of open drive bays (it has probably one — perhaps two — drive bays at the most). You may not be able to add any adapter cards, but this case does take up the smallest amount of space of any standard computer case. In fact, your friends may speculate that your computer has been working out nights at the gym.

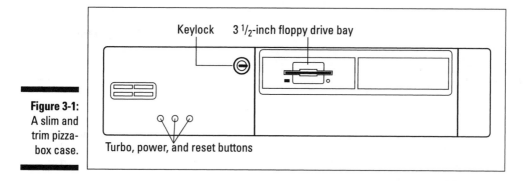

Figure 3-1:
A slim and
trim pizza-
box case.

Pizza-box cases are typically used for network workstations or as simple terminals, so I don't recommend that you buy one of these for your home computer. However, if you're building an economy-class machine and you want to save space as well as money, the pizza-box case may be fine.

Pizza-box cases don't offer much room for later upgrades.

Desktop case

The next case in our fashion show is the traditional *desktop case,* as shown in Figure 3-2. This case usually sits horizontally on your desk, just like those old ponderous PC-XT and AT cases did back in the ancient 1980s. Today's desktop case has gone on a diet, and the days of those behemoths are long gone. The desktop case is not as compact as the pizza-box case, although it's still not much bigger than two loaves of bread placed side-by-side; some new desktop cases can switch back and forth between horizontal mode and vertical mode, depending on the orientation you prefer.

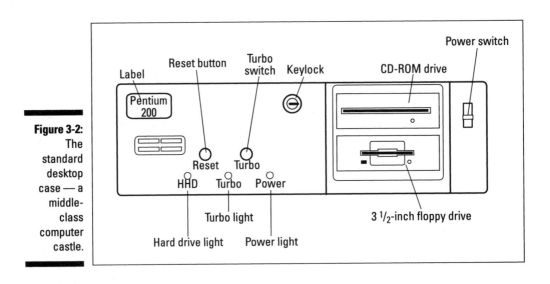

Figure 3-2:
The
standard
desktop
case — a
middle-
class
computer
castle.

The desktop case usually provides two or three open drive bays on the front, with one or two hidden bays. This case typically has room for a standard seven or eight adapter cards in the back. This setup is usually par for the course for a home computer, and, unless you're a power user, the desktop case is your case of choice.

Tower case

For the technogeek or power user who has everything, we have the Ferrari of cases — the brawny *tower case,* which sits vertically, like an old mainframe computer. As shown in Figure 3-3, many tower cases have four, or even five, open drive bays. If you're planning on stuffing your computer full of extras, this is the case for you. Like the desktop case, the tower case has room for a standard seven or eight adapter cards in back. Because of the weight and size of a fully outfitted tower case, it is designed to sit upright on the floor under your desk, where you can comfortably reach all the buttons and the CD-ROM drive.

Many manufacturers also produce a *minitower* case, which still sits vertically, like a tower case, but is designed to fit comfortably next to the monitor on top of your desk. An average minitower case has the drive bay capacity equal to that of a standard desktop case.

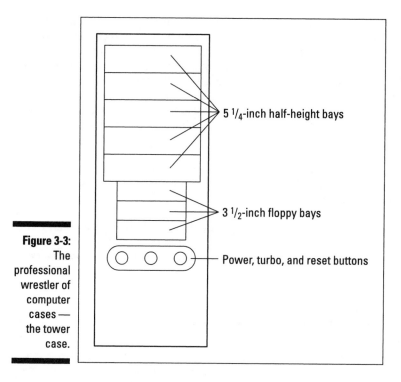

5 ¹/₄-inch half-height bays

3 ¹/₂-inch floppy bays

Power, turbo, and reset buttons

Figure 3-3:
The professional wrestler of computer cases — the tower case.

Feed me . . . feed me . . . feed me . . .

Your new computer will be hungry for power, and the *power supply* takes care of that need by reducing the voltage from your wall socket to something more easily handled by your computer. The power supply then pumps the juice to the computer's components through a number of individual power cables.

These cables end in a special connector you can insert in only one direction, so it's well-nigh impossible to make a mistake and damage a hard drive or CD-ROM because of an electrical short caused by a reversed connection. An ATX motherboard has only one power connector, and older AT motherboards require two power connectors. I show you how to connect both types later in this chapter.

Most cases are now sold with the power supply already installed; a prein-stalled power supply not only eliminates a step in building your PC but also ensures that you get a power supply of the proper rating. In addition, all the holes for the switches and cables match up.

The more powerful the CPU, the more power it generally draws — and the more powerful the case fan and the processor fan must be to cool it. Also, power users tend to stuff their computers full of all sorts of neat hardware toys, each of which draws its own power. For these reasons, I *strongly* suggest that you invest in a case that includes at least a 300-watt power supply if you're going to build a computer using a Pentium III or Athlon processor, especially if you're going to add a slew of internal extras, like a CD recorder and tape backup drive. (In fact, AMD already recommends at least a 300-watt power supply for the Athlon.)

If you buy a used case, make sure that it comes complete with a power supply and a working fan. You should also make sure that the power supply is UL listed and FCC approved.

A used power supply by itself isn't worth much, especially if it was built to fit a nonstandard case. *Never* open up a power supply to try to fix it or massage it to work in a particular case. *Live household voltage is not a welcome visitor within the human body.*

Keeping your computer cool

Because all the various devices and components in your computer produce lots of heat, your computer can actually shut down, lock up, or return errors if it gets too hot. Extended overheating reduces the operational life of your parts — especially your CPU — and leads to early failure. How does your computer keep its cool through this heat wave?

The answer is nothing elaborate or high-tech — in fact, it's just a fan! Your computer's power supply uses a fan to continually circulate air through the inside of the case. Smaller pizza-box cases and standard-size desktop cases are small enough to require only one fan. However, if you're thinking of buying a tower case and your computer will use an Athlon or Pentium III CPU (which run even hotter than the original Pentium and Pentium II processors), I highly recommend that you buy a case with *dual fans*. Dual fans are a definite requirement if this type of computer is going to stay on for many hours at a time or if it's jammed full of parts and devices. Ball-bearing fans are preferred because they last longer.

CPU chips now run so hot that they come equipped with their own dedicated fan, which sits on top of or beside the processor to keep it cool. This fan is connected to one of the power cables leading to the power supply. If a CPU overheats, it generally locks up your computer or returns some *really* strange results within your programs — and it will more than likely be permanently damaged.

Dust busting!

Conputers need an internal fan to keep all the sensitive electronics cool. This circulating air has a drawback: All the internal parts within your new computer get dusty over time — opening your computer's case every year or so in order to blow the dust off your motherboard, power supply, and all the various devices you've installed is important. Accumulated dust can act like an insulating blanket and cause chips and electrical parts to overheat.

Before you open your case to upgrade or clear off the dust, head to your local computer store or photography shop and grab some *canned*

air — you know, one of those spray cans that shoots a compressed stream of air for dusting off cameras and computer parts. Take particular care in dusting off your motherboard and the fan intake on your power supply (which is likely to be filthy). Canned air is also handy for cleaning keyboards and adapter cards. Help out your planet by making sure that you pick a brand that doesn't deplete the ozone layer, and don't make the mistake of buying one of those air horns that the football types use at the game. (Take my word for it: They don't work, and they annoy the neighbors.)

After your computer is running, it's also a good idea to place it where the fan exhaust isn't blocked by a wall or furniture. An open location provides a better airflow.

Buttons, lights, and other foolishness

Most cases today have a power light and a hard drive activity light — your motherboard runs these components. Some older computer cases also feature a *digital readout* of the computer's speed. These shameless consumer light shows are absolutely worthless (except as technoweenie ego-enhancers), and they're rarely used. A digital readout has to be manually configured, and not all motherboards support it, so don't spend any extra money to get one, unless you're the type who has seen all the *Star Trek* movies a dozen times each.

As for buttons, your case probably has a power button and a reset button; it may also have a turbo button (which is about as useful on today's computers as your appendix is for you). I actively despise key locks and, if your case comes with one, I recommend that you ignore it.

Your case should also include a simple speaker, which looks just like the speaker in an inexpensive pocket radio. Although you will definitely want to add a multimedia sound card and external speakers to your computer to take full advantage of today's software (see Chapter 9 for more about multimedia sound), this little internal speaker still performs an important task: If something is wrong when you start your computer, the speaker alerts you with a number of beeps.

Other than these standard items, your case can be as plain or as elegantly sculpted as you wish. Naturally, designer cases from Gucci cost you more, but you can subtly boast about your computer's good taste at parties, editors will want your picture in their fashion magazines, and you could become one of the "in" crowd. It could happen.

How about those slots?

Your case has a number of holes on the back, which are meant for *adapter cards.* Each of these slot openings enables you to screw in a bracket that attaches to an adapter card, holding the card firmly in place. If the card has any *external ports,* they are also visible through the back of the case.

Most cases have these slots open, although the slots need to be covered. Adding slot covers involves a little manual labor. If your slots are already covered, scoot to the next section; or, if you'll be installing at least one or two adapter cards in later chapters, leave one or two slots uncovered to save yourself the trouble of removing them again.

Keeping your computer castle secure

Even if security is a consideration, I *still* wouldn't use the key lock that comes on your computer case — it can be foiled by simply taking the cover off the computer and disconnecting the wire. Often, you find that cases manufactured by the same company have the same key pattern, so one key in an office may unlock half the computers in the building,. Also, keys tend to lose themselves easily.

If you need to prevent access to your computer while you get a cup of java or a can of caffeine-laden soda, use a Windows 98 screen saver with the password option. If you need tighter security, a number of encryption utilities on the market can prevent anyone from accessing your data, and they work completely through software, so you can forget about a silly metal key.

Another surefire security measure is to use a *boot password,* which prevents your computer from running unless you enter the correct password. Most motherboards can be configured to require a boot password through the BIOS menu.

Follow these instructions to close up the slot holes in the back of your case:

1. **Check the parts that came with your case to find the slot covers (*slot covers* are thin, metal strips with a bend at the top).**

   You should also find a number of screws that fit into the screw holes at the top of each slot opening.

2. **Lay your open case down on top of your work surface.**

   You should be able to clearly see the screw holes and the slot openings at the back of your case.

3. **Slide a slot cover over one of the slot openings so that the screw hole lines up with the screw hole in the case, as shown in Figure 3-4.**

4. **Insert and tighten the screw to hold the cover over the opening.**

5. **Repeat Steps 3 and 4 until all the slot openings are covered.**

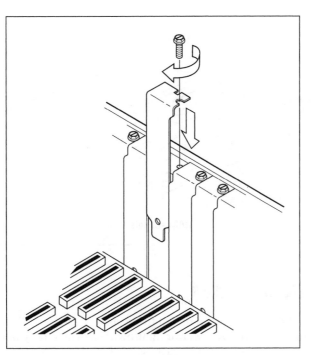

Figure 3-4:
Covering a vacant slot opening with a slot cover.

Your Best Friend Is Your Motherboard

Figure 3-5 shows the main features of the heart and soul of your computer —
its motherboard. The motherboard holds most of the electronics and circuits
your computer needs in order to follow your orders. Depending on the type
of processor you've chosen, the top of your motherboard has a big square or
slot socket to hold your computer's CPU chip and several rows of small slots
to hold your RAM modules.

Five years ago, buying a motherboard by itself used to be much harder. However, with the constant acceleration of CPU speeds and the requirements of
today's software, guys in the mall are now selling motherboards rather than ice
cream. Some companies that advertise in *Computer Shopper* magazine or operate Web-based parts stores sell nothing but motherboards. And you can generally buy a bare motherboard at your local computer store if it has a repair shop.

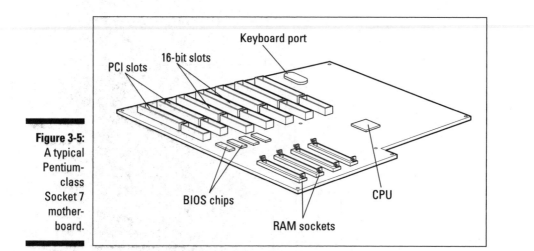

Figure 3-5:
A typical
Pentium-
class
Socket 7
mother-
board.

Keyboard port

16-bit slots

PCI slots

BIOS chips

RAM sockets

CPU

Motherboard sizes

Motherboards typically come in one of three sizes these days: Baby AT, AT,
and ATX (in order of size). A tower or minitower case generally holds any of
the three sizes, whereas a desktop case typically holds a Baby AT- or AT-size
motherboard.

Buying your motherboard first is a good idea, to ensure that you get a case
that accepts your board. If you've found a used case or motherboard, make
sure that whatever you buy fits your existing part. For example, an ATX motherboard requires an ATX case and an ATX power supply — an AT-size motherboard doesn't fit in an ATX case. Most Athlon and III motherboards require an
ATX case.

Don't give me any static!

Before you install your motherboard in your case, it's time for a short warning about the dangers of *static electricity*. Static can damage electrical components in the blink of an eye, and not even Thomas Edison himself could fix them. I won't launch into a terribly interesting discussion of how static was discovered in 400 B.C. by somebody we don't know with a piece of silk and a glass rod — for all I care, the discovery of static electricity could have been made by prehistoric man walking across a bearskin rug.

Instead, just remember this simple rule while handling motherboards, adapter cards, circuit boards, and other computer parts: Before installing any circuit board, adapter card, or part on your computer (or before removing it from the case), discharge any static electricty you may be harboring by touching something else

made of metal. You can also discharge static by touching your spouse on the earlobe, although I don't recommend this method.

If you follow this rule, you can forget that static electricity even exists! Typically, the metal chassis of your computer is a good choice, although you can also touch a metal table or chair. If your computer is plugged in with the cover off (which happens quite often when you're installing a hard drive or adapter card), you can touch the metal housing of your power suply for a perfect ground.

Antistatic strips are available too for keyboards and wrist rests that discharge static. However, the only time I ever worry about static is when I'm handling parts and circuit boards, so I don't use one of these items every day.

Motherboard features

While you're shopping for a motherboard, keep these guidelines in mind:

- ✔ **Stick with a bare minimum of a 233 MHz Pentium II.** You may have a strong temptation to jump on a great price for an original Pentium motherboard. No matter what the processor speed, however, you'll be buying yesterday's technology, and you won't have the Pentium-class power you need for running many current (or future) programs and operating systems. Even if the advertisement reads "A Good Pick for Windows 95 or Windows 98," say good-bye to the Pentium (as readers of the original edition of this book said good-bye to the 486).

  Okay, okay — so I guess if you were *given* a 233 MHz Pentium motherboard by your next-door neighbor, you can use it — but don't expect it to keep up with the latest software. Pentium III prices have dropped so significantly that even the Pentium II computer has all but vanished from store shelves.

- ✔ **Shop for a larger cache.** All Pentium-class motherboards offer a feature called *cache memory*. In effect, cache memory is a "waiting room" for data the CPU uses. The larger the cache, the better. Most motherboards that use a socket-style processor come with at least 256K worth of cache memory — if you're a power user, though, you should demand at least 1MB. (Depending on the CPU you choose, your processor may carry its own on-board cache as well.)

✔ **Consider an onboard drive controller.** Power users favor an *onboard EIDE drive controller,* an *UltraDMA/66 controller,* or a *SCSI controller* on a standard Pentium-series motherboard, which gives your computer faster performance and convenience. (See Chapter 7 for more information on EIDE and SCSI drives.) A motherboard with an onboard controller doesn't need a separate hard drive/floppy drive controller (therefore, you can save that adapter slot for another toy).

✔ **Spending extra for onboard ports is worth it.** Like an onboard drive controller, onboard serial and parallel ports save an adapter slot (jump to Chapter 5 for the lowdown on serial and parallel ports). In fact, some motherboards even have video cards built-in, although I prefer to add my own video adapter. If you buy an ATX motherboard, these ports should (by definition) already be on-board.

If you do get a built-in controller and onboard ports, you need to make sure of a few things. First, make sure that the controller supports *four* enhanced IDE devices (as an example, this type of controller enables you to run two hard drives, an IDE CD-ROM, and an IDE tape backup drive). Second, onboard serial and parallel ports should be capable of high-speed operation — the serial ports should use *16550 UART chips* so that you can use the latest high-speed modems, and the parallel ports should be ECP/EPP. The motherboard should also allow you to disable your onboard serial and parallel ports. This advice may sound like ancient Greek, but the salesperson on the other end of the phone should know exactly what you're talking about. If not, find a better source for your motherboard.

Of course, if you've already scavenged an EIDE hard drive controller or a high-speed port adapter card, you don't need these features built-in to the motherboard, and you can go with a cheaper board.

✔ **Make sure that your new motherboard has at least two PCI slots and one AGP slot.** If you're scavenging, you can use an older Pentium mother-board with standard ISA slots, although the newer PCI technology provides better performance for some adapter cards (for example, a PCI video capture card or a hard drive controller card). Your AGP slot, on the other hand, will be dedicated to your video card.

Every motherboard carries a set of chips called the *BIOS.* This time, the silly acronym stands for *Basic Input-Output System.* Your BIOS determines much of what your computer can do and also controls what happens for different types of input. For example, your BIOS keeps track of what hard drives and floppy drives you can use, what happens when you press a key on the keyboard, and how data is read and written to RAM. You can usually forget about your computer's BIOS and just let it do its work, but if your computer suffers a hardware failure or a really serious error, it's your BIOS that displays the error message. Most computers today use one of three or four brand-name BIOS chipsets, such as Intel, Award, Phoenix, or AMI.

✔ **Buy a motherboard with Flash BIOS.** You may see a board advertised as having "Flash BIOS," which sounds like the name of a hero from a science fiction film. This is actually a good feature; it enables you to update the capabilities of your computer with new features and bug fixes.

✔ **Shop for Plug and Play.** Here's another BIOS feature you should demand: *Plug and Play,* which enables your computer to automatically configure many common adapter cards. Windows 98 and Windows Me really take advantage of a motherboard with Plug and Play BIOS if you have it.

✔ **Random access memory.** All motherboards have a maximum amount of RAM (or *Random Access Memory*) they can handle. Unless NASA has picked you to control the next shuttle launch, a board that supports 256MB or 512MB (megabytes) of RAM should be sufficient. Real technonerds or ultrapower users may demand support for a gigabyte (1024MB) of RAM, although it's not likely that they'll ever use it all on a personal computer.

Grab Your Screwdriver and Install That Motherboard

It's showtime! Get ready to add your motherboard to your system case. Follow these steps:

1. **Protect your new motherboard from static electricity you picked up from your lava lamp or from Trixie, the family Persian cat — touch a metal surface beforehand.**

2. **Cover your work surface with a piece or two of newspaper and lay your open case down on top of the newspaper.**

   You should be able to clearly see the screw holes and the plastic spacer guides where the motherboard will sit. Check any documentation that came with your case for any special instructions.

3. **Hold the motherboard by the edges and lay it down inside the case in order to align it.**

   All the electrical components (like your CPU socket, memory sockets, and adapter slots) should be on top; the underside of the circuit board should have no components on it. To align the case, make sure that the adapter card slots line up with the slots cut into the back of the case, as shown in Figure 3-6.

4. **Now note which screw holes line up with the screw holes in your motherboard, and mark their position on a piece of paper.**

   Most cases use only two or three screws to hold the board, and the rest of the board is supported and held rigid by plastic spacers. These spacers usually slide under a metal tab or a metal guide — they serve to keep your motherboard away from any possible dangerous contact with the metal of your computer case. You may find in your motherboard manual additional help on locating these holes.

5. **Remove the motherboard from the case and add the plastic spacers to the holes (in your motherboard) that need them.**

   Figure 3-7 illustrates how you should push the spacers through the holes from the bottom of the board — the spacers should snap firmly into place.

6. **Before you install the motherboard, take a few minutes to check for any switches or jumpers that may need to be set.**

   Most motherboards are shipped with default settings that work fine, although it pays to check anyway. Older motherboards were configured with DIP switches (little banks of slide or rocker switches) and jumpers, which are pins you can connect with a small plastic-and-metal collar. (New Pentium-class motherboards are designed for people like you and me who hate poking and moving tiny things, so they rarely need any configuration.)

   Just in case: If you need to set a DIP switch, use a pen to push the plastic sliders into the correct order, as shown in Figure 3-8, where switches 4 and 6 have been set to On.

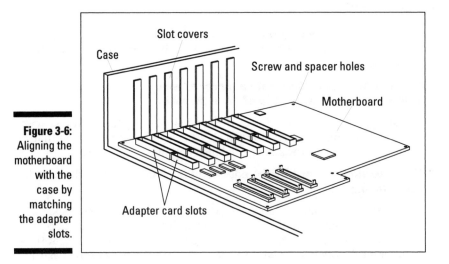

Figure 3-6:
Aligning the motherboard with the case by matching the adapter slots.

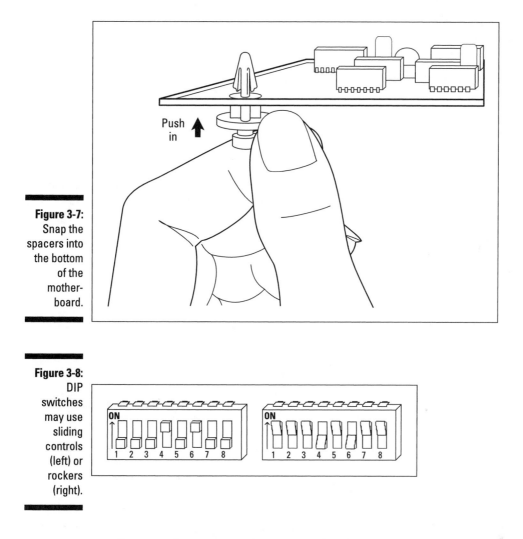

Figure 3-7:
Snap the
spacers into
the bottom
of the
mother-
board.

Figure 3-8:
DIP
switches
may use
sliding
controls
(left) or
rockers
(right).

If you need to set a jumper, use your fingers or a set of tweezers to lift the plastic jumper and seat it into the correct position — Figure 3-9 shows a jumper on pins 1 and 2 of jumper J1.

7. **Pick up your motherboard by the edges and slide it into place, making sure that all the plastic spacers are correctly positioned.**

Don't get upset if it takes a few tries, and don't bend or force anything — I've never installed a motherboard on my first attempt. Once again, make certain that the adapter slots line up with the slots in the case as before. After the motherboard is in, gently check each corner of the board to make sure that it's correctly seated and doesn't wobble.

Figure 3-9:
A pair of
tweezers
comes in
handy when
setting a
jumper.

8. **You're ready to lock it down. Put in the screws, but don't overtighten them — circuit boards tend to crack if you do.**

   Some boards come with thin, nonconductive washers for the screws, so don't forget to use them if they were included.

That's it! Congratulations — see, that wasn't that hard, was it?

You've completed your computer's basic chassis. In the next section, you connect the cables needed to provide power to the motherboard.

I Laugh at Pesky Wires!

The hard part of installing your motherboard is over, but the process isn't complete. You still need to connect the wires from the power supply as well as those wires to the buttons and lights on the front of your case. This is a good time to take care of these chores because your motherboard is easy to work with right now; you have unrestricted access to all the pins and connectors on your motherboard, with no adapter cards or cables hanging around to interfere with your work.

Special power switch instructions for an AT motherboard

Are you installing a scavenged AT motherboard? Your power switch isn't connected to your motherboard! Instead, the cable to be connected to the power switch on your case comes from the power supply itself, so check the documentation that came with your case and power supply to determine what type of connector it uses. Some cases have a power switch mounted on the back — you don't have a power switch wire in this case because the switch is internally wired to the power supply. If you're installing an ATX motherboard (virtually all new motherboards are ATX these days), the power switch does indeed plug directly into the motherboard.

Pumping power to your motherboard

The first connection you make is the most important — connecting the motherboard to the power supply. To connect the two cables that supply power to the motherboard, follow these steps:

1. **If your case is plugged in to a wall socket, unplug it first.**

2. **Locate the two power connectors on your motherboard.**

   Again, if you need help in finding the power connectors, check your motherboard manual. Can you see why I recommend that you save all the documentation for your hardware? If you're installing an ATX motherboard, the two power cables are combined into one cable, and the plug is designed to connect only one way, so things are easier — yet another reason to build a PC with an ATX case!

   If you're installing an older AT motherboard, the two power cables for your motherboard look different from all the other cables that sprout from one side of the power supply — they have long, flat connectors. Although these connectors work only one way, two of them are on an AT motherboard. Which one goes in which plug?

3. **If you're installing an AT motherboard, align the two cables so that the black wires are next to each other, as shown in Figure 3-10, and you should have the connectors in the right configuration.**

   Just line up the pins and press down gently until the connectors snap in place.

Figure 3-10:
The right way to connect the power cables to your motherboard.

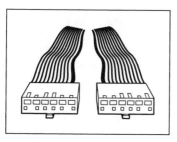

Connecting power cables may seem kind of scary the first time you do it, but even if you connect the cables on an AT motherboard in the wrong order, you won't hurt your motherboard — it just won't work. To fix it, simply swap positions on the cables.

Flashing lights, clicking switches, and a beeper to boot

Follow these steps to connect the motherboard to the various switches and lights (and your all-important PC speaker) on your case:

1. **Check the documentation that came with your case to determine which wires lead to which lights and switches.**

   Typically, you get to play "match the colors." For example, the connector on the green and white wires may be for the turbo button, and the red and white wires may be the PC speaker.

   Are you using a secondhand case without any documentation? If so, you can still determine what's connected to what with a bit of electrical detective work. Follow the wires back to their source, and jot down what switch or light each one is connected to — and don't forget to save that piece of paper for the next time you perform surgery on your computer.

2. **After you determine which connector is which, refer to your motherboard manual for the location of the following pins.**

   On most motherboards, these words (or an abbreviation) are also printed right next to the pins, making it easier to locate them if you don't have a copy of the manual:

   - **Power Light or Power LED:** This is the power light on the front of the case.

   - **Turbo Switch or Turbo Sw:** If your motherboard has a turbo switch connector, these two pins should be connected to the turbo switch wire. The turbo switch lets you select between your computer's top speed, or *turbo mode,* and a much slower speed. Years ago, running at a slower speed helped the computer run older PC software, like the first PC games. Most computer owners *never* leave turbo mode anymore, although it takes awhile for computers to evolve. If your case doesn't have a turbo switch, all the better!

   - **Turbo Light or Turbo LED:** This is the turbo light on the front of the case; it's normally lit, indicating that your computer is running in turbo mode. Your case may not have a turbo light.

   - **HDD Light or HD LED:** This is the hard-drive activity light on the front of the case; it lights whenever your computer accesses your hard drive, so it's flickering just about all the time.

   - **Reset:** This is the reset switch on the front of the case; you press it when your computer is locked up.

- **Key Lock:** This leads to the key lock on the front of your case; if your computer is locked with the key, your keyboard is disabled. The key lock is another anachronism from the ancient days of the 1980s, and thankfully most cases today have eliminated this irritating little feature; I've never used it, nor has anyone else I know. Unless you have some pressing need for this type of security, *don't spend extra money to get it* — if your case has a key lock, feel free to leave its wires disconnected.

- **Speaker or Spk:** This wire should lead to your computer's internal speaker — even if you plan on adding a sound card later, you need to connect the speaker. It provides audio error messages that can help you diagnose problems with your computer — in fact, you use these audio error messages in the next chapter.

3. **Attach each of the cables to their corresponding pins on the motherboard by pushing the connector onto the pins, as shown in Figure 3-11.**

Figure 3-11:
Connecting
cables from
your case
to your
mother-
board.

For most cables, it doesn't matter which way the connector is facing; if a connector needs to be reversed, you can fix it in the next chapter, when you run your first tests.

Chapter 4

A Bag of Chips: Adding RAM and Your CPU

- -

In This Chapter

▶ Evaluating today's CPUs

▶ Plugging in your CPU

▶ Adding system RAM

▶ Figuring out the type of bus slots you have

▶ Testing your work

- -

*A*fter you install the motherboard inside your computer's case, your PC may still be missing one or two very important parts: its brain (the *central processing unit,* or CPU) or its memory (the *Random Access Memory,* or RAM). When you run a computer program, your computer's CPU actually performs the calculations and executes the commands stored in that program. Your computer's RAM acts as a work area for the program, storing data, changing it, and retrieving it as required by the program. (Athlon, Duron, Pentium II and Pentium III PCs use DIMM memory — short for *Dual Inline Memory Module,* if you hadn't guessed — and older Pentium-class computers use SIMM memory, short for *Single Inline Memory Module.*)

As an example, if you run an address book program on your computer, your CPU can use the instructions within the program to search for names or print address labels, and your computer's RAM stores all those names and addresses until you exit the program.

It's a good idea these days to buy a motherboard with the CPU and RAM modules preinstalled — you don't need to worry about compatibility problems or installation hassles with this type of motherboard. (There are differences in socket types, voltage requirements, and physical measurements within both the Pentium and Athlon lines of CPU chips, so not every motherboard accepts every CPU.) If your motherboard comes with these chips preinstalled, you can skip most of this chapter and visit your local miniature golf course for a heady 18 holes. Don't forget, though — I need you back here to test your chassis in the last section of this chapter.

If you need to install either your CPU or your memory, this chapter will attach itself to you like a sucker fish to the side of an aquarium, and you'll have to follow the appropriate steps and then test your chassis.

FYI about CPUs

You can choose from a number of CPU models these days, and you may be able to save a little money while shopping if you're faced with a decision between manufacturers and speeds. Therefore, let's review the general characteristics of the current crop of computer cranium components! I take them in order of price and power, starting with the low-end processors.

I mention this question earlier in this book, but the question bears repeating: What's the difference between a 450 MHz Pentium III CPU and a 600 MHz Pentium III CPU? No, it's not a trick question! Because the processors are the same type, it's the *speed* (expressed in megahertz, or MHz). When you're shopping for the processors I describe in this section, make sure that you get at least the speed I recommend in Chapter 2. Alternatively, you can simply buy the fastest possible processor you can afford.

Celeron, Duron, and Cyrix III processors

These three processors were designed for the "price-conscious consumer." In other words, although you get lots of bang for your buck from these CPUs, they're not as advanced and don't have the extra punch of their more expensive brethren. Don't get me wrong, though: Any one of these three processors is still more than speedy enough to power a typical family PC.

The Intel Celeron: The darling of the low-cost crowd

The Celeron, designed by Intel as a cheaper alternative to the Pentium II (and, later, the Pentium III), works quite well if you're building a midrange computer for use with an office suite — or if you plan to explore the Internet. The Celeron has a lower amount of cache memory, so it's not as efficient as the Pentium III, and its raw megahertz speed rating is typically slower than a full-blown Pentium III. Although almost all Celerons are Slot 1 processors, make sure that you're buying the right version for your motherboard. Intel has produced a number of different variants in the past few years, and a new version is also available for Socket 370 motherboards. In other words, be careful not to buy a "vertical" chip for a "square" socket!

The AMD Duron: A bare-bones hot rod

Because the Duron was designed by AMD to compete directly with the Celeron, the Duron is significantly more efficient than a Celeron CPU of the same speed. Moreover, the Duron also has a faster megahertz figure than the current crop of Celerons. (At the time this chapter was written, the Duron was available in 600 MHz, 650 MHz, and 700 MHz versions). Unlike the Celeron, which handles data at 66 MHz or 133 MHz (that's the *bus speed*), the Duron has a 200 MHz bus; the faster the bus speed, the faster the CPU can send and receive data to other system components, like your video card and system RAM. On the downside, because it's a stripped-down Athlon, it typically also runs hotter. I therefore recommend that you pick up a bigger fan and power supply than those necessary for a Celeron. Like its bigger brother, the Athlon, the Duron CPU is a Socket A processor.

The VIA Cyrix III: The other guy

The Cyrix III is a somewhat radical departure from the other two processors in this category. It's a Socket 370 processor, so it's a flat-socketed processor that looks more like an older original Pentium chip or an AMD K6-2 CPU from days past. Although the Cyrix III has a higher bus speed at 133MHz than most older variants of the Celeron, it's not as speedy as the Duron, and its internal architecture is not as advanced as either the Duron's or the modern Celeron's. I usually recommend either the latest Celeron or the Duron over the Cyrix III.

Pentium III and Athlon processors

In this section, I cover the big CPU twosome that dominates the current PC scene. The Pentium III and the Athlon are suitable for midrange to high-end power-user systems. Either of these processors is my first recommendation for most folks playing the latest computer games, working with digital video or music, or using demanding business applications.

The Intel Pentium III: King of the hill

The Pentium III is the most popular CPU on the market, and with good reason: It's a fantastic all-around CPU. Although it's not quite as fast in raw speed as the Athlon, it's efficient, it runs with a wider range of motherboards, and it doesn't require the extra cooling and heavier power supply of the Athlon. It's a great choice for just about any PC. The Pentium III, a Slot 1 processor, runs on a motherboard with a 133 MHz bus.

The AMD Athlon: The tyrannosaurus rex of processors

The AMD Athlon is the fastest, most efficient, and most advanced CPU available at the time this chapter was written. It's the first processor generally available with a 1-*gigahertz* model. (Yes, friends and neighbors, I really do mean *one thousand megahertz!*) The Athlon outperforms the Pentium III in many respects and has a maximum bus speed of 266 MHz. But wait: Before you close this book and head to your Web browser, you should know that the Athlon is *not* the right choice for everyone. Like any sports car, the Athlon is significantly more expensive and, as I mention earlier in this chapter, requires a heftier fan and a 300-watt power supply to run in a well-outfitted PC. Plus, only a few motherboards are available that are approved for use with the Athlon. I would recommend it for technowizards who want absolutely the best performance available in a CPU or for those folks who want to look forward to three or four years of use before they plan to buy another motherboard or build another PC. The Athlon CPU is a Socket A processor.

The future

Although these next two processors are months from release and their names may change before they appear in any store, I can still introduce you to them. These incredible next-generation CPUs will leave the current crop of Pentium III and Athlon models in the dust!

The Intel Itanium

Talk about a monster: The Itanium will be the first Intel 64-bit CPU, with 4MB of onboard cache (rather than the "measly" 256K, 512K, or 1MB on today's fastest processors) that can handle as much as 16GB (that's gigabytes) of RAM. The Itanium will be able to perform six *billion* operations per second. I'd say that ought to set any technowizard's heart beating faster!

The AMD "sledgehammer"

The upcoming AMD CPU, code-named SledgeHammer, is another 64-bit processor that will deliver supercomputer performance. Not much information has been released about this chip, although AMD is already proud of the CPU's internal bandwidth. AMD swears that this chip will be capable of transferring 6.4 gigabytes per second between the CPU and its onboard cache. That's more than *20 times* the bandwidth of today's Athlon!

Your Monster Needs a Brain

Suppose that someone who upgraded a PC donated a 450 MHz Pentium III CPU to your cause — hey, it could happen, right? Or, more likely, you found a CPU for sale online at a great price. Anyway, you need to install your CPU on your motherboard — that's where it belongs, and the pins on a CPU can be damaged easily by small children and dogs (or a cat in an exceptionally bad mood).

For a novice, the CPU installation process is probably one of the scariest moments in the entire project. If you feel that you need professional help on this one, bring your case (with motherboard installed) and CPU to your local computer repair shop, or ask a computer guru you know to handle the CPU installation. Ask the expert to install the CPU, and watch the process closely — after you've seen it done correctly, it's not a big deal at all.

Installing a Slot 1 CPU

If you're installing a Celeron, Pentium II, or Pentium III processor in a Slot 1 motherboard, follow these steps:

1. **Touch your computer chassis to dissipate any static electricity.**

2. **Haul your open computer chassis onto your work surface.**

   If the computer is plugged in, unplug it now.

3. **Locate the CPU slot connector, bracket, and pegs on your motherboard.**

   Having problems finding that pesky CPU slot? Your motherboard manual should include a schematic that indicates where the CPU slot is hiding out. On many motherboards, the slot bracket has already been installed; if you need to install it, align the bracket with the matching holes in the motherboard and use the fasteners included with the motherboard; thumb pressure should be enough to push them into place. Figure 4-1 shows how a typical Pentium II processor is held in place by the bracket.

4. **Attach the two C-clips onto both ends of the CPU housing.**

   Okay, I know this thing is starting to look much like a junior high science project — but take my word for it, these clips provide the support to make sure that your CPU is rock-solid (as shown in Figure 4-2).

5. **Carefully slide the CPU into the bracket.**

   Note that the C-clips, fan, and heat sink should be facing the pegs you've already installed in the motherboard. To make sure that your alignment is correct, take a look at the entire CPU assembly from the top and the side.

6. **Slide the latches on the C-clips to lock them, and slide the latches closed on the top of the processor assembly.**

7. **If required, attach the power cable for the processor fan to the connectors on the motherboard and the CPU itself.**

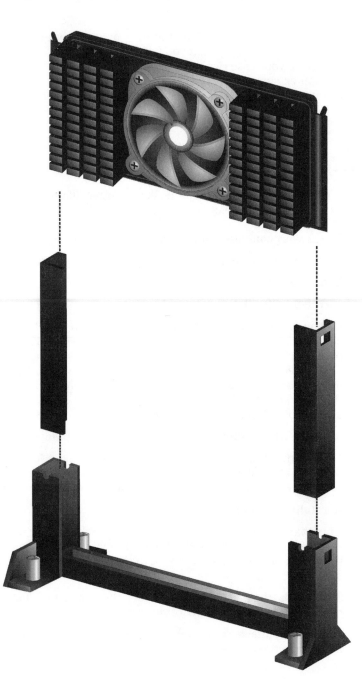

Figure 4-1:
The
bracket — a
good, solid
foundation
for any
Slot 1 CPU.

Figure 4-2:
The C-clips
join the
Slot 1 party.

Installing a Socket A CPU

If you're installing an Athlon or Duron processor in a Socket A motherboard, follow these steps:

1. **Touch your computer chassis to dissipate any static electricity.**

2. **Unplug your computer and lift the computer chassis onto your work surface.**

3. **Locate the CPU slot connector and processor guides on your motherboard.**

   If you need help, check your motherboard manual for a schematic that shows the layout of the slot connector.

4. **Push in the retention latches on the top of the processor until they click in their recessed position.**

   The latches are at the top corners of the processor.

5. **Push the heat sink support clip between the first and second rows of fins at the bottom of the heat sink.**

   The locking slots on the clip should be facing up.

6. **Slide the processor between the processor guides, as shown in Figure 4-3.**

   If the plastic processor guides are folded down, unfold and extend them first. To make sure that your alignment is correct, take a look at the entire CPU assembly from the top and the side before seating the CPU.

   Be careful not to accidentally crease or bend the thermal sensor ribbon on the motherboard, and make sure that it's not blocking the connector on the bottom of the processor!

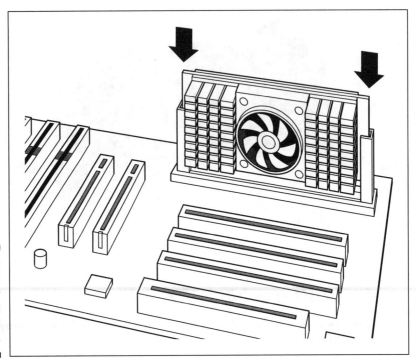

7. **Press down firmly on the CPU to seat it in the processor socket.**

8. **Pull out the retention latches at the top corners of the processor, as shown in Figure 4-4.**

   The latches will click into place in their extended position.

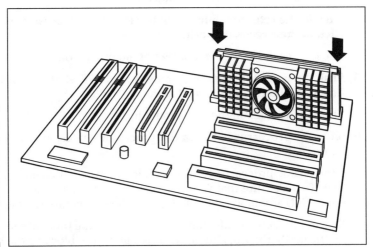

9. **Slide the heat sink support clip onto the grooves in the heat sink.**

   The clip clicks into place.

10. **Attach the power cable for the processor fan to the connectors on the motherboard and the CPU itself.**

    Again, check your motherboard manual for the location of the fan power connector.

Installing a Socket 7 or Socket 370 CPU

If your motherboard uses a Socket 7 or Socket 370 processor, like the AMD K6-2 or Cyrix III, follow these steps to install your CPU chip:

1. **Don't handle anything until you touch a metal surface first.**

   I'll bet that you just finished pulling a load of fuzzy socks out of your clothes dryer, didn't you?

   Touching a metal surface, like your computer's chassis, conducts static electricity away from your body. Static electricity can damage sensitive computer components!

2. **Haul your open computer chassis onto your work surface.**

   Don't plug it in yet.

3. **Locate the CPU socket on your motherboard.**

   The CPU socket is a big square that looks like it can hold two or three thousand pins. If you need help finding the CPU socket, refer to the schematic in your motherboard's manual. Pentium and AMD K6/K6-2 motherboards typically feature special sockets called ZIF *(zero insertion force)* sockets for the CPU; unlike older motherboards that used 386 and 486 processors, ZIF sockets allow you to easily install or remove CPUs without requiring force.

   Unfortunately, the CPU is not one of those parts that was cleverly designed to fit only one way, but at least the nice folks at the plant give you a marker to help during installation. Figure 4-5 shows two typical Socket 7 CPU chips and two different types of sockets. See the stubby corner on the chip? That corner should point in the same direction as the socket's marker. Depending on the motherboard, the matching corner on the socket may be stubby as well, or it could have a small dot or a tiny groove. If you're the least bit unsure about how to line up the CPU chip, check your motherboard manual.

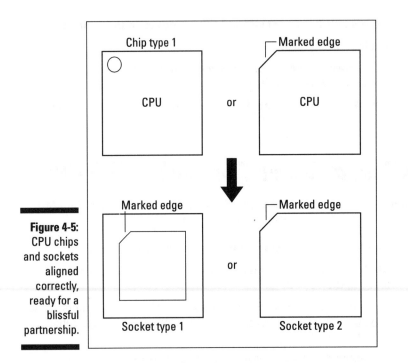

Figure 4-5:
CPU chips
and sockets
aligned
correctly,
ready for a
blissful
partnership.

4. **If your motherboard has a ZIF socket for the CPU, raise the lever on the side of the socket.**

   Your motherboard manual should show you how to lift the lever; this step "unlocks" the ZIF socket so that you can insert the chip.

5. **Carefully place the CPU chip on top of the socket.**

   The edges of the chip should match the edges of the socket, and the stubby corner should match the socket marker. Look at the chip from the top and the side to make sure that the pins you can see are on top of their matching holes.

6. **Okay, take a deep breath and relax — then use your fingers to gently push down on the edges of the chip.**

   Apply even pressure to the top of the CPU. After some initial resistance, the chip should settle into the socket. Press evenly on the CPU until the pins aren't visible from the side.

7. **If your motherboard has a ZIF socket for the CPU, lower the lever on the side of the socket.**

   Push the lever down to "lock" the ZIF socket so that the CPU chip is held in place.

Never, never, *never* try to force a Socket 7 CPU into a motherboard — if it doesn't feel like it's correctly seated and all the pins fit, back off and check your motherboard manual to make sure that the chip is aligned correctly. If the CPU is not correctly aligned and you try to force it into the socket, you'll bend some of the pins (which can be fixed, but only by an experienced technician). In the worst case, you'll break a pin — if this happens, you may as well bury in your backyard whatever is left and get another CPU.

All processors made these days have built-in fans on top or on the side of them to keep the chip cool; the fan is clamped or glued to the top or side of the chip. This fan may have a separate power cable you need to connect, or it may draw power directly from the chip — refer to your CPU documentation to see whether you need to connect the fan to your power supply and how to do it.

Add RAM Until the Mixture Thickens

If you bought RAM with your motherboard, it should come preinstalled. If you bought your RAM chips separately or you scavenged them, here are the rules of the game:

✔ Most motherboards sold these days accept RAM in the form of 168-pin *SyncDRAM* (short for *Synchronous Dynamic RAM,* often called *SDRAM*) DIMMs. Check your motherboard manual for any special requirements before ordering DIMMs to populate your board. Figure 4-6 illustrates a typical DIMM, just waiting for someone to reach out and install it.

Figure 4-6:
Is it a potato chip? A chocolate chip? No, it's a DIMM chip.

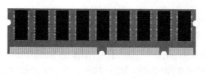

✔ Older Pentium motherboards used *EDO* (short for *Extended Data Output*) 72-pin SIMMs. Once again, your motherboard should specify what types of memory can be installed.

✔ To avoid mix-ups and stragglers, it's better to order all your RAM at one time from the same dealer. In general, RAM modules made by different manufacturers are supposed to work together as long as they're all rated at the same speed, although I've heard horror stories on the Internet about compatibility problems. Whenever you can, order the same brand from the same dealer.

✔ Check the design you created in Chapter 2 for the recommended amount of RAM you should use — but don't forget the old maxim, "The more RAM, the merrier!" This is especially true with Windows 98, and Windows NT — the more RAM you can add, the better and faster your system runs.

✔ In the days of the 486 and the original Pentium, SIMMs were typically grouped in pairs, although most of today's motherboards can accept one or two DIMMs.

Ready to install your DIMMs? Good — follow these steps:

1. **Touch something metal to banish the static monster.**

2. **Cover your work surface with a piece or two of newspaper and lay your chassis down on top of the newspaper.**

   Don't plug it in yet.

3. **Locate the DIMM memory slots, which you can generally find at one corner of the motherboard, close to the CPU itself.**

   If your motherboard was designed by Picasso, check the manual, which should include a schematic drawing to help you find the memory slots. You should also find instructions on which bank of slots to fill first — make sure that you add the memory in the order specified by the manual. (The banks are usually marked on the motherboard itself, just to avoid confusion.) In general, most people fill bank 0 first, and then bank 1, and so on.

4. **Position the motherboard so that the DIMM memory slots are facing you — the slots should look like those shown in Figure 4-7.**

   The clever little locking mechanism uses friction to lock the DIMM firmly into place. Notice that the notches cut into the connectors at the bottom of the module match the spacers in the memory sockets; you can't install DIMM chips the wrong way — this notch is an example of good thinking on someone's part.

Figure 4-7:
A DIMM
socket,
ready for
action.

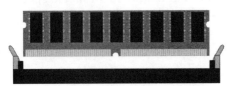

5. **Align the metal "teeth" at the bottom of the module with the socket and push down lightly to seat the chip, as shown in Figure 4-8.**

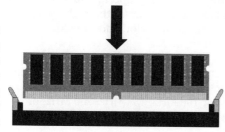

Figure 4-8:
Inserting the DIMM chip safely into its socket.

6. **As the module moves into place, make sure that the two levers at each side of the socket move toward the center, as shown in Figure 4-9, until that clever little locking mechanism clicks into place.**

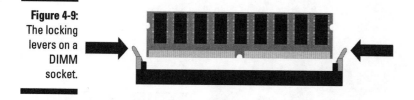

Figure 4-9:
The locking levers on a DIMM socket.

That's it! When correctly installed, the DIMM should sit vertically on the motherboard, and the two levers should be flush against the sides of the module.

Time to Meet Your Bus

While you have your case open and you can see everything clearly, take a moment to determine what type of *bus slots* you have. (And note that it has nothing to do with the processor and motherboard's bus speed.) If you add any internal adapter cards to your computer, they fit into these bus slots (becoming, in effect, an extension of the motherboard itself). If you're confused about which types of slots you have — most motherboards you buy today have an AGP slot, three or four PCI slots, and one or two ISA 16-bit slots — check your motherboard manual. This information becomes really important really quick because you'll need to buy the proper type of adapter card for many other parts in your computer; if the card doesn't match your available slots, you can't use it!

These slots are a series of long, parallel connectors on your motherboard, and most motherboards come with anywhere from five to seven slots. Figures 4-10, 4-11, and 4-12 illustrate the three most common types of slots on Pentium III and Athlon motherboards: the superfast AGP video card slot (more about this high-speed slot in Chapter 6), the high-speed 32-bit PCI *(Peripheral Component Interconnect)* bus slot, and the older, slower 16-bit ISA (or *Industry Standard Architecture*) slot.

Figure 4-13 illustrates an 8-bit slot, which dates back farther than either of the other slots. You're not likely to see one on a Pentium III or Athlon motherboard — especially if it runs at 100 MHz, 133 MHz, 200 MHz, or 266 MHz bus speed — but such slots are easily confused with PCI slots.

However, if you do scavenge an older scanner or peripheral that uses a proprietary 8-bit card, you can use that card in a 16-bit ISA slot without problems.

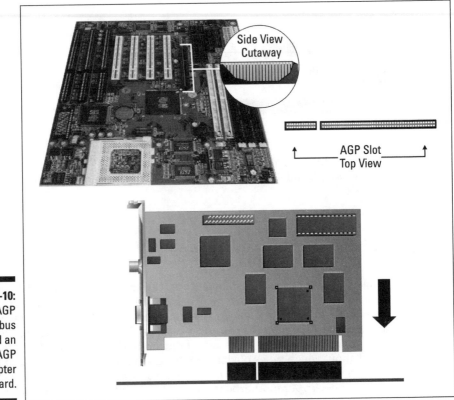

Figure 4-10:
An AGP
video bus
slot and an
AGP
adapter
card.

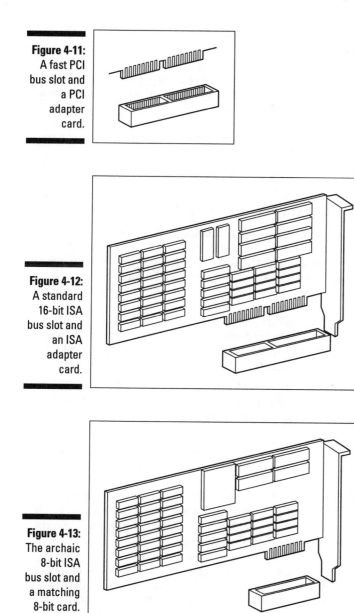

Figure 4-11:
A fast PCI bus slot and a PCI adapter card.

Figure 4-12:
A standard 16-bit ISA bus slot and an ISA adapter card.

Figure 4-13:
The archaic 8-bit ISA bus slot and a matching 8-bit card.

Fire That Puppy Up!

Time to test your work and see how well you did. Although your computer doesn't even have a monitor or keyboard connected yet, you can still check out your assembly so far. Follow these steps:

1. **Plug the three-prong power cord that came with your computer case into the matching connector on the power supply.**

   Go ahead and push this one in pretty firmly — you don't want it to wiggle free.

2. **Plug the power cable in to your friendly wall socket.**

3. **Push the power switch on the front or back of your case.**

If you connected your cables correctly to the motherboard, your switches are hooked up correctly (both of which are covered in detail in Chapter 3), and your CPU and RAM chips are installed correctly, the following should happen:

✔ The power light should be lit. (If it doesn't light and the fan on your power supply is turning, reverse the connector attached to the Power Light pins on the motherboard; for all the information on motherboard connections, refer to Chapter 3.)

✔ If you have a turbo light, it should be lit. (If it doesn't light, reverse the connector attached to the Turbo Light pins on the motherboard; Chapter 3 contains instructions for making connections to your motherboard.)

✔ The fan on the CPU should be spinning. (If not, check to make sure that you've plugged in the cable from the fan to your power supply.)

If the preceding components are in working order, your motherboard is receiving power and the power and turbo lights are correctly connected. (If none of these things is happening, switch your computer off and reverse the order of the power cables connected to your computer.)

Your computer may blurt out a series of beeps. Don't worry — it's merely trying to tell you that it can't find a video adapter, keyboard, and other such components (you install and attach those elements in later chapters). In fact, the beeps are your friends, and you can use them later in the assembly process to help you diagnose problems. For example, if the machine emits one long beep followed by three short beeps, you have a video problem. If your PC sounds eight or more long, continuous beeps, it's telling you that it's encountering a memory problem.

That's about all the testing you can do at this stage. After your chassis passes all these tests, you're ready to add more components to your computer.

Chapter 5

The Three PC Senses: Your Ports, Mouse, and Keyboard

*I*n today's world of graphical user interfaces (read that as "Windows 98, Windows 2000, and Linux"), a keyboard is no longer enough. To get the most from modern computer programs, you need to drag and drop and double-click — in other words, your computer needs a mouse (or other pointing device). In fact, pointing devices have been around for more than a decade, and they were standard equipment on other computers (like the Atari ST and Commodore Amiga) long before the arrival of Windows 3.0 on the PC. Most computer geeks prefer the speed of keyboard commands, but, for better or worse, the mouse is here to stay. Both your mouse and keyboard connect to your new computer through special connectors plugged into connector *ports* on the front or back of the case. Your computer needs a port for sending information to your printer as well as a port for sending and receiving data through a modem. Although some of these ports have changed over the years, others are virtually unchanged since the arrival of the first PC.

In this chapter, you find out how to add ports to your computer (if required) and how to connect your keyboard and mouse, as well as the many different types of pointing devices available today. You also find out more about high-speed serial ports and why you need them for today's faster modems.

If you bought a new motherboard, it should have several of these ports built-in already (for example, all motherboards have a built-in keyboard connector). However, older "antique" motherboards may require you to buy an adapter card that adds COM ports and a printer port to your computer. If you installed an ATX motherboard into an ATX case, your ports are already set! If your motherboard came with ports built-in but without connectors, you still need to attach the port connectors to the motherboard and then add the ports to your case — so don't skip this entire chapter; instead, jump to the section "Connecting Built-In Ports" in this chapter.

Pursuing Your Port Preferences

Prepare to be amazed at the variety of ports you can add to your computer! Your computer definitely needs the first three or four ports mentioned in the following list, although the rest are optional ports that handle the special hardware power users just love:

✔ **Keyboard port:** Keyboard ports come in two varieties — one type fits the IBM PS/2 connector shown in Figure 5-1. An older type of keyboard port accepts a round connector, which is larger than the PS/2 connector. Most motherboards have a keyboard port that accepts the smaller PS/2 plug. If you want to use a keyboard that has a good feel to it but uses the older-style, round connector (usually called an *AT connector*), you can pick up a converter that lets you plug the older keyboard into a PS/2-style port.

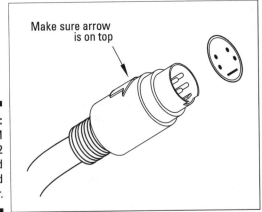

Make sure arrow is on top

Figure 5-1: The IBM PS/2 standard keyboard connector.

✔ **Serial port:** This type of port is commonly called a *COM port* (short for *communications port*). In the past, computers used serial ports to handle your modem and your mouse (if you're a real technological old-timer, you may have even used this type of port to plug in a strange type of printer called a *serial printer*). In current computers, serial ports are primarily reserved for external modems, connections to devices like digital cameras, and some exotic types of joysticks and game controllers.

A serial port is typically assigned one of four standard COM port designations, like COM1 or COM2, which identifies that particular port to the computer. With as many as four COM ports on the same computer, you can run multiple modems on the same computer. Most motherboards with built-in ports (and serial port adapter cards you add to the motherboard) offer two serial ports. These ports used to come in two different varieties (a male 9-pin version and a male 25-pin version), but the 9-pin serial port is much more popular today. (By the way, a *male* connector has pins, and a *female* connector has holes for those pins.)

High-speed external modems — that is, modems that run at 14.4 Kbps or faster — require a high-speed serial port to run at top speed. Older serial ports simply can't handle such a fast stream of data. When buying a motherboard or serial port adapter card, make sure that it features *16550-class high-speed UART chips* (that's the technonerd description of a *high-speed serial port*). For more information on high-speed UART chips, head for Chapter 10, where I discuss modems in detail.

✔ **Parallel printer port:** Although it's hard to believe, one type of port hasn't changed very much since the early days of PC-XT and AT-class computers. Parallel printer ports look and operate pretty much as they did in the early 1980s; their primary purpose in life is to provide a connection for your printer. (Lately, however, parallel ports are also doing double duty as connections for external devices, like scanners, Zip drives, and even CD-ROM drives.) Unlike serial ports, parallel ports transfer data on several wires rather than on just two. If you're shopping for a motherboard or port adapter card, just make sure that it has at least one high-speed *bidirectional parallel port.* Parallel ports are female and accept 25-pin connectors, and these ports must be bidirectional if you're going to connect those external devices. Unfortunately, parallel ports are often mistaken for the older 25-pin serial port (sounds like a case for more computer case labels, as I suggest at the end of this section) — unless you're using a scavenged serial card from an older computer, you probably won't run into a 25-pin serial port.

✔ **PS/2 mouse port:** As I mention earlier in this chapter, older computers enabled you to connect the mouse using one of the serial ports. However, most motherboards and adapter cards now feature a dedicated mouse port — this type of mouse port doesn't take up an actual serial port.

If you scavenged a used mouse designed for a serial port, you can still use it on your computer. Just check the manual for your motherboard or port adapter card and find out how to disable the PS/2 mouse port (you probably need to set a DIP switch or a jumper, or your motherboard's BIOS configuration utility may have a setting that disables it). Your serial mouse should run fine when it's connected to your COM1 serial port, after you've installed the software drivers that came with it; however, if

you want to use both a scavenged serial mouse and an external modem
and you have only one serial port, it's time to shop for a new serial port
adapter card with two serial ports.

✔ **USB port:** USB is short for *Universal Serial Bus,* and this high-speed port is
truly shaping up as a universal method for attaching all sorts of peripherals to your computer. The first version of the USB port could accommo-
date as many as 127 devices (probably even enough for Bill Gates), and it
provided transfer rates of as much as 12 megabits per second — the
2.0 USB standard goes even further, moving data at speeds of as much as a
blistering 480 megabits per second (and it's backward-compatible with
version 1 USB hardware). Plus, any peripheral you plug into a USB port is
automatically recognized by Windows 98 and Windows 2000 (as it should
be), and you can remove that same device without rebooting your computer. USB is becoming popular as the connection of choice for scanners,
joysticks and controllers, digital cameras, and even printers. If you're
shopping for a new motherboard, make *sure* that it comes with USB ports,
and you can kiss port confusion goodbye!

✔ **FireWire port:** Otherwise known as your friendly neighborhood IEEE-
1394 High Performance Serial Bus, a FireWire port transfers data as fast
as 100 megabits per second, which has made it a popular choice for connecting expensive toys that generate lots of data, like digital cam-
corders, videoconferencing cameras, superfast scanners, and color laser
printers. Like USB, FireWire is automatically recognized by Windows 98
and Windows 2000; it supports as many as 63 devices. (Although the
USB 2.0 port may surpass FireWire in a speed race, FireWire allows your
computer to control digital devices as well, so it's likely to hang around.)
If you're planning on editing digital video or participating in videoconferencing, consider adding a FireWire port to your PC.

✔ **Game port:** If you plan to add a sound card to your computer, it may
also have a game port for your joystick or gamepad. If not, most "multiple I/O" port adapter cards also provide a game port onboard along with
the standard serial and parallel ports. Game ports have 15 pins, and one
port can connect two standard two-button IBM joysticks.

✔ **MIDI port:** You use this type of specialized port for connecting MIDI-capable
musical instruments to your computer; MIDI ports are usually added along
with your sound card, and a MIDI port can also do double-duty as a game
port. (You find out more about both sound cards and MIDI in Chapter 9.)

✔ **Infrared port:** If you have a laptop computer with an *infrared port,* you
may want to consider adding one to your new computer. An infrared
port lets you transfer data and files between two computers without the
need to string cables between the two machines. An infrared port comes
in handy if you travel often and you like to keep your data synchronized
between your laptop and desktop systems. Infrared ports are typically
installed on an adapter card, with some sort of external infrared sensor.

✔ **SCSI port:** If you install a SCSI adapter card in your computer (which I
cover in Chapter 11), the card also offers an external *SCSI port* to connect scanners, CD recorders, and other SCSI devices.

The versatile parallel port

You can use parallel printer ports to connect any other types of devices than just a parallel printer. Many parallel port devices are arriving on the scene, like Zip removable cartridge drives, parallel port scanners, and even video capture hardware. Rather than require you to open your case and add a new adapter card, these devices simply plug into your parallel port, and then you plug your printer into the device. Old-timers like me (who remember the days of 8-bit computers) will recognize this method of connecting computer peripherals — we used to call it *daisy-chaining.* (Look for the parallel port to become obsolete in the future, though, because the USB port will in all likelihood eventually take its place.

Even though you may remember *now* which port is which, I heartily recommend that you create labels for your ports after you install them. If you label your ports, you eliminate any identification problems in the future.

Of Keyboards, Mice, and Men (And Women)

"Grandpa, in your day, did they really have only one kind of mouse and one kind of keyboard?" Things have really changed — now you can choose from a dizzying array of pointing devices and keyboards (and even combinations of both).

The mouse has mutated

If you're at a loss about which pointing device is best for you, here are some guidelines to steer you in the right direction:

✔ **Standard mouse:** The basic mouse is still around; it comes in two-button and three-button varieties. Some mice even carry smaller buttons on the sides! If you do pick a mouse that has sprouted more than two buttons, you may be able to program the additional buttons (for example, the software that came with my trackball enables me to program the middle button to double-click). A mouse is still a good pick for a traditional pointing device, although it's harder to use for delicate work, and a mouse requires lots of desk space. These pointing devices tend to get dirty often. You should clean your mouse at the first sign of skipping or sloppy response.

Some newer mice have a wheel between the buttons, which enables you to scroll Web pages and documents up and down by turning the wheel with your finger — nice!

✔ **Wireless mouse:** This type of mouse doesn't trail cords around behind it, and many computer owners find this feature desirable. Going wireless also enables you to control a presentation with much more freedom than a standard mouse. Be prepared to feed this monster new batteries every so often, though, and check the box to see just how far you can actually stray without worrying about losing the signal.

✔ **Trackball:** As shown in Figure 5-2, this pointing device resembles an upside-down mouse: Rather than move the housing around, you move the ball with your finger or thumb. Trackballs are a little harder to use at first; they stay in one place, however, so they require much less desktop space.

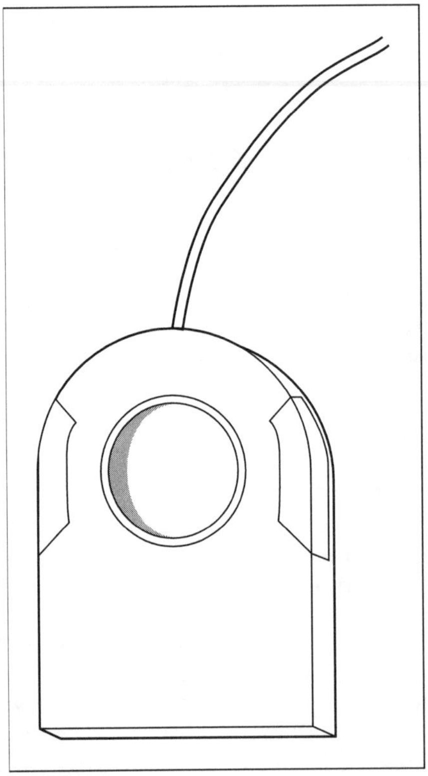

Figure 5-2:
A typical
trackball.

If you decide on a trackball for your computer systems, consider buying my favorite pointing device: an *optical trackball.* These units are much more expensive than standard trackballs, but they never require adjustment or cleaning, and they have fewer moving parts than standard trackballs or mice. These trackballs use balls covered with a pattern of dots, and optical sensors in the body of the trackball "read" these dots to determine movement.

✔ **Touchpad:** This pointing device has been very popular on laptops, but it's also available for desktop computers. To use a touchpad (shown in Figure 5-3), you move your finger across its surface, and the mouse follows your movements on-screen. To click, you can either press a button on the touchpad or tap the pad surface twice in quick succession. No pen or other stylus is required. Like trackballs, touchpads take up very little space, and they don't require cleaning, although they do need to be adjusted every few months by running a special program. Some people feel that a touchpad is better for fine detail work on a computer.

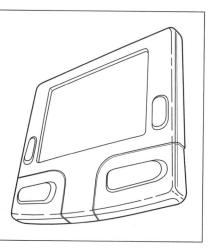

Figure 5-3:
Okay, so a touchpad looks a little strange, but it works!

✔ **Drawing tablet:** This pointing device is a larger version of the touchpad — a drawing pad is designed specifically for computer art and drafting. It allows freehand drawing on the tablet, which then appears on the screen; depending on the size of the tablet, you can even use a ruler or stencil. The drawing tablet can also double as a regular touchpad when you're not drawing.

✔ **Fingertip mouse:** Another pointing device that started out on laptops is the fingertip mouse — there's really not much to it other than a tiny button about the size of a pencil eraser that sits in the middle of a smooth case. (Many laptops feature a fingertip mouse in the middle of their keyboards.) To use a fingertip mouse, you nudge the button in the direction you want the cursor to travel on-screen. The longer you push, the farther the cursor travels; the harder you push, the faster it moves. To click, you press a button on the case. As with a touchpad, you need to adjust a fingertip mouse from time to time by running a program.

The key to keyboards

One keyboard is *not* just like another! For example, if you've been given an older 84-key keyboard, I suggest hanging it up in the barn as a good luck charm along with the horseshoes. You can tell these keyboards because they don't have a separate set of cursor control keys. If you're using any version of Windows, you need at least a standard 101-key keyboard.

However, some more-expensive keyboards have additional features that can make your life at the computer considerably easier. For example:

✔ Windows 98 supports extra keys — in fact, one even looks like the Windows logo! These keys drop down menus within programs, display the task list, print special characters, and much more.

✔ Recognizing the evils of carpal tunnel syndrome, many keyboards today are ergonomically designed. This design usually includes a wrist rest and a more human-friendly shape. The popular Microsoft Natural Keyboard is a good example (as shown in Figure 5-4).

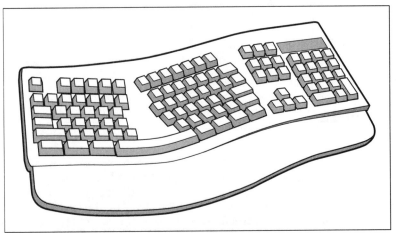

Figure 5-4: Catch the wave! The Microsoft Natural Keyboard helps reduce wrist strain.

✔ Need every inch of desk space? Consider a keyboard with a built-in trackball or touchpad. These integrated keyboards reduce hand movements and make you a more efficient, meaner typing machine.

✔ For the couch potato who has everything: Look Ma, no wires! The *wireless* keyboard enables you to lounge on your futon while composing that Great American Novel — but don't forget the batteries, and these keyboards are quite expensive.

If you decide to use a wireless keyboard or mouse, rechargeable batteries are the smart power user's investment! Although you pay more up front for the special reusable batteries and the charger unit, you more than make up for that in savings over the years!

✔ Many computer *multifunction* keyboards look more like your car's dashboard these days — buttons have been added to allow you to check your email, visit certain Web sites, display help for your operating system and applications, connect to the Internet, and control your CD-ROM or DVD drive! (One of my computers even has a rotary volume control on the keyboard, which I find much handier than the volume control on the Windows taskbar. Besides, it reminds me of my old stereo receiver.)

Although these keyboards are very convenient, remember that a multifunction keyboard requires its own proprietary software; if you've scavenged one of these keyboards and you didn't get the software, all those extra buttons become window dressing. Also, you have to "program" many of those keys on your multifunction keyboard. Sounds a little strange, doesn't it? What you're doing is identifying what function each of these specialized keys is supposed to perform. (Luckily, you should have to do this only once.)

If you're using a desktop case, I recommend a *keyboard shelf,* which looks much like a drawer that fits under your computer. The shelf slides out to give you access to the keyboard. After you're done typing, you can simply push the shelf back inside the unit. This device saves desk space, and it puts your keyboard at the proper typing position.

If you're buying a new keyboard, always try it out before you pull out your credit card. Computer people can be very finicky about their keyboards, and typing a long document on a bad keyboard is roughly equivalent to poking a soggy sponge repeatedly with your fingers.

Installing a Port Adapter Card

If your motherboard doesn't have built-in serial and parallel ports, it's time to add your port adapter card. These cards typically have one serial and one parallel port on the side of the card itself, and you can add cables that take up another slot on the back of your case to add a second serial and parallel port. Other cards offer USB and FireWire ports instead. Check the manual that came with your port adapter card to determine what connectors are actually on your card and which must be added separately.

Your adapter card manual should also fill you in on any DIP switch or jumper settings that have to be configured — now is a good time to do so, before your card is mashed in between three or four other cards and you have to be a contortionist like the Great Zambini to reach it. I do have good news about most port adapter cards: The factory default settings are usually just what you need, although it never hurts to check first.

To install your port adapter card, follow these instructions:

1. **Don't handle anything until you touch a metal surface.**

   Have you been shuffling your feet through that deep, plush carpeting all day? You're talking Static City!

2. **Haul your open case on top of your work surface.**

   Do not plug it in yet.

3. **Locate an adapter card slot of the proper length at the back of your case.**

   PCI cards use the short slots, and 16-bit cards are twice as long. Because most port adapter cards are 16-bit, I'll bet that you need a 16-bit slot. Also, make sure that any notches cut into the connectors on your card match any spacers within the slot — these spacers help ensure that you don't stick an 8-bit card into a PCI slot. Found an empty slot of the right length? Good! Move along to the next step.

4. **Take your trusty screwdriver and remove the screw and the metal slot cover at the back of the case, as shown in Figure 5-5.**

   Stick both these parts in your parts box — you may need a slot cover to close your case if you decide to remove an adapter card.

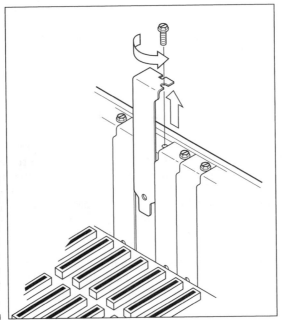

Figure 5-5:
To open a slot, you must first remove the metal cover from your case.

5. **Pick up the adapter card by the top corners. Line up the connector on the bottom of the card with the slot on the motherboard, as shown in Figure 5-6.**

   The card's metal bracket should align with the open space created when you removed the slot cover.

   Does the adapter card have extra connectors that aren't positioned above the slot? If so, you're trying to fit a 16-bit card into an 8-bit or PCI slot. Look for a slot that has matching connectors and notches.

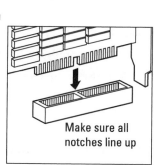

Figure 5-6: Make sure that the connectors on the bottom of the card line up with the slot.

Make sure all notches line up

6. **Houston, are we go for launch? If so, apply even pressure to the top of the card and push it down into the slot on the motherboard.**

   Although you don't hear a click, you should be able to tell when the card is firmly seated. The bracket should be resting tightly against the case.

7. **Add the screw you removed in Step 4 and tighten down the bracket, but don't overtighten it.**

Your computer is now equipped with at least one external parallel port and one external serial port — and depending upon the port adapter card, you may also add a USB port, a FireWire port, a game port, or a PS/2 mouse port as well.

Connecting Built-In Ports

If your motherboard came with built-in serial, parallel, and USB ports, you don't need to add a separate adapter card — but you *do* still need to attach the external ports to the back of your case and connect them to your motherboard. The external ports should look something like metal slot covers, but they also have one or two ports on the outside and separate ribbon cables for each port.

If your computer uses an ATX motherboard and case, your ports are already connected. You can skip this section with a smile.

To install these ports, follow these instructions:

1. **Don't handle anything until you touch a metal surface.**

   Put down that slick-plastic handheld video game; you may be carrying static now.

2. **Remove the screw and the metal slot cover at the back of the case and save both these parts in your parts box.**

3. **Insert the slot cover with the ports into the vacant slot.**

4. **Add the screw you removed in Step 2 and tighten down the bracket.**

5. **Check your motherboard manual and find the connectors for the built-in ports.**

   These connectors are similar to the motherboard connectors for your reset button and turbo switch.

6. **Attach the cables to the connectors on your motherboard as instructed by your motherboard's manual.**

   Pin 1 on the motherboard connector should align with the marked wire on the cable; this marking is usually a red stripe or red lettering.

Connecting Your Keyboard and Pointing Thing

It's time to add those all-important parts that let you argue directly with your computer: your mouse and keyboard. As I mention earlier in this chapter, computers use one of two different types of keyboard connectors, and a mouse can be connected to a serial port or a separate mouse port — the steps you follow are determined by your motherboard and what it provides.

Installing a keyboard

Connecting the keyboard is as easy as plugging in the cable through the case and into the keyboard port, although you should know about a couple of tricks. To install your keyboard, follow these instructions:

1. **Locate the keyboard port on the back of your case.**

   If you have an older keyboard, the port should be as thick as your little finger. If you have a PS/2 keyboard port, it should be about the thickness of a pencil eraser. If your keyboard connector is the same size as the keyboard port, rejoice and continue. If the connector is the wrong size, grumble to yourself, visit a local computer shop, and ask for an adapter to make an older keyboard fit a PS/2 keyboard port (or the other way around).

2. **Place the tip of the keyboard connector into the port and rotate it slowly while applying light pressure.**

   The connector should fit into the port only one way, so you should be able to feel when the pins line up. If your connector has a little arrow or a flat area on the outside, that indicator usually points "up" (although not every motherboard has the decency to define "up" the same way).

3. **When the keyboard connector is correctly aligned, push it in firmly.**

Installing a mouse (or other pointing thing)

Check your motherboard manual to determine whether it has a PS/2 mouse port onboard, and follow the appropriate set of steps that follow.

If your computer doesn't have a PS/2 mouse port:

1. **Locate a 9-pin serial port on the back of your case.**

2. **Align the 9-pin connector on the end of your mouse with the serial port.**

   The connector can go on only one way.

3. **When the connector is correctly aligned, push it in firmly.**

   If you want, you can tighten the connector by turning the knobs on the connector clockwise. Some connectors use screws instead; you need a very small screwdriver to tighten these connectors. If the connector feels like it is seated firmly, you can leave it as is.

If your computer does have a PS/2 mouse port, follow these steps:

1. **Locate the port on the back of your case.**

2. **Place the tip of the connector into the port and rotate it slowly while applying light pressure.**

   The connector should fit into the port only one way, so you should be able to feel when the pins line up. If your connector has a little arrow or a flat area on the outside, that marker usually points "up" (although the direction that "up" takes seems to vary in the eyes of some engineers).

3. **After the connector is correctly aligned, push it in firmly.**

Check It Once, and Check It Twice!

Even though you've added all your ports, you really have no way to test them — but all is not lost. You can test your keyboard right now. Push the power switch on the front or back of your computer case.

If you've connected your keyboard correctly to the port on your motherboard, all three keyboard lights should flash — the Num Lock, Caps Lock, and Scroll Lock indicators. If these indicators light up, your keyboard is correctly installed. If these lights don't illuminate, remove the keyboard connector from the keyboard port and try plugging it in again. If you still have no luck, try another keyboard to make sure that the port is working, and check your motherboard manual to make sure that you're connecting the keyboard to the keyboard port. (Remember that it's the same size and shape as your mouse port.)

If you install an external modem, you use your external serial port in Chapter 10. If you install a printer, you use your printer port in Chapter 14.

Chapter 6

Images 'R Us: Adding Video and Your Monitor

As you're building your computer, you'll be dazzled by more features, functions, acronyms, and assorted hoo-hahs surrounding your *video display* than just about any other component of your computer system. Computer components such as your mouse and your keyboard remain largely unchanged since the 386-class computers of old — but today's multimedia applications and operating systems demand monitors and video cards that deliver photographic-quality color and sharp detail. Game players and multimedia technojocks will also spend more money for advanced 3D graphics and good-quality digital video.

In this chapter, I help you understand all the buzzwords and acronyms that surround the technology behind all those video features so that you can make an intelligent decision on what to buy. I give you the inside information about your video subsystem, which has two parts: the *video adapter card* that fits inside your computer, and the *monitor* that displays the images. You find out how to select the features you need and how to install your video components.

I'm Okay, You're a Video Card

Your video card plays an important role in your computer: It sends the visual output produced by a program to your monitor, which displays the output on its screen. That visual output may be alphanumeric characters that form words, high-resolution graphics like a photograph, or even the shape of a monster in your favorite PC action game.

Get set — in this section, I take you on a whirlwind tour designed to help you find the video card that's exactly right for your applications.

Full speed ahead!

Unless you've been living under a rock in the Mojave Desert for nearly a decade, you've probably encountered a Windows program running on a computer. Graphical operating systems like MacOS and Windows were designed to make computers easier to use by making the displays more visual.

You probably agree that the graphical *point-and-click interface* is a good development, but when this type of interface was introduced, computers were nowhere near ready to handle the graphics. The first Windows programs ran abysmally slow, and the splashy graphics took too long to display — hence the popular nickname for Windows 3.0 became WinDoze.

By the way, I have a copy of Windows 2.1, the precursor of Windows 3.0. It runs on antique 80286 PCs. Windows 2.1 takes up a whopping seven floppy disks, and they're the old 720K disks to boot!

However, as time went by and Windows slowly developed into the operating environment of choice, computer hardware designers decided to tackle the problem of slow graphics by beefing up the standard PC video adapter. These enhancements would enable the computer's CPU to concentrate on running programs and performing calculations. With the arrival of the *accelerated graphics card,* technonerds around the globe breathed a collective sigh of relief. Finally, graphics were moving full speed ahead!

Accelerated cards have a separate processor onboard to handle complex graphics functions, like drawing 3D objects and displaying menus (which means that your CPU doesn't need to worry about these tasks). Although accelerated cards used to cost dramatically more than standard video cards, they've dropped so far in price that most brand-name video cards offer acceleration these days. As you're shopping for a fast video card, keep these guidelines in mind:

✔ If you plan to invest in an accelerated video adapter, you get the best performance from an AGP (short for *Accelerated Graphics Port*) video card. If your motherboard doesn't support AGP, by all means get a PCI video adapter card. Sticking a fast video card in a 16-bit ISA slot is a little like forcing a thoroughbred horse to pull a plow: It will do the job, but you're holding it back. Only the AGP bus (or, if you're using an older motherboard, the PCI bus) provides the superfast throughput your new video card needs in order to work its magic. (Chapter 3 includes more information on selecting a motherboard with support for AGP and PCI adapter cards.)

✔ Most video card manufacturers provide benchmark figures advertising the speed of their accelerated cards; you can use these figures for speed comparisons. As an example, 3dfx, the maker of my Voodoo 3 video card, measure the card's speed in *WinMarks* (a well-known benchmark figure for graphics hardware under Windows).

✔ Make sure that your new card is fully supported with drivers for Windows 95 and Windows 98, Windows NT, OpenGL, Direct3D (and yes, even OS/2). With the right software drivers, just about any operating system can benefit from the same accelerated video adapter. If you're looking for a specific software driver, I heartily recommend The Driver Zone, at www.driverzone.com (a Web site that provides links for just about every manufacturer and every type of computer component I've ever seen).

If you're trying to save money by scavenging a video card from a 486-based computer, you can certainly use that older card. However, I urge you to replace it whenever possible with up-to-date technology — this section shows you what features to look for in a video card. You'll end up saving time because of the faster video display, and you'll prefer working at your computer with an AGP video card designed for an Athlon, Celeron, or Pentium III computer (or a PCI video adapter designed for a Pentium computer).

Catching a ride on the magic bus

If you're familiar with the history of motherboards and the various bus architectures that have been used in computers, you're probably lots of fun to talk to at parties. With all this technical knowledge at your disposal, you may also know that 486 computers used a nifty bus called the *VESA Local Bus,* which was faster than the original 16-bit ISA standard bus.

VLB was the forerunner of PCI, offering the fastest access to your system's CPU and RAM, and it was used for the same purposes that PCI is used for in older Pentium machines: connecting your video adapter card and hard drive controller card to provide the fastest possible flow of data. Unfortunately, VLB wasn't fast enough and has faded into the ancient history of yesterday's technology; VLB isn't suitable for use on a Pentium motherboard. The PCI bus, which is roughly 30 percent faster, has been declared the winner for hard drives, and an AGP bus delivers the fastest video performance.

"Will 3D video transform my entire existence?"

Maybe! You may have seen 3D computer graphics on television or in the movies, but what good is a 3D video card for someone who's not running an expensive graphics program like AutoCAD? Computer gamers will tell you that there's no better piece of hardware to improve 3D games like Unreal Tournament, Halo, Quake, and Mechwarrior. With a 3D video card, objects in these games look so realistic that you can practically reach out and touch them, and these games will run much faster, too.

If you're a nut for computer graphics, you may have already entered the world of 3D — if not, here's a quick introduction. Today's 3D video cards take care of *rendering* — that's the computer term for *drawing* objects in three dimensions and overlaying a pattern on the surface of the object. For example, a square wooden block is originally rendered as a simple cube object, but when a wood grain pattern is added, it suddenly looks just like a wooden block. Of course, that wooden block can just as easily become a complex object, like a tentacled mercenary with a phased plasma rifle from the planet Quark. Modern 3D computer games work with your 3D video card to realistically render your enemies, who then proceed to try to "render" you (limb from limb, if you get my drift).

A 3D video card handles the complex math necessary to produce 3D images (just like an accelerated video card does for Windows), enabling your CPU to focus on handling the program. Figure 6-1 illustrates my favorite rendering program, TrueSpace, with a representative cool 3D graphic (in this case, a giant walking robot).

A 3D video card speeds up just about every operation in today's hottest computer games (as well as "serious" programs like TrueSpace, Photoshop and other multimedia bigwig applications), so an advanced 3D video card is worth every penny. Most popular 3D video cards use chipsets from three top manufacturers:

- ✔ **3Dfx:** One of the first 3D cards to appear on the scene, the current crop of 3dfx cards uses the Voodoo 5 chipset, which features not one but two on-board processors working together. Although the Voodoo 3 and Voodoo 4 chipsets are now considered old news, they're still great with most games, so scavenge them when you can.

- ✔ **NVIDIA:** Home to the older Riva TNT and TNT2 (both of which have been big favorites of computer gamers for years), NVIDIA has recently raised the stakes in the 3D world with the introduction of its new GeForce2, which is described by the company as an honest-to-goodness GPU (short for *graphics processing unit*). The GeForce2 chipset is found on the most powerful 3D video cards now available.

> ✔ **ATI:** The ATI Rage series of 3D video cards has been a mainstay for years in the retail PC world because they're cheap and reasonably powerful. However, the company has released its new RADEON GPU chipset to compete head-to-head with the Voodoo 5 and the GeForce2, so it's also a 3D video card to compare.

Speaking of comparisons, what should you look for in a 3D video card? Here's a quick shopper's checklist:

> ✔ Look for the most on-board RAM you can afford. Most cards feature anywhere from 16MB to 64MB.

> ✔ Check common benchmarks between cards to determine which is actually faster. As an example, the WinMarks figure I mention earlier in this chapter can help determine which card is truly the fastest at performing a standard rendering test. You typically find these benchmark figures in the card's specifications on the box or on the company's Web site.

> ✔ Your card should offer full OpenGL and Direct 3D support. These two drivers are the most popular for today's computer games and rendering programs.

> ✔ The deeper the color depth and the higher the resolution, the better. Find out more about these features in the next section.

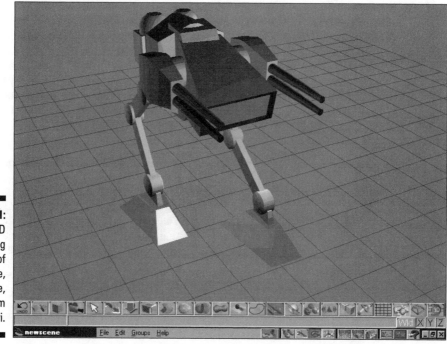

Figure 6-1:
My 3D rendering program of choice, TrueSpace, from Caligari.

Thanks for the memory

Your computer's motherboard isn't the only part of your computer that has its own RAM — your video card needs memory as well. In essence, your video adapter uses RAM to store colors and pixel values; the more RAM on your video card, the more colors you can display and the higher the video resolution you can use. I recommend a minimum of 4MB of video memory for a PC running an office suite and Internet applications or a minimum of 16MB if you're running graphics-intensive games and applications on a 3D video card.

Because these factors are important in selecting a video card, I attack them separately.

More about colors

In the early days of computers, you were lucky if you could display 4 or 16 colors on the screen at one time — these old standards were called CGA (for *Color Graphics Adapter*) and EGA (for *Enhanced Graphics Adapter*). People were satisfied with CGA and EGA colors for a surprisingly long time — mostly because computer hardware in those days cost a fortune, and why would anyone need more colors to run (chortle) *DOS* programs? Even game players were happy with 16 colors (and some still say that the games had more depth and imagination back then because games didn't rely on flashy graphics).

With the arrival of the VGA *(Video Graphics Array)* standard of 256 colors and the debut of Windows 3.0, everything changed. Suddenly, the rush was on for flashier and more realistic color. Most computers now use the SVGA *(Super Video Graphics Array)* standard, and today's sophisticated cards can provide more than 16 million colors on the screen at one time. That's true photographic-quality color, and if you've never seen a high-resolution image with that many colors, you're in for a real treat. When you're shopping for a video card and monitor, make sure that you demand SVGA.

How deep is your color?

You hear technonerds talk about color depth all the time, especially when they argue about the Web. *Color depth* refers to the number of colors in an image; popular color depths are 16 colors, 256 colors, 64,000 colors, and 16 million colors. Most graphics on the Web use a color depth of 256 colors — the lower the color depth, the less time it takes to download the image to a Web browser. Yet some people who create Web pages like to use 16 million color graphics because those graphics look better. The battle rages on.

If your video card has less than 2MB of RAM, you probably can't display 16 million colors in Windows — although you can always use 256 colors (and you can upgrade most video cards with additional memory later). If the primary application for your new computer involves scanning or editing graphics (or you just want the best available color), you should look for a card that offers 4MB of video RAM or more so that you don't need to worry about upgrading.

More about resolution

Extra video RAM lets your monitor display images at a higher *resolution*. To explain resolution, I need to introduce you to a single dot on your monitor — it's called a *pixel*. The display on your monitor is built from thousands of pixels arranged in lines, each pixel displaying a certain color. Your video system's resolution is expressed in the number of pixels displayed horizontally and the number of lines displayed vertically. For example, a resolution of 640 x 480 means that the monitor displays 640 pixels horizontally across the screen and 480 pixels vertically. To keep it simple, most people just refer to horizontal x vertical.

At lower resolutions, graphics look big and chunky, with ragged edges and blocky shapes. Any resolution lower than 640 x 480 (the standard resolution for Windows 3.*x*, Windows 95, and Windows 98) is pretty much unusable these days.

At higher resolutions, like 800 x 600 or 1024 x 768, you can fit more images, data, icons, and information on your screen at one time — suddenly, you can work on an entire brochure in your desktop publishing program without "zooming out." Or, you can fit more of your favorite Web page on your screen without scrolling. Details look better, too, and you can work more efficiently.

But wait — it couldn't be that easy, could it? Nope, you're right: There's a trade-off between resolution and the number of colors within Windows. If you have less than 2MB of video RAM, you can still pick a higher resolution, but you'll probably drop back to 256 colors (or even 16 colors). If you're looking for more colors, you can increase the color depth, although your resolution also will have to drop.

Why? Because both these desirable features — extra colors and higher resolutions — demand more RAM, and if your older video card has only 1MB of RAM, you have to decide how best to divide things up. The best choice is probably somewhere in between — perhaps a resolution of 800 x 600 and 256 colors.

If your work relies heavily on graphics, extra RAM is well worth the investment. Figure 6-2 illustrates the Settings tab on the Windows 98 Display Properties dialog box, where you specify both the color depth (in this case, called Colors) and the resolution you use within Windows.

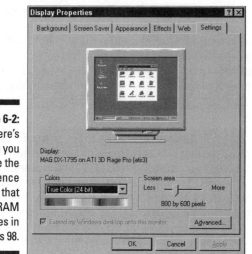

Figure 6-2:
Here's
where you
can see the
difference
that
extra RAM
makes in
Windows 98.

Look out! Aliens from the planet MPEG!

Yep, video cards are just chock-full of acronyms, and this one is a real winner: MPEG stands for *Moving Pictures Expert Group*. Now that's a trivial fact you can toss around to your friends, right? At least the name suggests something of value — MPEG is the buzzword for digital video on your computer.

If you plan to use your computer extensively to display or edit digital video, make sure that your video card has *hardware MPEG support,* which can decode MPEG digital video all by itself without bogging down your CPU. Digital video will run smoothly — even at full screen — and you can see more detail at higher resolutions with MPEG support.

"What else do I need from a video adapter?"

By this time, you may be shrugging your shoulders in disgust, thinking that you'll probably have to pay $1,000 for a good-quality video adapter that has acceleration, 3D support, at least 16MB of RAM, and hardware MPEG decoding. Perhaps you'll have to take a second mortgage on the house?

Fear not, good citizen! As an example, an XPERT@Play card from ATI has all these features and even a few more — and you can pick it up at a local computer store for $100 (other comparable cards are around the same price). Not a bad price for a power-user part, eh?

Digital Video 101

"What exactly is digital video, and why do I need a video card that displays it?" Well, like the digital audio stored on audio CDs, you can also store video in digital format. In fact, this technology has been around as long as the laser disc.

On the computer, however, digital video has come of age only within the past three or four years. A big breakthrough occurred when Windows arrived and became the PC operating system of choice because it contained support for digital video in the Microsoft AVI format. (DOS had no built-in support for displaying video.) Computer games and the Web have also helped to popularize digital video on the computer screen.

The big drawback with digital video has been the sheer amount of space it takes up — a few minutes of uncompressed digital video (recorded at full-screen resolution with stereo sound) can easily take up 200MB or 300MB of storage space on your hard drive. (This massive storage space required for digital video is one of the reasons for the popularity of the CD-ROM, which can store as much as 680MB of computer and audio data.)

Notice that I said "uncompressed" a second ago? That's where MPEG comes in — it's one of two or three compression formats that greatly reduces the sisze of a digital video file. The video is compressed (or *encoded*) as it's recorded, and then an MPEG software program decompresses (or *decodes*) it on your computer. That takes time and quite a bit of your CPU's resources, and it's the main reason for slow, stuttering video playback on older computers — or video playback in a window the size of a postage stamp.

Knowing about a few other features can help you determine which video card to buy — along with the 3D features I mention earlier in this chapter, here's a short checklist of features that add value to any video card:

- ✔ **Higher refresh rate:** If you're one of those who spend hours at the PC, your eyes will feel much better at the end of the day if your video card offers a refresh rate of 75 to 85 Hz. (I discuss refresh rate in more detail later in this chapter, in the "Feeling refreshed?" section.)

- ✔ **Support:** Before buying a video card, check the company's Web site. Some questions to ask: How often does the manufacturer update its drivers for the card you're considering? Does it offer tech support over the Web, or will you end up getting put on hold, waiting for "the next available customer service rep"?

- ✔ **Bundled software and Windows utilities:** Most video adapters available today include bundled software on CD-ROM. The software usually highlights the top features of the video card (for example, a 3D video card typically includes one or two games that take advantage of the card's 3D hardware). Other favorites are multimedia encyclopedias and educational multimedia software for kids. The best cards have utilities that add functionality to Windows, like enabling you to quickly change the resolution of your desktop. Look for the software bundle that best fits your needs.

✔ **TV output:** If you create business presentations or broadcast-quality animation on your computer, how can you display your work on your television (or transfer it to videotape)? The easiest method is to buy a video adapter that can display output on a TV, VCR, or videocamera as well as on a monitor.

A video card with *TV output* is not the same thing as a *TV card* (an adapter that enables you to watch TV in a little window on your monitor). Although a TV card is just the thing for sports fanatics and those who refuse to miss their soaps, don't expect to be able to watch TV just because your video card has TV output. See Chapter 15 for more on TV cards.

✔ **Video panning:** If you have the necessary RAM, some cards enable you to *pan* your screen around a huge image or document, rather like a movie camera pans to keep an actor in view while he moves from one part of the set to the other. This feature lets you view the whole image or document, even though it's so big that it doesn't fit all on one screen. If you're going to edit large graphics in Photoshop (or edit large documents or brochures in a desktop publishing package), video panning may be a valuable feature for you.

✔ **DPMS support:** A video card with DPMS (short for *Display Power Management Signaling*) support can shut down your monitor to save energy in case you leave your computer unattended for a preset amount of time. (This feature requires a DPMS monitor, which I cover later in this chapter.)

DVD details

You may have already noticed a new type of video disc that has entered the public eye: *DVD,* which is acronym-speak for *Digital Video Disc.* This type of disc, the new generation of CD-ROMs, is predicted to eventually replace the VHS tape for home movie distribution.

Why? First, single-sided DVDs hold about seven times the data of a standard CD-ROM — an incredible 4.7GB (gigabytes) — so they have the storage capacity required to hold even the longest movies. (Double-sided DVDs will hold a whopping 17GB!) Plus, DVDs carry Dolby Digital surround sound, and there's even plenty of room for niceties like subtitling in multiple languages. Finally, DVDs use a new form of MPEG encoding, MPEG-2, which provides a picture as good as commercial satellite TV (much better than your average VHS tape). Make sure that your video card has hardware MPEG-2 support to take advantage of DVD (some manufacturers label their cards as "DVD ready" to make this clear).

For complete coverage of DVD drives meant for PC use, see Chapter 8.

Staking Out Your Visual Territory

Luckily, there's less to remember about your computer's monitor than there is about your video adapter — although it's still just as important in providing you with the best possible display. In this section, I discuss the selling points of a good monitor.

Like a keyboard, a monitor is something you really need to try in person. You need to *see* the monitor and its display with your own eyes before you buy it — often, the only difference between two monitors with similar prices is that one simply looks better to you.

If you live in a larger town with at least one or two computer stores, visit each store and take a look at the monitors they offer. Before you decide to buy, write down the brand name and model number of the monitor and see whether you can buy it online or through mail order in *Computer Shopper* for less.

Whichever monitor you choose, it *must* be capable of displaying SVGA graphics. Without an SVGA monitor, even the best video card and the most powerful Pentium III computer will look like those old "Pong" games from the early 1980s. (Luckily, it's getting harder to find a VGA monitor these days, for exactly that reason.)

"Should I toss my 14-inch monitor?"

You can buy a monitor in several different sizes (all measured diagonally, like a TV): 14-inch, 15-inch, 17-inch, 19-inch — even all the way up to a 21-inch monitor (which is especially useful for those doing desktop publishing or computer-aided drafting). Which is the right size for you?

You can compare the size of your monitor to the size of your car. A 14-inch monitor is like a '71 Volkswagen Beetle, and a 21-inch monitor is like a BMW sports sedan. They both do the same job — driving you where you want to go — but one is faster, bigger, and more fun to drive (as well as much more expensive). You can stretch out in the BMW, and it has all the latest controls and a gaggle of automatic functions that keep everything in sync — it's the same with the 21-inch monitor.

In general, the larger the monitor, the easier it is on your eyes, especially if you'll be chained in front of your computer for hours at a time. At the same resolution, the 17-inch monitor displays the same images as the 14-inch, but the image is physically bigger and the details stand out more clearly. As you increase the resolution of your desktop (to 1024 x 768 or so), the monitor size becomes more important — the smaller monitor needs to shrink everything in order to fit the entire desktop on its screen.

Ever heard the old adage "How big is a 19-inch TV?" Computer monitors suffer from the same inaccuracy; although two monitors may both be advertised as 17 inches, one of them may have an *actual viewing area* of 15.9 inches, and the other may have a viewing area of 16.1 inches. As you may expect, the second monitor displays more than the first. The first monitor probably looks the same size, but you'll probably be paying for more plastic case than usable screen area. When you're shopping for a monitor, it's worth paying a few dollars more for the monitor with a larger actual viewing area.

For games and general home use, a 15-inch or 17-inch monitor is fine; if you plan to do graphics-intensive work for several hours at a time, however, I would point you toward at least a 17-inch or 19-inch monitor.

Dot pitch: Sounds like a cartoon character

While shopping for a monitor, you can use another important figure for comparison: a monitor's *dot pitch*. Rather than go into an exhaustive technonerd discussion of electron guns, cathode-ray tubes, and magnetic fields, just keep this in mind — the lower a monitor's dot pitch, the more detailed and precise the display. (In fact, dot pitch refers to the distance between pixels; the smaller the dot pitch, the closer the pixels and the more detailed the image.)

Although more expensive monitors boast a .24 or .26 dot pitch, typical SVGA monitors have a *.28 dot pitch,* which is fine for most computer users. Any dot pitch higher than .28 loses a noticeable amount of detail, resulting in a grainy appearance at higher resolutions — the higher the dot pitch, the worse the image becomes.

Feeling refreshed?

Another feature to look for while shopping for a monitor is a high *refresh rate,* which refers to the number of times per second your video adapter card redraws the image on-screen. Always look for a monitor with a refresh rate of at least 60 Hz, and the higher the refresh rate, the better. Although the human eye can't see it, most monitors redraw each pixel on the screen 60 times a second (for a refresh rate of *60 Hz*). The screen is drawn line by line, starting at the top left corner; Figure 6-3 shows you this process.

Although you can't see the screen being redrawn, the human eye *can* discern the difference between 60 Hz and 70 Hz — the more times the screen is redrawn every second, the sharper, clearer, and more stable the image appears. The best monitors now have average refresh rates of between 75 Hz and 80 Hz. If you plan to spend long hours in front of your monitor, you'll probably feel less fatigued and your eyes will be in better shape if your monitor offers a higher refresh rate. Your video card needs to support a higher refresh rate, too.

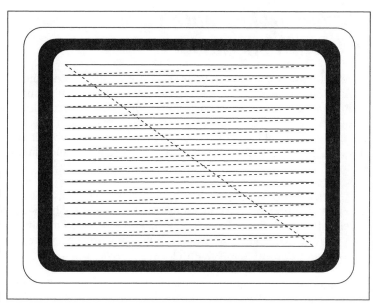

Figure 6-3:
Can you imagine repeating this path 60 times a second?

Common refresh rates for today's PCs are 72 Hz, 75 Hz, 80 Hz, and 95 Hz. (I recommend anything above 75 Hz.) However, some very expensive high-performance monitors (commonly used for computer-aided drafting) can handle refresh rates over 100 Hz. If your monitor and video card have Windows 95 or Windows 98 drivers, your computer can automatically set the optimal refresh rate for your particular hardware combination.

Remember that the best judge of a monitor's display is your own eye, so use it!

Attack of the dot-pitch piranha

There you are, shopping for a monitor at your local computer chain store. The salesperson swoops down like a vulture and leads you to a remarkably cheap 19-inch monitor. "Isn't this a great deal?" he crows. "You get a 19-inch monitor for about the same price as a 17-inch!"

Here's your response: Stare him straight in his beady little eyes and ask him, "Okay, slugger, what's the dot pitch on this great deal?" If his answer is something outrageous, like "a .39 dot pitch," you can bet that the monitor probably

won't reach a higher resolution than 800 x 600 — and the display won't be very readable, either! AT best, you may find a monitor like this one suitable for playing MS-DOS computer games at 640 x 480 resolution, although using it under Windows will eventually drive you insane from the grainy, smudgy-looking fonts.

These cheap monitors are usually an off-brand because no major monitor manufacturer (like NEC, Sony, or MAG Innovision) would want to produce such a monster.

Interlacing has nothing to do with sneakers

You're not quite finished with your trip through the world of monitors yet — you have another important feature to look for while you're shopping. Many monitors advertise that they can display higher resolutions *noninterlaced,* and others say that they can provide the same resolution *interlaced.* For example, one model I saw on a recent trip to the local computer store can achieve a "high resolution of 1280 x 1024 interlaced." Which monitor is better?

If you guessed *noninterlaced,* you can go celebrate (later, though, after you finish this chapter). Noninterlaced monitors can display high-resolution images without the flickering associated with interlaced monitors and are much easier on the eyes after several hours of work with your PC. I recommend a noninterlaced monitor, and I use one myself.

Because an interlaced monitor actually skips every other line on the screen as it refreshes your display (as shown in Figure 6-4) and the phosphorescent coating inside the monitor tube stops glowing quickly, an interlaced monitor can demonstrate a flickering effect as it refreshes the monitor screen. This flickering can range from "barely noticeable" to "absolutely horrifying" (depending on the resolution you've chosen), and can cause headaches or lead to eye fatigue. Because an interlaced monitor doesn't have to work as hard as a noninterlaced monitor, it is generally less expensive.

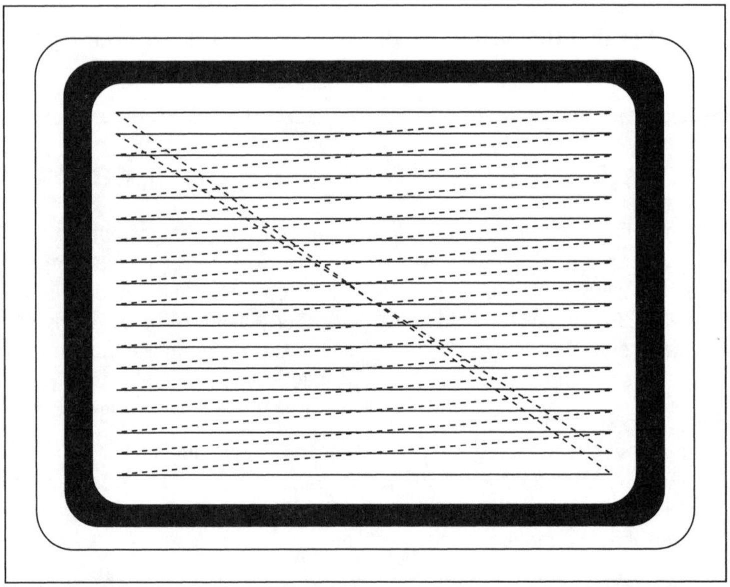

Figure 6-4:
An interlaced monitor skips lines when it redraws the screen.

TECHNICAL STUFF

Time to redraw . . . time to redraw . . .

"Why does the computer have to redraw the image?" Good question. Thank goodness that it doesn't require a degree in electrical engineering to answer the question, or else I'd be seriously stuck.

The image you see on your monitor's tube is actually emitted by a glowing phosphorescent coating on the inside of the tube. This coating glows as it's being hit with a stream of electrons. However, while the electrons are focused on another portion of the screen, the pohospho-rescent coating dims and then stops glowing entirely. So the monitor must redraw the image constantly to keep it stable.

Because your choice in monitors depends on how the display looks to you, I recommend actively shopping for your monitor rather than simply choosing something with "the best price for the most features" from a mail-order cata-log. Even the most expensive monitor may flicker or look blurry to you. It's a very personal decision.

What else makes a great monitor?

When you're familiar with the major features of a good monitor, you're almost ready to go shopping. In this section, I list a number of extra features you should look for while selecting the monitor that works best for you. Keep in mind that these features can appear on a good 14-inch monitor as well as on an expensive 17-inch model:

✔ **Flat tube:** If you can imagine writing a document, playing a game, or answering your e-mail on the surface of a basketball, you get some idea of why computer owners crave monitors with screens as flat as possible. Old monitors with curved tubes tend to distort the display, especially if you're doing fine detail work, like drafting or desktop publishing layout.

✔ **Flat panel:** Although they're still much more expensive than standard tube monitors, these color displays are a dream come true. Flat-panel monitors use the same liquid-crystal technology as laptop computer screens, so they require only 15–20 percent of the depth of a regular monitor. With a flat-panel monitor, you get truly flat edge-to-edge display with no distortion and gorgeous color. Flat-panel screens also give off very little heat and use much less electricity, and, unlike a monitor with a tube, a flat-panel display emits virtually no radiation (so it's easier on your eyes, and you can spend longer periods of time in front of your computer without discomfort). Once available only in 15-inch models, larger 17-inch and 19-inch flat panel displays are hitting the market now that the price of the technology has started to drop.

✔ **Antiglare coating:** As a general rule, whatever you create or do on your computer should shine — *not* the monitor itself! An antiglare screen can be a big help in a brightly lit office or in an office that has a large number of windows. If you decide on a monitor that doesn't have an antiglare coating, you can still buy an antiglare panel and attach it to your monitor later.

✔ **Energy Star/DPMS-compliant:** Most Pentium-class motherboards sold these days have a power management system named *Energy Star* built-in. (Before Energy Star became a standard, these motherboards used to be called *green* or *power-saver* boards.) You can configure an Energy Star motherboard to power down the computer while you're off getting doughnuts. If your monitor is Energy Star-compliant, your computer can shut the monitor down too. When you return, press a key or move your mouse to wake up your computer, and congratulate yourself on saving both your money and your environment.

Some video cards can also perform this power-down function for your monitor — see whether your card's manual mentions that it's Energy Star/VESA DPMS compatible. If so, follow its instructions for enabling the power-saving features.

✔ **Low radiation:** Computer monitors emit electromagnetic radiation — depending on what you read, you may feel that computers also attract Bigfoot or UFOs — but the radiation is real. Your monitor is responsible for virtually all the electromagnetic emissions from your computer, which makes sense when you think about it: You're sitting in front of a big glass tube, on the other side of which are three big electron guns shooting a bazillion electrons at hyperwarp speed right at your head. Before you decide to go back to using an abacus, let me reassure you — computer monitors are safe to use! However, many monitors are designed to further reduce electromagnetic emissions to a standard called *MPR II,* set by the Swedish Board for Technical Accreditation, or the more stringent European TCO standard. If you plan to spend hours every day in front of your monitor, it's reassuring to know that you won't get a sunburn.

✔ **Digital controls:** Older monitors have thumbwheel controls, which you use to adjust everything from contrast and brightness to vertical and horizontal positioning. This method is fine, until your 4-year-old starts messing with them. Technonerds like me favor more precise digital controls with OSD (short for *On-Screen Display*) — they make fine-tuning your monitor's picture more like setting your VCR, with easy-to-follow menus that appear on the monitor itself.

Most monitors with digital controls also offer separate programmable configurations you can store in memory. If a particular program changes the characteristics of your screen, you can load a special configuration to take care of it rather than manually adjust your monitor each time.

✔ **Color configuration:** Does that pink really look like pink to you? If your monitor supports *color configuration,* you can change the hue of the colors displayed by your monitor. This feature is a real killer for users who do desktop publishing and image editing — they can adjust their colors to match the Pantone color chart used by printers.

✔ **Built-in speakers:** Built-in speakers aren't for everyone — they usually add a considerable amount to the price of your monitor, and the stereo separation from speakers that are only a few inches apart is pretty dismal. (Remember that the sound card has jacks that enable you to add your own external speakers, which typically sell for less than $50 a pair — for more information, see Chapter 9.) However, if you're looking for convenience and you want to save desktop space, you can investigate a monitor with built-in speakers.

✔ **Tilt/swivel pedestal:** Older CGA and EGA monitors usually came with little pop-up legs, but any good-quality monitor you buy today should have a base that tilts and swivels. Your neck will thank you! If you've scavenged an older VGA monitor without a base, you can also pick up a tilting *monitor stand* at most computer stores.

Take it from someone who spends hours a day writing at the keyboard — elevating your monitor correctly is very important. You should be able to sit down at your keyboard and type naturally, with your monitor at eye level and at least two feet distant from your eyes. With a properly positioned monitor, you should be able to work without undue strain on your neck or your eyes.

✔ **Warranty:** Because you can use an SVGA monitor with just about any IBM-compatible computer you may build in the foreseeable future, it's worth paying extra for a longer warranty. Most top monitors these days have a three- to five-year warranty; economy models typically offer only a one-year warranty.

Installing a Video Adapter Card

In this section, I show you how to add your video adapter card to your chassis. Your video adapter card will have one VGA port on the side of the card itself.

A word about configuration: Some video cards have a set of DIP switches on the outside of the card that configure settings like color or monochrome mode, and you should set them now. Other DIP switch settings may enable multiple monitors or adjust the refresh rate. Check your video card's manual for any switch or jumper settings you need to adjust.

Most video cards on the market today are called *jumperless* or *Plug and Play* — these video cards configure themselves automatically for your computer. For example, Windows 95 and Windows 98 can usually set up a Plug and Play video card automatically. If you have one of these video cards, congratulate yourself for your good choice — although it's still a good idea to check your manual for any last-minute instructions that may apply to your operating system.

To install your video adapter card, follow these instructions:

1. **Touch a metal surface before you handle your video card (or anything else on your computer).**

   Let me guess: You've been making balloon animals to amuse your kids? If so, your skin is now one big conductor for static electricity, and that static could damage your video card.

2. **If your computer chassis is plugged in, unplug it.**

3. **Locate an adapter card slot of the proper length at the back of your computer case.**

   If you have an AGP video card and a Pentium II or Pentium III motherboard, you should be able to easily locate the single AGP slot (it's usually in the middle of the motherboard). If you have a 32-bit PCI video card and a Pentium motherboard, you should use one of the shorter adapter card slots (these should be PCI slots). If you have a 16-bit ISA video card, use one of the longer adapter card slots. (Need help identifying what type of card slots you have? The section "Time to Meet Your Bus" in Chapter 4 illustrates these slots.)

   Most video adapter cards meant for Pentium-class computers these days fit only in an *AGP slot* or a *PCI slot*. If you're unsure whether you need a 16-bit ISA slot, an AGP slot, or a PCI slot, check your video card's documentation.

4. **When you locate the slot, take your favorite screwdriver and remove the screw and the metal slot cover at the back of the case.**

   Stick both parts in your spare-parts box.

5. **Pick up your video adapter card by the top corners. Line up the connector on the bottom of the card with the slot on the motherboard.**

   All the connectors and any notches on the video card should line up with the slot; the card's metal bracket should align with the open space created when you removed the slot cover.

   Does the adapter card have extra connectors that aren't positioned above the slot? If so, you're trying to fit a 16-bit card into an 8-bit or PCI slot. Look for a slot that has matching connectors and notches.

6. **If everything is lining up as it should, apply even pressure to the top of the card and push it down into the slot on the motherboard.**

   Although you won't hear a click, you should be able to tell when the card is firmly seated; and the bracket should be resting tightly against the case.

7. **Add the screw to the corresponding hole in the bracket and tighten down the bracket, but don't overtighten it.**

Connecting a Built-In Video Port

Along with serial and parallel ports, some motherboards these days also have their video adapter built-in. If your motherboard has video support onboard, you don't need to add a separate video adapter card — but you do still need to attach the video port to the back of your case and connect it to your motherboard. The video port should look something like a metal slot cover, but it also has a port on the outside and a cable that leads to the motherboard.

To install a built-in video port, follow these instructions:

1. **Touch a metal surface to discharge any static electricity on your body.**

   Why are you working on your computer right after unloading the dryer? Never handle any internal component of your computer until you touch a metal surface to discharge static.

2. **Remove the screw and the metal slot cover at the back of the computer case.**

   Stick both of these parts in your parts box.

3. **Insert the video port's slot cover (with the connector) into the vacant slot.**

4. **Add the screw and tighten down the bracket.**

5. **Check your motherboard manual and find the connector for the built-in video support.**

6. **Connect the cable as instructed by your motherboard's manual.**

Connecting Your Monitor

Connecting your monitor to your computer is a simple task, and, luckily, the VGA video port and cable connect only if they're correctly aligned.

Is a screen saver really necessary?

Do you need to protect your monitor by using a screen saver? This question is asked so often by new computer owners that I'd like to answer it for you here: The answer is No. Modern VGA and SVGA color monitors don't suffer from *burn-in,* as did the old monochrome monitors that were originally paired with IBM PCs, XTs, and ATs. Burn-in was a particularly horrible fate for a monochrome monitor; if left on for hours on end with the same display, the image would be literally *burned* into the monitor tube. That shadowy image would be visible even while you worked on other programs. Even today, you still see one of these ancient relics from time to time.

However, if you run Windows 95 or Windows 98, you get one or two screen savers for free anyway — those screen savers do come in handy:

✔ If you need a simple measure of security at your home or office, you can password-protect a screen saver, which prevents anyone else from using your computer. Be careful, though — it is still possible to bypass the screen saver by rebooting the computer (turning it off and then on again).

✔ You can configure some screen savers to display a scrolling message, which is perfect for letting fellow works know where you are and when you'll be back.

✔ Some screen savers are humorous enough to keep you from losing your cool on a particularly bad day.

To connect your monitor, follow these instructions:

1. **Locate the VGA video port on the back of your case.**

   Although the port is about the size of a serial port, notice that the VGA port has 15 pins.

2. **Align the connector on the end of the monitor cable with the video port.**

   The angled edges on the connector are designed to make sure that it goes on only the right way.

3. **When the connector is aligned correctly with the video port, push the connector in firmly.**

4. **If you want, you can tighten the connector by turning the knobs on the connector clockwise.**

   Some connectors use screws instead, and you'll need a very small screwdriver to tighten these connectors. If you feel that the connector is in firmly, you can leave it as is.

5. **Plug the three-prong power cord that came with your monitor into the matching connector on the back of your monitor's case.**

   Push the plug in firmly to make sure that it doesn't pop out.

6. **Plug the monitor's power cable into your friendly local wall socket.**

   If your wall socket accepts only two prongs — indicating that it isn't grounded — I would heartily recommend that you relocate your computer to a socket that *is* grounded (rather than sticking an adapter plug on the cable).

In case you noticed, the connector on the monitor end of your monitor's power cable and the connector on the computer end of your computer's power cable are very similar — in fact, they're interchangeable. Interchangeable cables were one of the first things that someone designed correctly for the IBM line of personal computers. Interchangeable cables let you grab whatever standard power cable is around, and use it on either your computer or your monitor. Most technotypes have at least one or two spare power cables in their parts box.

"Hey, I Can Finally (Kind of) Boot!"

That's right, you're finally going to see something on the screen after completing this chapter's tests. You can also visually check to make sure that your CPU and RAM chips are correctly recognized by your motherboard at this point.

If you've unplugged your PC, plug it back in now. Push the power switch on your monitor, and then push the power switch on the front or back of your case.

To make sure that all your stuff is recognized correctly by your computer, you should turn on your monitor and any external parts, like your modem or printer, before turning on your computer (or at the same time). The easiest and most convenient way to do this is to connect all the power cables from your various computer devices into the same surge protector; this way, you can turn the entire system on or off with a single flip of one switch, and your entire system is also protected against indirect power surges from lightning strikes or alien encounters.

If you've correctly installed your video adapter and connected your monitor cable, the following should happen:

- ✔ You should see a message on your screen, which identifies either the video adapter or the motherboard. It doesn't matter which you see — the important thing is that your monitor is displaying the message. (If your monitor doesn't display any text, check the installation of your video card, make sure that the monitor cable is firmly connected, and check to make sure you plugged your monitor in. Also, make sure that you've set both the contrast and brightness on your monitor to *medium.*)

- ✔ After a few seconds, you should see your computer counting the amount of RAM on your motherboard. Actually, your computer is testing your computer's RAM, so watch to make sure that you have all the memory you should have and that no error messages are displayed. (If your computer returns an error message about your system memory or RAM, go to Chapter 4 and check your RAM to make sure that you installed it correctly. You may also need to consult your motherboard's manual to make certain you picked the right bank to add RAM.)

- ✔ If the RAM test goes okay, your computer will probably show a screen detailing all the parts it can find (like what CPU you have), how much RAM you have, and how many ports it can locate. (If your computer locks up, return to Chapter 4 and double-check your CPU installation.)

At this point in the boot process, your computer tries to find a hard drive or floppy drive and promptly gets very upset when it doesn't find them. Poor thing — your computer will probably beep once or twice and then sulk in frustration. Turn off your computer and pet the case affectionately, and reassure your half-assembled chassis that you will be adding a hard drive and floppy drive in the next chapter.

If your machine completed this test, you've successfully added your video adapter and monitor to your system — good going!

Chapter 7

Make Room! Your Hard Drive and Other Storage Devices

• •

• •

*P*ermanent storage. Your new computer needs a warehouse to store all those programs and all that data you'll be using: For that, you need to add a hard drive. You could simply run your trusty Web browser, jump to your favorite online hardware mega-super-colossal-mall and buy the first hard drive you see. If you're looking for the best value, however, you should take your time and consider your options. To make an informed choice while you're shopping (and to make the installation easier), you need to know which hard drive features and specifications are most important.

A hard drive isn't the only magnetic storage device you need for your computer. In this chapter, I also introduce you to floppy disk drives, tape backups to protect you against the loss of your valuable data, and even removable magnetic storage that lets you carry anywhere from 250MB (megabytes) to a whopping 2.2GB (gigabytes) of data — in your pocket!

"Be Vewy Quiet . . . I'm Hunting for Hawd Dwives!"

Shopping for a hard drive that's suitable for your system? Then get ready because the acronyms are going to flow fast and free through this section. You'll find out more about what types of hard drives will fit in your computer, and the advantages and disadvantages of each breed of hard drive.

Today's technology twosome

Luckily, today's PCs use only two major types of internal hard drive technology:

- **Enhanced IDE:** This type of hard drive (commonly known as *EIDE*) is the successor to the IDE (or *Integrated Drive Electronics*) throne; the *enhanced* part simply means that these drives are even smaller, run even faster, and have even more storage capacity. As you can guess from its name, an IDE drive carries onboard most of the electronics that used to be located on a hard drive controller card. Enhanced IDE is the single most popular hard drive technology, and this type of drive is used in just about every PC manufactured today. Most EIDE adapter cards can control a maximum of four EIDE devices (including hard drives, tape backup drives, and CD recorders).

  Figure 7-1 illustrates the business end of a modern EIDE drive. Note the appearance and position of the power connector, the ribbon cable connector, and the master/slave jumper set. (You need to be familiar with all three components when you install your hard drive.) Of course, these components may be in different spots on your hard drive, but they're there — check your hard drive manual for their exact location. The master/slave jumper is particularly important; the setting you choose for this jumper determines whether the drive is the primary (or master) drive or the secondary (slave) drive in a PC with two hard drives. If you have only one drive, you should select Master drive in a single drive system. Your hard drive manual provides the settings for the master/slave jumper.

- **SCSI:** To be more precise, I should say SCSI-2, although most technoids simply shorten the name. SCSI is short for *Small Computer Systems Interface,* the power user's dream. A typical SCSI drive can move data many times faster than its EIDE counterpart, and the larger SCSI drives can hold an amazing 50GB or more. SCSI hard drives are often found on network server computers and powerful graphics workstations. (The SCSI hard drive used to be the standard for all Macintosh computers — something to remember for your next technotrivia game.)

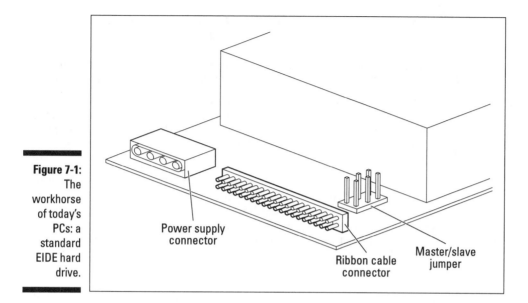

Figure 7-1:
The
workhorse
of today's
PCs: a
standard
EIDE hard
drive.

Power supply
connector

Ribbon cable
connector

Master/slave
jumper

SCSI speed isn't limited to hard drives, however: A typical SCSI adapter can connect as many as seven SCSI devices to your computer (including scanners and CD recorders). Some variants of SCSI can support as many as 15 devices. (Unfortunately, you really do pronounce it "scuzzy.") For complete details on SCSI and what it can do for your PC, jump to Chapter 11.

A hard drive genealogy

Hard drives have been one of the computer parts that have developed more quickly over the years, and the hallowed family of older acronyms is proof. In fact, the following acronyms are so old that I don't even bother spelling them out.

In the beginning, computers used *MFM* and *RLL* drives — big, heavy clunkers that actually used voice coil magnets (the kind of magnets used in stereo speakers). These hard drives took up half the computer's case. Most of us old-timers fondly remember an MFM drive thrashing around on our desktops. You can't buy one of these drives these days — unless you jump into a time machine.

The next arrival was the *ESDI,* a hot, new item that took hard drives to faster speeds and larger capacities. ESDIs needed new controllers, and every power user jumped on the bandwagon. Again, you can promptly forget about them.

IDE drives were next on the horizon, and some are still around. These drives were much smaller, lasted longer, and ran faster than earlier models. You can still find IDE drives on some 386 and most 486 computers.

"Okay," you say, "SCSI wins, right?" Wrong, believe it or not — EIDE is the hard drive of choice for three important reasons:

- ✔ EIDE drives and adapter cards are typically less expensive than SCSI hardware, which makes EIDE more popular with computer manufacturers.

- ✔ Not every computer application sees a dramatic performance increase from SCSI hardware; for example, your word processor doesn't perform any better with a SCSI drive than with an EIDE drive because hard disk access isn't important while you're typing.

- ✔ Third (and I think most important), SCSI adapter cards, drives, and devices can be the most aggravating beasts on the face of this planet to install and configure. Unlike EIDE, where a single jumper is all you have to set, a SCSI device chain requires correct termination and a unique SCSI ID number for each device. Many a computer guru has snapped from the frustration of trying to force a cantankerous SCSI card to work properly — usually these cards get thrown off a local bridge and float to the bottom, where they even irritate the fish.

With an EIDE drive, you need to set only a jumper or two and make sure that your cable is correctly connected, and you're ready to rock.

Other improvements have been made to EIDE — for example, *Ultra IDE drives* (sometimes called Ultra DMA or DMA/66 drives), which can move data in bursts of 66MB per second, although they require a special controller card. If you're building an original Pentium PC, stick with an industry-standard EIDE drive; if you're building a faster Pentium II or Pentium III PC, spend the extra money for Ultra IDE/Ultra DMA.

Don't give up entirely on SCSI, though — I describe it in detail in Chapter 11 and even show you how to install it. In fact, you can mix both SCSI and EIDE hardware in the same computer; if you find that you need a SCSI device chain after your computer is up and running with an EIDE drive, you can add it.

More stuff about hard drives

What specifications does a smart shopper look for in an EIDE drive? Here are a few:

- ✔ **Storage capacity:** No big mystery here — the more storage capacity, the more data you can store on a drive. Although an obsolete MFM drive of 50MB was considered overkill in its day, modern EIDE drives hold anywhere from 4GB to 40GB (a gigabyte is equal to 1,000MB). Hard drive capacities are always increasing over time.

On average, most home computers running Windows 98 need at least 2GB of hard drive space. For an office computer, the size of your hard drive is more dependent on what type of programs you run; some office software suites take up 300 or 500MB all by themselves. My personal recommendation? It's always a good idea to buy a drive so large that you can't imagine ever running out of space — believe me, my friend, you'll fill it up! I would suggest a drive of *at least* 6GB.

✔ **Access time:** A drive's access time (often called seek time) is a measure-ment of how fast the drive can read and write data — the lower the number, the faster the drive. This time is measured in milliseconds (abbreviated as *ms*), and it's usually listed next to the drive in advertise-ments. Naturally, the faster the drive, the more expensive it is (just once, I'd like the best of something to be the cheapest).

Today's fastest EIDE drives have access times of around 7 ms, although any speed from 9 ms to 12 ms should be fast enough for your Pentium computer. If you're a power user with a Pentium II or Pentium III proces-sor, stick with a drive below 10 ms.

✔ **rpm:** At last, an acronym that most of us understand! Yes indeed, this is your old friend, *revolutions per minute,* and it measures the speed at which the platters within your hard drive are moving. In general, the faster the rpm, the faster the drive can retrieve data. Before you strap a tachometer onto your drive, however, you should know that rpm is not as accurate as *access time* in predicting a drive's performance. A fast EIDE drive can hit more than 7,200 rpm, and I would recommend a drive that averages at least 5,400 rpm.

✔ **Size:** Most EIDE drives are 3½ inches, which means that they fit in a stan-dard 3½-inch bay (these are usually reserved for floppy disk drives, but they can be covered). If you have an open standard half-height 5¼-inch bay in your case, you need a drive cage kit to enable the 3½-inch drive to fit. A *drive cage* is simply a metal square that holds the smaller 3½-inch drive inside; in turn, the cage is fastened to the computer chassis as though it were a 5¼-inch device.

Some larger 50GB SCSI drives still use a full-height drive bay, although you're not likely to encounter this type of drive in the EIDE world.

✔ **Cache:** A hard drive's cache (sometimes called a buffer) holds data that's used frequently (or will soon be needed) by your CPU. With a disk cache, the hard drive itself doesn't have to actually reread that data over and over. As you may guess, the larger the cache, the better (and usually the more expensive the drive). I recommend a drive with at least a 512K cache.

✔ **Warranty:** A hard drive is one of the few parts in your computer that is both complex and has moving parts of its own, and a typical hard drive has a half-life of three years or so under normal use. The standard indus-try warranty for hard drives is three years, although you can find drives with warranties as long as five years.

Are you considering using a scavenged drive? If so, consider the condition of the drive carefully before deciding to use it. For example, if the drive is more than three or four years old (or if it's been used for several hours every day for two or three years), it's already well past middle age, and it's probably not fast enough for a Pentium II or Pentium III system. In essence, you'll be slowing down your entire computer if you use it. Also, older drives usually hold well under 1GB (a *gigabyte*), and perhaps as little as 500MB. With the size of today's Windows operating systems, a lower-capacity hard drive under 1GB doesn't give you much room for additional programs or data files. I urge you to consider a new hard drive that uses the latest technology.

The Ancient Floppy Still Lives — and Why

Once upon a time, long before modems and networks, only one way existed to transfer information from one computer to another, back up your computer files, or store data offsite: the floppy disk. The floppy disk was an icon, a universally recognized symbol that everyone revered, and if you didn't have a drawer full of floppies — well, Bucko, you just weren't *with it!*

Why aren't floppies trendy anymore?

A number of things have led to the gradual decline in importance of the floppy disk:

- Floppy disks are the most fragile of magnetic media. Even the plastic case of a 3½-inch floppy disk isn't much protection, and floppy disks are infamous for simply "losing" data through exposure to magnetic fields, heat, and simple old age. (Never, *never* put floppy disks on top of your stereo speakers. The next time you play Jimi Hendrix, they're goners!)

- The development of really big programs — programs that simply won't fit economically on 40 floppy disks — produced the perfect environment for the arrival of the CD-ROM.

- Floppy disks are as slow as watching paint dry; a program that takes 20 seconds to load from a floppy is loaded in less than a second from a hard drive. It's not practical to run a program from a floppy drive or access files regularly from a floppy.

So, why are floppy drives still standard equipment on computers?

Squeezing more space from a skinny hard drive

If you can't afford an 20GB hard drive, you can find another way to extend the storage capability of a smaller drive. DOS 6.22, Windows 95, and Windows 98 provide a nifty feature named *disk compression.* The Windows version is named DriveSpace. This utility enables you to create additional space on your hard drive by compressing your data so that it fits in a smaller amount of space. Whenever your computer needs that data, it's automatically decompressed on the fly and supplied to whatever program wants it.

Depending on what kind of data you store, you can nearly double the amount of space on a hard drive (some types of data compress better than others). Some computer owners are a little uneasy at using DriveSpace, especially because previous DOS-based disk-compression techniques had a tendency to "forget" data unless they were treated exactly right. If your computer is running under Windows 95 and Windows 98, however, I can recommend DriveSpace as a nearly foolproof way to immediately gain more hard drive territory. Refer to your Windows manual for more information on DriveSpace. If you're running another operating system, there may be a version of Stacker, a commercial compression program, that you can run.

Floppy drives are still standard equipment on computers partly because of the universal nature of 3½-inch floppy disks; they've been around for so long and everyone's so used to them that no computer manufacturer wants to take the plunge and produce a computer without a floppy drive. (Unless, of course, you're interested in a new Macintosh computer like the G4 or the iMac — but if you are, why are you reading this book?)

Another reason for the continued survival of the 3½-inch floppy is that all computer users still need some form of removable storage, and floppy drives are cheap. Better forms of removable media have been developed (for example, the Orb, Zip, and Jaz drives I mention later in this chapter). However, those types of drives are more expensive to produce, and they're not universal enough, yet.

IBM once attempted to make 2.88MB disks a standard, but that concept was met with hoots of derision by most of the computing world. By that time, digital video and audio had arrived on the Web and on CD-ROM, and even a small digital video or digital audio file probably wouldn't fit on a single floppy disk, even if that floppy could hold 2.88MB.

Also, important data still resides on 3½-inch floppies around the world.

Selecting a floppy drive

There really isn't much in the way of features to look for when you're buying a floppy disk drive.

If you have older 5¼-inch 1.2MB floppy disks you still need to read, you might consider an *over and under* floppy drive combo, which fits both a 3½-inch drive and a 5¼-inch drive in the same half-height 5¼-inch drive bay. Otherwise, you need a standard 3½-inch high-density 1.44MB floppy drive.

Don't Forget Your Controller Card

Many motherboards sold these days feature more than just integrated serial ports and parallel ports. Your motherboard may already have a built-in hard drive and floppy drive *controller.* If your motherboard does not have a built-in *enhanced IDE controller,* it's time to go shopping for one. A controller directs the flow of data to and from your hard drives, floppy drives, and any additional devices.

Today's Pentium III CPUs gulp files from your hard drive as fast as it can send them, so — like your video adapter — your EIDE hard drive controller should definitely use a 32-bit PCI bus, which is much faster than an ISA bus. If your motherboard doesn't have PCI slots, you'll have to settle for a 16-bit ISA controller that fits in an ISA slot.

Here are two other features you should consider for your controller (whether it's built-in to your motherboard or a separate adapter card):

- ✔ **Secondary IDE support:** When IDE was first introduced, no one imagined that anyone would need more than two hard drives or IDE devices, so the original IDE specification called for only two drives. People rapidly got upset and there was talk of revolution, so computer hardware manufacturers decided to create a secondary IDE port for computers that needed more than two drives. Because many CD-ROM drives are IDE devices, check to make sure the controller (or motherboard) you're buying can support four IDE drives.

- ✔ **Cache:** A controller memory cache stores data that's used often, or will probably be required by your CPU very soon; it improves performance because the CPU can retrieve the data from the memory cache, which is much faster than rereading it from the drive. Don't spend any extra on a caching controller, however, unless you're a power user or you plan to use your computer as a network server or something equally taxing — home PCs and simple office PCs really don't need such high-speed disk access.

Selecting a Tape Drive

One thing that floppy disks were once good for was backing up your hard drive. Of course, in those days a hard drive held 50MB or 75MB, so you needed only a box or two of 3½-inch high-density floppies to do the job. However, no one would even consider backing up one of today's 16GB or 24GB hard drives on 1.44MB floppy disks — no one deserves punishment like that. As a result, many computer owners don't back up their data.

Now, consider that statement carefully because, unfortunately, it's true. The vast majority of computer owners in the world have absolutely no recourse if their hard drive fails or if they happen to delete the wrong file or directory. If your data is important to you — and I'm certainly assuming that it is — can you really afford to lose it all in a few seconds?

(If you answered No, keep reading. If you answered Yes, I'm wondering why you need a computer in the first place.)

Three popular solutions exist for backing up your data easily: a tape backup unit, a Zip or Jaz drive, and a CD recorder. I discuss the Zip and the Jaz drive in the next section, and I attack CD recorders in Chapter 8. For now, I concentrate on backing up your hard drive to tape.

Tape drives vary widely in speed and capacity. Older QIC-80 models, which used to be the standard, maxed out at about 250MB per tape (with compression — the tape actually held only 120MB, but the backup software automatically compressed the data as it was written to tape, so you could squeeze as much as 50 percent more data onto one tape). Typical speeds were about 10MB per minute, although some drive manufacturers offered proprietary tape drive adapter cards that can boost speeds to as much as 19MB per minute.

However, even backing up 250MB at a time has become anachronistic, so the QIC-80 standard was updated to a technology named *Travan,* which can hold anywhere from 800MB to 8GB of compressed data per tape. These drives can typically save data at anywhere from 40 to 60MB per minute. Figure 7-2 shows a typical Travan drive.

Most Travan drives are internal drives and take up a single half-height bay. Although some Travan drives require a separate controller card (which should be provided along with the drive), most either connect to your floppy drive cable or act as another IDE or SCSI device. Some external tape backup units connect to your parallel port; these external tape drives are good for office use or if you have both a laptop and a desktop computer and want to back up the data on both of them, although they're typically much slower than an IDE or SCSI model. You can pick up a Travan drive for less than $200.

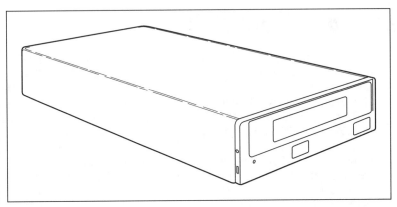

Figure 7-2:
A standard Travan internal tape drive, which holds as much as 8GB of data per tape.

The Cadillac of tape backup units is the DAT drive (short for *d*igital *a*udio-*t*ape), which is several times faster than a Travan drive in both backing up and restoring files. DAT tapes can also hold anywhere from 2GB to 24GB of data on a single tape, so if you're looking for a backup solution with the least amount of tape swapping, DAT is your choice. As you may expect, these drives are more expensive, averaging about $500, and most of them demand a SCSI adapter card before you can use them. (Find out more about SCSI in Chapter 11.) DAT tapes are far more reliable than older magnetic backup tapes, and they're faster than Travan drives.

Whichever method you choose to back up your data, I *strongly* urge you to make it a habit to back up once a week or once a month, depending on how often the important data on your drive changes.

I back up my entire system to tape once a week. However, to back up individual files conveniently, you can still use floppy disks. Although they can only hold 1.44MB, floppy disks work well to back up smaller files you're working on — Word document files or address book data, for example. These files are small enough to fit easily on a single floppy, and no fancy backup software is required. For example, I simply copy the latest versions of the files I'm working on to a floppy, and copy the files back to my hard drive in case I do something really dumb. Remember, however, that you can't rely on floppy disks as permanent backup!

Hey, You Just Removed Your Media!

In this section, I tell you about two drives that enable you to take anywhere from 250MB to 2.2GB of data and run with it — or mail it, or toss it to a coworker, or even lock it in a safety deposit box. I'm talking about two popular removable-media drives from Iomega: the Zip drive and the Jaz drive as well as the Orb drive, from Castlewood Systems. A removable-media drive enables you to insert and remove cartridges (or, in some cases, actual hard drive platters) so that you can take your data with you.

The Zip drive: The floppy with muscle

Iomega caused a minor revolution a couple years ago by introducing the *Zip drive,* which uses a cartridge very similar in size and shape to a standard 1.44MB 3½-inch floppy. The original Zip drive held 100MB; the new model holds 250MB of data and accesses that data much faster than your old friend, the floppy drive. The Zip features an average seek time of 29 milliseconds.

Although each Zip disk sells for anywhere from $10 to $15, the ability to store 250MB means that you finally have a means for carrying those digital video and audio files, or perhaps the contents of an entire Web site — all on a disk you can carry in your pocket. Technonerds around the globe breathed a sigh of relief at the same time.

Figure 7-3 illustrates the parallel port version of the Zip drive, which simply connects to your printer port. Only one small program is really necessary to run the drive under DOS, Windows 3.1, Windows 95, Windows 98, Windows 2000, Windows Me, or Windows NT. And, unlike with a software driver, you can load the program at any time. However, if you install the entire set of Zip drive utilities, you can password-protect a disk or catalog the contents of all your disks so that you can locate a single file easily.

Figure 7-3:
An Iomega Zip removable media drive caught napping.

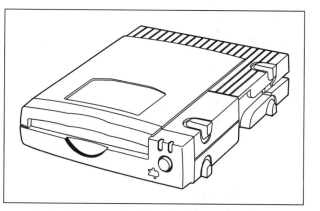

The Zip drive is also available in a SCSI version, which is 20 to 30 percent faster than its parallel port sibling. At the time this chapter was written, both versions were about $150, although the SCSI version naturally requires a SCSI adapter card. (Chapter 11 provides all the details on SCSI.)

Although Zip disks hold less data than a Travan tape drive, they're faster — many computer owners therefore use Zip drives for backing up portions of their hard drives. Recognizing this, Iomega includes a simple-to-use backup and restore program with both versions of the Zip drive.

The Jaz drive: The technoid's storage weapon

Soon after the introduction of the Zip drive, Iomega started producing the *Jaz drive,* and other hard drive manufacturers cringed — this drive stores 2GB on a single cartridge. Unlike the Zip drive, the Jaz cartridge is actually a removable hard drive platter. Basically, when you're carrying a Jaz cartridge, you're carrying the guts of a hard drive with you — without all the hard drive electronics. When you insert the cartridge, the rest of the machinery is moved into place, and — wham! you've got a hard drive. Figure 7-4 illustrates the Jaz drive.

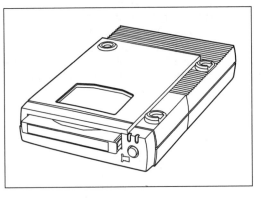

Figure 7-4: A SCSI Jaz drive is a portable boss at 2GB per cartridge.

Although Jaz drives are SCSI-only, they've got an average access time of about 12 ms, which is only a millisecond or so slower than a regular fast hard drive. Jaz drives are therefore perfect for presentations and digital video. The external Jaz drive (which weighs a whopping two pounds) simply plugs in to the external SCSI port on your SCSI adapter card.

The internal Jaz drive (which fits inside your computer case) currently sells for a little under $300. The external (portable) Jaz drive sells for around $400. Cartridges usually run around $120 each.

Do you really need removable storage, or are you just fascinated by toys?

To be absolutely honest, you don't absolutely need a removable storage drive, unless your primary application fits one of these criteria:

✔ If you plan to send or receive files that can't be efficiently sent over the Internet or by floppy disk (because the files are just too big). Fir example, publishers and printers love to use the Zip and Jaz drives to send desktop publishing files.

✔ If security is an issue and you want to protect your data, the best way to do so is to take your data with you or lock it up — Jaz and Zip drives make taking your important data with you easy.

✔ If you want to store information without filling up your hard drive, a Zip or Jaz drive can act as a warehouse for archiving data.

Yes, any technonerd would long to add one of these drives to his or her system!

The Orb has landed

If you want a removable media drive with 2.2GB of capacity and a wealth of connection options, you're asking for the Orb drive, from Castlewood Systems (www.castlewood.com). Orb cartridge drives are available with parallel port, USB, and SCSI external connections and with internal IDE and SCSI drives. At a street price of around $175 to $200 for the internal versions (and around $25 per cartridge), the Orb is an economical choice, too. Its cartridge isn't much bigger than that hoary floppy, and it's sturdy enough to mail or ship across town or around the world.

The average access time for an Orb drive is close to that of a traditional hard drive — so, like the Jaz drive, it's a good choice for retrieving digital video and sound files for your multimedia projects. You can also use an Orb drive as a fast backup unit for selected directories on your hard drive; a simple backup application is included with the drive.

If you're running multiple operating systems — for instance, Windows 98 and Linux on the same PC — removable cartridge drives like the Orb and the Jaz make it easy to store files you use with "that other operating system" when you're not using it. For example, a friend of mine stores his Linux source code and compiler files on a Jaz drive so that they don't take up valuable space on his hard drive — and he can carry them with him when he travels out of town!

Connecting Your Drive Controller Card

Remember that your EIDE controller may be built into your motherboard — if so, congratulate yourself. Then skip to Step 8 of this section and continue to the installation of your EIDE hard drive and floppy drive (covered in the following sections).

Ready? Then follow these steps to install your drive controller card:

1. **Oh, my goodness — you've been struck by lightning! Now is not the time to install a computer component; in case you can't wait, however, touch a metal surface before you handle anything. This action discharges any static electricity your body may be carrying.**

2. **If your computer chassis is plugged in, unplug it.**

3. **Locate an adapter card slot of the proper length at the back of your case.**

   Most EIDE controller cards for Pentium computers fit only in a PCI slot. If you're unsure whether you need a 16-bit ISA or PCI slot, check your card's documentation.

4. **After you locate the adapter slot, unsheathe your mighty screwdriver and remove the screw and the metal slot cover at the back of the case.**

   Stick both parts in your spare parts box. Return your screwdriver to your tool belt.

5. **Pick up your controller card by the top corners. Line up the connector on the bottom of the card with the slot on the motherboard. All the connectors and any notches should line up with the slot, and the card's metal bracket should align with the open space left when you removed the slot cover.**

6. **If the connector on the bottom of the card lines up with the slot, apply even pressure to the top of the card and push it down into the slot on the motherboard.**

   Although you don't hear a click, you should be able to tell when the card is firmly seated, and the bracket should be resting tightly against the case.

7. **Again, your screwdriver answers the call! Add the screw and tighten down the card's bracket until it's snug.**

8. **Check your controller (or motherboard) manual for the location of two connectors: You should find one connector on the controller or your motherboard for the primary hard drive and one connector for the floppy drive. Attach the ribbon cables that came with your controller or motherboard to these connectors, as shown in your manual.**

   Make sure that you connect the correct cable to each connector — the floppy drive cable usually has a twist in it toward the end that connects to the drive.

For any ribbon cable connector you attach to a drive or adapter card, Pin 1 on the male connector must always match the hole for Pin 1 on the female connector. In almost every case, Pin 1 on the male connector is the pin in the upper-left corner of the connector. "Okay," you say, "but how can I tell which side of the ribbon cable is Wire 1?" No problem — every ribbon cable has one wire that's painted red or somehow marked with a design (or lettering, perhaps). That wire is Wire 1, which should always connect to Pin 1. Figure 7-5 illustrates this phenomenon.

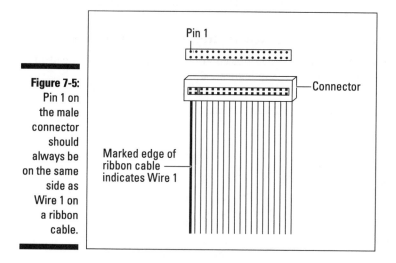

Figure 7-5:
Pin 1 on the male connector should always be on the same side as Wire 1 on a ribbon cable.

Installing Your EIDE Hard Drive

Installing an EIDE drive is a pretty simple procedure. Follow these steps to install your hard drive:

1. **Just finished combing your hair? Now that you look marvelous, touch a metal surface before you handle your drive; this action discharges any static electricity you may have picked up.**

2. **If your computer chassis is plugged in, unplug it.**

3. **If you're installing only one drive, check the jumper settings on your hard drive to make sure that it's set for *single drive, master unit*.**

   This setting is the default factory setting for most drives, although it never hurts to be sure. If the jumpers aren't set correctly, move them to the correct positions for *single drive, master unit*. If you're installing two devices (or a second device on a PC that already has one EIDE hard drive), your EIDE hard drive must be set as *multiple drives, master unit*, and the other device should be set as *multiple drives, slave unit*.

4. **Select an open drive bay for your hard drive.**

   Depending on the size of your drive, it may fit in a 3½-inch bay, or you may have to use a 5 1/4-inch half-height bay. If you want to fit a 3½-inch drive into a 5¼-inch half-height bay, you need a drive cage kit, which contains rails that fit on the side of the hard drive, bringing its total width to 5¼ inches. If the drive is the same size as the open bay, you don't need a cage kit and you can simply add the screws.

5. **Does your drive need a cage kit? If so, now is the time to attach it. Use the screws that came with your drive to attach the cage rails onto both sides of your drive.**

6. **Slide the drive into the selected bay from the front of the case.**

   The end with the connectors should go in first, and the electronic stuff should be on the bottom, as in Figure 7-6.

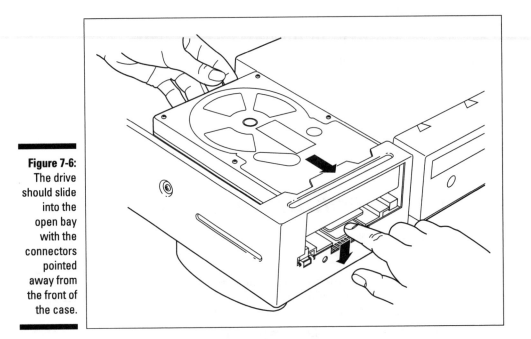

Figure 7-6:
The drive should slide into the open bay with the connectors pointed away from the front of the case.

7. **Carefully slide the hard drive back and forth in the drive bay until the screw holes in the side of the bay line up with the screw holes on the side of the drive. Use the screws that came with the drive (or your cage kit) to attach the drive to the side of the bay.**

   You generally use four screws to secure the hard drive to the bay.

8. **Connect one of the power cables from your power supply to the power connector on the hard drive.**

   This connector fits only one way. Press it in firmly to make certain that it doesn't pull out.

9. **Connect the ribbon cable coming from the controller card (or your motherboard if it has a built-in controller) to the back of the hard drive.**

   Remember: The wire with the markings is Wire 1 — if you're unsure which pin on the drive's connector is Pin 1, check your drive's manual. The connector should fit snugly, so after it's correctly aligned, press it all the way on. Many drive and cable manufacturers now help solve this problem by blocking one hole and one pin on the two connectors (a trick called *keying*), so that the cable fits only one way!

Well done! You don't have to be an electrician to install a hard drive.

Installing Your 3½-inch Floppy Disk Drive

Follow these steps to install your 1.44MB 3½-inch floppy disk drive:

1. **Now that you're done dusting the furniture and building up static, touch a metal surface before you install your floppy drive; this action discharges any nasty static electricity you may be carrying.**

2. **If your computer chassis is plugged in, unplug it.**

3. **Select an open drive bay for your floppy drive. All cases come with at least one 3½-inch bay especially for your floppy drive, so use that one.**

   If you have a computer case from the planet Quark that doesn't have a 3½-inch drive bay, you can even use a 5¼-inch half-height bay if you get a *drive cage kit*.

    Is your 3½-inch drive bay sitting vertically so that it's sideways in the case? Never fear — you weren't sold a mutant case; floppy drives work both horizontally *and* vertically. Smile knowingly to yourself and continue the installation.

4. **Slide the drive into the selected bay from the front of the case. (The end with the connectors should go in first.)**

   If you're installing the drive horizontally, the button that ejects the disk should be on the bottom; if you're installing the drive vertically, it doesn't matter which way it faces.

5. **Slide the floppy drive back and forth in the drive bay until the screw holes in the side of the bay line up with those on the side of the floppy drive. Use the screws that came with the floppy drive to attach the drive to the side of the bay.**

   You generally use two screws to secure the floppy drive to the bay.

6. **Connect one of the power cables from your power supply to the power connector on the floppy drive.**

   To avoid mistakes, this connector fits only one way. Push it in as far as possible.

7. **Connect the ribbon cable coming from the controller card (or your motherboard if it has a built-in controller) to the back of the drive.**

   If you're installing this floppy drive as your drive A (the standard configuration for PCs), use the last connector on the cable (the one after the twist in the cable). This connector goes on only one way and should fit snugly. When the connector is aligned correctly, press it all the way on.

Installing Your Internal Tape Backup Drive

Did you decide to install a Travan or DAT tape drive for backups? Good idea — you'll be happy you did after you've filled up several gigabytes of hard drive space. Follow these steps to install an internal IDE tape backup drive:

1. **Silk sheets on the bed? Say no more — touch a metal surface before you touch the inside of your computer. This action discharges any static electricity that may be hiding on your person.**

2. **If your computer chassis is plugged in, unplug it.**

3. **Select an open drive bay for your tape drive.**

   If your tape drive fits in a 3½-inch drive bay, use that drive bay. Otherwise, you can use a 5¼-inch half-height bay and a drive cage kit.

   Unlike a 3½-inch floppy drive, your tape drive *must* sit horizontally in your computer case so that you can't use it in a vertical drive bay.

4. **Slide the tape drive into the selected bay from the front of the case. (The end with the connectors should go in first.)**

   Check your drive manual for the correct orientation. (Most units have some sort of label on the front that tells which end is up.)

5. **Slide the tape drive back and forth until the screw holes in the side of the bay line up with those on the side of the drive. Use the screws that came with the tape drive (or your cage kit) to attach the drive to the side of the bay.**

   You generally use four screws to secure the tape drive to the bay.

6. **Connect one of the power cables from your power supply to the power connector on the drive.**

   This connector fits only one way, which makes life easier for everyone. Make sure that you push it in tightly.

7. **Most tape backup units connect to your floppy ribbon cable (or the drive comes with its own ribbon cable, and your floppy drive plugs into that).**

   Check your tape drive manual to see which method your drive uses, and follow the instructions for connecting the cable.

Configuring Your Hard Drive and Testing Everything

In this section, you configure your new hard drive and format it.

 You need a copy of the full MS-DOS 6.22 installation disk set for this section. It doesn't matter whether you plan to run Windows 98, Windows NT, or OS/2 later on — for now, DOS enables you to check your computer and format your EIDE hard drive.

Setting up your PC and configuring your hard drive

To get started with your hard drive setup, make sure that the monitor and keyboard are connected and your computer is plugged in. Then follow these steps:

1. **Before you turn on your computer, insert the first disk of the MS-DOS installation disk set into your floppy drive.**

   Also, check your motherboard manual and see what key or key combination displays your computer's _CMOS setup_ screen. (CMOS stands for _complementary metal oxide semiconductor_ — it's a type of RAM that stores data even after your PC is turned off.) Usually, the key you press to display this screen is the Delete key (or perhaps F1). If you can't find the key, don't panic — all motherboards display the setup key when you turn on the computer — just watch closely and be prepared to press the key.

2. **Push the power switch on the front or back of your case.**

3. **When you see the screen prompt to enter your setup screen, press the indicated key.**

   Although the screen that appears varies with every motherboard, you should see a menu with at least one entry for `IDE HDD Auto Detect` or `Hard Drive Auto Detection` or something similar. Use your cursor keys to select that function and follow the on-screen instructions — your motherboard should identify your hard drive's characteristics automatically.

4. **After you enter the hard drive settings, select the standard settings screen and set your drive A as a** `3½-inch 1.44MB floppy drive.`

   On this same screen, set the computer's internal clock with the current date and time.

5. **Exit setup — make sure to save the values you entered.**

   Usually, you see a separate menu item to "save values and exit." Your computer should now reboot.

Your PC can now recognize its hard drive and floppy drive. For your floppy drive, that's all that's necessary; however, your hard drive must now be formatted before your computer can access it.

Formatting your hard drive

At this point, your new computer knows that it has a hard drive and a floppy drive and the specifications of those drives. However, the hard drive isn't partitioned or formatted — so, when you reboot your PC, it can't access the hard drive (and you can't load that fancy operating system you've been hankering to use). After what will seem like an agonizing wait, your computer beeps and informs you that there's been a hard drive failure. Smile quietly to yourself, insert the first disk of your MS-DOS installation set, and continue the boot process by pressing the indicated key; the floppy drive should spring to life, and eventually the DOS prompt appears.

If you have a scavenged drive that already has existing data, it should boot correctly if it was drive C (the primary hard drive) on the original PC. I would still recommend that you partition and format it, however, to ensure that the formatting will be completely compatible with your hard drive controller.

Ready to format your hard drive? Good for you — I'll make an honest-to-goodness computer guru out of you yet! In effect, formatting prepares your hard drive to hold data by creating areas to store information on the magnetic surface, as well as a directory that stores the location of all the files you save to your hard drive.

If the MS-DOS installation program appears, just press Escape and exit out of it — you can't install DOS until the drive is partitioned and formatted.

1. **Type** FDISK **at the DOS prompt and press Enter.**

   The FDISK program appears. This program enables you to prepare your drive for formatting as well as divide a single physical hard drive into multiple drive letters. Your drive must be partitioned (in nontechnoid terms, divided into one or more drive letters) before you can format it.

2. **Press Enter to select option 1 and then select the option Create Primary DOS Partition.**

   When prompted by FDISK, indicate that you want to create one huge partition.

3. **After FDISK creates the partition and it has been activated, press Esc to exit FDISK and return to the DOS command prompt.**

   This action rudely reboots your computer. Your computer once again complains that it can't find a hard drive. Once again, press the indicated key and allow DOS to boot from the floppy disk.

4. **When the DOS prompt appears, type the innocent-looking command** FORMAT C: /S **and then press Enter.**

   This command tells DOS to format your new C: drive, and the /S part specifies that DOS should copy over the necessary DOS system files that enable your computer to boot from the hard drive. If you're installing the first hard drive in your computer, FDISK assigned your drive the identifying letter C:, which is reserved for the first hard drive in a system.

   If your new drive was assigned a different letter by FDISK, you must specify that letter rather than C. For example, if you're installing a second hard drive, you already have a working C: drive, and FDISK probably assigned your second hard drive the letter D:, so you would substitute D: for C: in the previous command.

   Although you're formatting this drive because it's brand-new, you should never, never, *never* type the command **FORMAT** at the DOS prompt on a PC that's already working — unless you know *exactly* what you're doing, like formatting a floppy disk in drive A. It's not considered funny to type the command on someone else's machine, either — you could end a friendship very quickly that way. If you execute this command and answer Y at the prompt, you lose every bit of information on a drive — it's like wiping a blackboard clean.

5. **Now that I've scared you to death, go ahead and do just that: Press** Y **at the confirmation prompt.**

Remember that because your drive is brand-new, there's nothing on the drive you need to worry about losing.

6. **When the hard drive formatting step is complete, your computer reboots.**

While the BIOS message is on the screen, remove the MS-DOS installation disk from the floppy drive, and stand in awe as a computer you built *yourself* boots from its own hard drive for the very first time!

At this point, you need to decide on an operating system. In Appendix A, I introduce you to MS-DOS, Windows 95, Windows 98, Windows Me, Windows 2000, Windows NT, OS/2, Linux, and Unix (whew!) and explain what each operating system can do for you.

Part III
Adding the Fun Stuff

The 5th Wave By Rich Tennant

"WELL, RIGHT OFF, THE RESPONSE TIME SEEMS A BIT SLOW."

In this part . . .

You add all the fancy bells and whistles that any multi-media computer needs these days, such as a DVD drive, a stereo sound card that plays MP3 music, and a modem for the Internet. Get ready to blast 3D invaders, surf the Web, or listen to audio CDs while you work on a spreadsheet!

Chapter 8

Putting the Spin on CD-ROM and DVD

*I*t's becoming hard to remember the days of old — I'm speaking of the prehistoric time long ago, before computers had CD-ROM drives. (As scary as it sounds, some young folks don't remember a computer *without* one!) You already know that a modern multimedia computer requires a CD-ROM drive for games, digital video, interactive encyclopedias, and silliness like talking bears — but you can actually do much more than that in the world of CD-ROM. Today's technology even enables you to record your own data CD-ROMs and audio CDs or watch DVD movies with Dolby Digital surround sound!

In this chapter, I explore all the CD-ROM and DVD hardware that's available, and I discuss the features that help you determine which drive is right for your new computer. After you install your drive and the software it requires, you're ready to access the world of multimedia — and don't forget to take a few minutes to explain to the younger generation the historical relevance of floppy disks.

Discovering the Details about CD-ROM

Ready for a long, highly technical discussion of bits and bytes, reflected laser light, and variable speed motors?

If so, you're reading the wrong book! The good thing about CD-ROM technology is that you don't *have* to know anything about how it works; most drives are built in the same manner, you use them the same way, and they perform equally well. (The irritating exception to this rule is the CD recorder, which sometimes requires precise configuration and a bit of prayer to work correctly.)

However, a number of extra features often help determine the price of your CD-ROM drive, and I discuss them in this section.

Name your interface

Just as with hard drives, you can choose from two standard connection interfaces for your new internal CD-ROM drive:

- ✔ **IDE:** Most CD-ROMs today use the same IDE technology as the most popular type of hard drive, so you can connect your CD-ROM drive to the same controller as your hard drive. (I talk about IDE technology in Chapter 7.) Enjoy this kind of convenience because it doesn't happen very often in the PC world.

- ✔ **SCSI:** You may want to choose a SCSI CD-ROM drive for its pure, raw, unadulterated speed — just like the SCSI hard drives I discuss in Chapter 7. SCSI CD-ROM drives transfer data much faster than their IDE counterparts. Previously, most CD recorders required a SCSI interface, although today's IDE CD recorders are rapidly taking the favored spot. (For more details on the SCSI interface, jump to Chapter 11.)

Many CD-ROMs are bundled with sound cards as part of a multimedia kit — generally, the sound card from such a kit has a built-in IDE interface for the CD-ROM, so you can use the connector on the sound card rather than the IDE connector on your controller card or your motherboard.

Additionally, you have two interface choices for connecting an external CD-ROM drive:

- ✔ **USB:** Is it any wonder that the USB port is so popular these days? Here's yet *another* peripheral you can connect — and, as with the other USB hardware I discuss throughout this book, you don't have to reboot your PC when you add or remove your external USB CD-ROM.

- ✔ **FireWire:** Because an external FireWire CD-ROM drive is superfast, you can compare it favorably to an internal SCSI CD-ROM drive: It transfers data faster than the common USB standard, so these drives can usually read faster as well. Naturally, if you're looking for an external CD recorder with the best performance, FireWire is your best bet. However, FireWire ports are still somewhat rare on all except the most expensive PCs, so if your computer doesn't have one, you have to add a FireWire port adapter card.

The great CD-ROM speed myth

If you're shopping for a CD-ROM drive, you're going to be pelted with numbers: 12x, 16x, 24x, and 48x, for example. Those numbers aren't size figures for NBA basketball shoes — the number in front of the *x* indicates how fast the CD-ROM can transfer data.

Original single-speed CD-ROM drives could read data from the disc at about 150 kilobytes per second; the *x* figure indicates a multiple of that original speed. For example, an *8x* drive (usually pronounced *eight speed* by CD-ROM racing enthusiasts) can read data eight times faster than the original single-speed drives. So, an 8x CD-ROM drive can transfer about 1,200 kilobytes per second from the disc to your computer.

Okay, so where does the "myth" come in? Well, most of today's games and applications really don't *need* the whopping-fast transfer rate of a 32x or 48x CD-ROM drive. Because these faster drives cost a pretty penny (compared to the more mundane and inexpensive 8x and 16x drives that were common a couple of years ago) and because the typical CD-ROM game or application is still likely to recommend a 8x drive, the biggest benefit of these drives ends up being that they give technoweenies a chance to brag about their speedy drives. (Coincidentally, this is the reason that most retail computers still come with 24x drives — those manufacturers know the fact behind the myth as well as you do!)

TECHNICAL STUFF

What really goes on in my CD-ROM drive?

Okay, if you absolutely *must* know, your CD-ROM drive uses a laser to read a long series of tiny pits in the surface of a disc. These pits represent digital data — a string of zeros and ones — which your computer can recognize as program data or music. In fact, your computer CD-ROM drive is internally very similar to a regular audio CD player. Ready for a totally useless fact? If you unraveled all the pits in a typical CD-ROM, they would stretch over three miles!

How does the laser read these microscopic pits? The laser light is directly reflected from the smooth areas of the disc (called *lands*), and the pits scatter the light and do not reflect it. A lens in your CD-ROM drive picks up the reflected light and therefore can tell the difference between pits and lands. The reflective surface on a CD-ROM is actually a thin layer of metal, which gives the disc a shiny appearance.

Because most programs and games don't need the blazing speed of a 32x or 48x CD-ROM drive, most computer owners are still quite satisfied with a 16x drive. If you want to save some money by buying or scavenging a used 16x drive for your new Pentium III computer, I say that you can go for it with a clear conscience.

Don't get me wrong. High-speed drives are nice in certain situations. For example, a 48x drive installs one of those huge 500MB office applications or 3D games to your hard drive much faster than a 16x drive — so a fast drive can save you time. Also, a faster drive is practically a prerequisite for watching full-screen digital video from a CD-ROM or videodisc, where a higher transfer rate prevents skipped frames or jerky animation. If your primary application revolves around digital video or you have the spending money and simply hate waiting, a fast CD-ROM drive is probably a better choice.

The battle of the drives: Internal versus external

As I mention earlier in this chapter, CD-ROM drives using the IDE interface are internal drives; they fit in an internal half-height drive bay in your computer case (just like a floppy or hard drive). However, if you're using a SCSI CD-ROM drive, you can also buy an external kit that includes a separate case and power supply (so SCSI owners can choose either an internal or an external CD-ROM drive).

External CD-ROM drives can be very convenient if you have a laptop computer that has a SCSI interface card but no internal CD-ROM drive. You can connect the external CD-ROM drive to your laptop's SCSI port, carry the drive with you when you travel, and then simply reconnect the drive to your desktop computer when you return to your home or office.

External drives also eliminate much of the heat inside your case because the laser used within the CD-ROM drive generates more heat than just about any other part in your computer. Naturally, external drives are more expensive because you're also paying for a separate case, power supply, and external cable.

If you need an external CD-ROM drive to share among more than one PC and they all have USB ports, you're in luck! A portable USB CD-ROM drive will be a perfect fit for your needs.

Laptop owners can also choose an external CD-ROM drive that uses the PCMCIA (commonly called a *PC Card*) connector; however, if your card slots are already stuffed full with a modem card and a network card, I recommend, again, a USB drive.

What's the difference between an audio CD and a computer CD-ROM?

Like everything else in the computer world, of course, the answer is hidden by acronyms! An audio CD (or *compact disc*) holds digital audio in a standard international format called Red Book. On the other hand, a computer CD-ROM (short for *compact disc-read/only memory*) is written using the Yellow Book standard. (You absolutely do not need to remember this type of trivia, and you won't be tested on it.) An audio CD player can't read a CD-ROM, but a computer CD-ROM drive *can* read both audio CDs and computer CD-ROMs.

"I have no USB port on my older laptop!" Don't panic! For about $100, you can pick up a *parallel port external kit* that transforms any internal IDE CD-ROM drive into a drive that connects to your parallel port (just like the external Zip drive I discuss in Chapter 7). These kits are notoriously slow, and they require you to run special driver software — but if you can't add an internal CD-ROM drive to your PC or laptop, your computer doesn't have USB, and you'd rather not install a SCSI adapter, you may want to consider a parallel port external kit.

If you can't play just one CD-ROM at a time. . . .

The development of computer CD-ROM drives has paralleled that of audio CD players since the beginning. When audio players first arrived, you could play only one disc at a time; soon, however, the basic pull of consumer convenience created the need for players that could hold more than one CD (even though you can still play only one at a time). Typically, you end up arranging several discs on a tray of some sort or loading a cartridge with CDs that you then load into the player.

Sure enough, the multiple CD-ROM changer for your computer has arrived — except that it's usually called a *jukebox* for short (in honor of those vinyl-playing Wurlitzer dinosaurs that everyone wants for the den). Jukeboxes are available in several different sizes, including half-height internal drives that can switch between four discs. Drives with a higher capacity don't fit internally, so they sit outside the computer in an external case. Although a jukebox holds multiple CDs, it can read from only one CD at a time.

External jukeboxes are usually SCSI devices, so make sure that you get everything you need when buying a jukebox, including a SCSI adapter (if you don't have one), an external SCSI cable, and all the software drivers for your operating system.

Another way to access multiple CD-ROMs is the *tower CD-ROM drive array*. Nothing really exotic here: A tower system is simply a large external case that holds anywhere from four to eight half-height internal SCSI CD-ROM drives, including a separate power supply and fan. Sounds a little clunky, right? Well, don't laugh too hard; unlike jukeboxes, tower CD-ROM arrays can read from each of those CD-ROMs *simultaneously!* Tower arrays are typically used on office networks, web servers, and larger bulletin-board systems that need immediate access to a wide range of CD-ROMs. For a small office, a tower system enables one person to retrieve an image file from one disc at the same time another person is searching a database on another CD-ROM.

Will that be caddy or tray?

The earliest computer CD-ROM drives all used a flat plastic cartridge called a CD-ROM *caddy*. (Sorry, Tiger — it won't help you choose the right club for that difficult par 3 on the 17th.) This type of caddy holds the disc inside the drive and helps keep the disc away from dust and fingerprints. (You could store a disc in the caddy, if necessary.) Figure 8-1 shows a caddy CD-ROM drive.

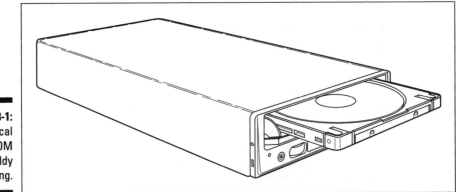

Figure 8-1: A typical CD-ROM with caddy loading.

As CD-ROM technology advanced, however, more and more drives turned to a motorized tray system for holding the CD-ROM. As you can see in Figure 8-2, a tray CD-ROM drive looks more like a standard audio CD player. You press a button to extend the tray, and then you press the button again to retract the tray and load the disc into the innards of the drive. Of course, this procedure is much more convenient than opening a plastic caddy each time you want to load a disc, so tray drives are preferred by the hip multimedia crowd — caddy drives are practically extinct.

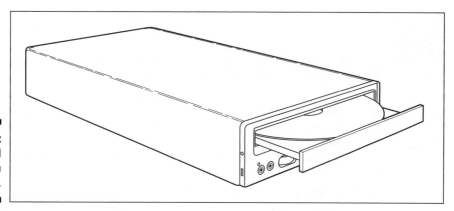

Figure 8-2:
A CD-ROM
drive with
tray loading.

If you've scavenged an older caddy CD-ROM drive, however, there's no reason to toss it; caddy drives work just as well and last just as long as tray drives. In fact, many CD recorders still use caddies because caddies provide the precise alignment required for CD recording, even after years of use.

If your CD-ROM drive ever swallows your CD and won't eject it, it's time to straighten a paper clip. Locate the emergency manual eject hole — it's an unmarked hole under the tray (about the diameter of a piece of wire). Stick the end of the paper clip into the manual eject hole and push firmly; the caddy should pop out of the drive. This trick works with both tray and caddy drives.

Other CD-ROM features to covet

In actual operation, you can find very few differences between an expensive, name-brand CD-ROM drive and a cheaper drive of the same speed from a smaller manufacturer. Both drives read and transfer at about the same speed, and both can be controlled from within your applications. (For example, you can eject a disc from within your audio CD program with either drive.)

So which features really make a difference? Here's a checklist that helps you separate the wheat from the chaff as you're shopping for a CD-ROM drive:

> ✔ **Access time:** If you're not careful, you can easily confuse a CD-ROM drive's *access time* with its *transfer rate* (measured as 8x or 16x, as I discuss in the section "The great CD-ROM speed myth," earlier in this chapter). Access time is the actual time required for your CD-ROM drive to locate a specific file on the disc. Older drives have access times of about 150 milliseconds, and today's faster CD-ROM drives average an access time of around 80 to 40 milliseconds.

Several high-speed CD-ROM drives on the market now offer dramatically faster access times; these *multilaser* CD-ROM drives use more than one laser beam to read multiple tracks from the surface of the disc at one time. If you're looking for the best possible performance for games and digital video on CD-ROM, look for a multilaser drive.

In Chapter 7, I discuss how access time is important when choosing a hard drive. Most hard drives have access times of around 7 to 11 milliseconds (much faster than a standard CD-ROM's 80 milliseconds), which is another reason that hard drives are still the champions of the multimedia world. Besides, you can both read and write data on a hard drive, whereas a typical CD-ROM drive can only read data.

✔ **MultiRead:** If you'll be using your drive to read recorded CDs, pick up a *MultiRead* drive (check the drive's feature list, or look for the logo on the box or on the front of the drive). Because a MultiRead drive can reliably read from both CD-R and CD-RW discs, you don't encounter data errors in trying to load that photo of Uncle Phil your aunt sent you on a recorded CD.

✔ **Audio controls:** When the first CD-ROM drives appeared on the market, many of them didn't even have a stereo headphone jack or a volume control — after all, who knew that playing audio CDs through a multimedia computer system would become so popular? Manufacturers have learned their lesson, though — most drives now include a headphone jack and volume control. More expensive drives come with everything necessary for dual use as an audio CD player and a computer CD-ROM drive: separate channel connectors for your stereo, track displays, and even a full collection of control buttons, like skip track, pause, and play.

✔ **Cache (a.k.a. data buffer):** Just like a hard drive, a CD-ROM drive uses a special set of onboard RAM chips to hold data your computer needs often, or will probably need soon. The larger this cache, or buffer, the fewer interruptions you experience in the transfer of data. If you plan to use your CD-ROM drive for digital video, consider a CD-ROM drive with a megabyte or more of cache RAM.

✔ **Support:** CD-ROM drives are finicky beasts, so check the company's Web site and make sure that your drive is supported by a complete range of drivers for DOS, Windows 98, Windows NT, and Linux. Find out how often the drivers are updated for the model you're considering; it's better to buy a CD-ROM drive from a manufacturer that regularly updates its drivers. Does the company offer tech support via the Web, or will you end up spending your two bits calling long-distance for support over the telephone?

What You Need to Know about DVD

If you keep your eye on the latest in consumer electronics, you've probably already heard about DVD, which is short for *digital video disc;* some folks are starting to say that the acronym stands for *digital versatile disc.* (Although it's probably an urban legend, I've heard that a computer novice recently asked a computer salesman for a PC with a "digital voodoo disc.") DVDs look very similar to standard audio CDs or computer CD-ROMs, but they can store much more data. They also feature a higher transfer rate than standard CDs. The first generation of DVDs holds a hefty 4.7GB (that's the equivalent of seven standard CD-ROM discs), and the DVD specification allows for discs holding as much as a whopping 17GB each!

Before you get really upset at the computer hardware industry for replacing your traditional CD-ROMs with this new voodoo, here's the good news: A DVD drive can read your standard audio CDs and computer CD-ROMs, so you don't need two drives. However, older DVD drives can't read discs created by a CD recorder.

Although DVD drives work the same as a CD-ROM drive, they use a different type of laser, and the pits carrying the encoded data on the surface of the disc are smaller and more tightly packed together. The denser the data, the more data a single disc can hold, as shown in Figure 8-3.

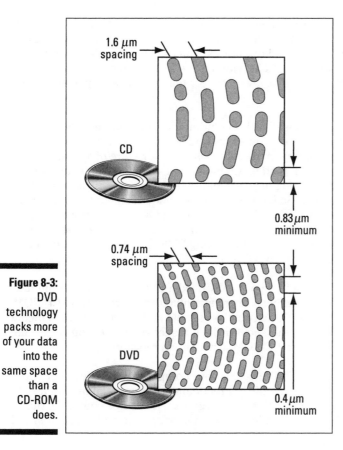

Figure 8-3: DVD technology packs more of your data into the same space than a CD-ROM does.

"Why on earth do I need that kind of space?" you may ask. DVD technology is rapidly replacing VHS tape in the video rental market. Although today's digital video takes up gigabytes of space, the quality of the digital video is much better than VHS. In addition, a typical Hollywood movie fits nicely on a single DVD, with room to spare. A CD-ROM simply doesn't have the capacity for all that digital video.

The extra room on a DVD even enables manufacturers to include such luxuries as running commentary from the director, multiple language versions of the same film, or parts of the film that were edited out in the big-screen version.

DVD movies also feature Dolby Digital surround sound — although if you want to watch movies on your computer, you need a separate adapter, called an *MPEG-2 decoder card,* to play DVD movie discs (or a video card that includes the same feature). (For more information on decoders, see the section "The whole decoder thing explained," later in this chapter.)

"Do I need DVD for my computer?"

If you've played one of the latest computer games, it's probably obvious why DVD is becoming more attractive: A single CD-ROM simply doesn't have the storage space required by today's hottest games. For example, it's not uncommon for a sophisticated 3D video game to ship on two or three discs. DVD ends the irritation of disc swapping for millions of game players (at least for a few years, anyway).

Although DVD may be considered revolutionary for the home video market, it's pretty much MOTS for computer owners. Sorry about that — acronyms have begun to take over my brain. MOTS is short for *more of the same.* Computer DVD drives can read much more data and do it faster, although discs are used for the same purposes: multimedia games, educational titles, digital video, and audio. (So far, I've heard no announcement that DVD will replace those irritating free CD-ROM discs you get in the mail from every online service and Internet provider. I use those free discs as coasters for parties, or you can make a really interesting DMFYBC; that's short, of course, for *digital mobile for your baby's crib.*)

So how long will it take before you really need a DVD drive in your computer? That depends on how quickly software manufacturers switch from CD-ROM to DVD technology. CD-ROM distribution should still be the preferred media throughout the next few years. So, for the foreseeable future, you're certainly safe in selecting a standard CD-ROM drive for your system.

If you do decide to add a DVD drive to your computer, make sure that your PC has the horsepower to handle it. I recommend a bare minimum of a 233 MHz original Pentium CPU with MMX. Of course, the faster your CPU, the better. (Chapter 4 explains the Intel Pentium, Pentium II, and Pentium III CPU models in detail.) Your video card should be capable of displaying 16 million colors at a resolution of at least 800 x 600, and you need an SVGA monitor with at least a .28 dot pitch. (See Chapter 6 for more information on video cards and monitors.)

The whole decoder thing explained

You can buy a DVD drive kit without a hardware decoder adapter card (or a video card with a built-in decoder), although you won't be able to enjoy DVD movies. The digital video on DVDs is compressed by using the MPEG-2 standard to save space, and the *MPEG-2 decoder card* decompresses the video and handles the Dolby Digital audio. Without the decoder card, you can't watch the same discs that you can use in a home DVD movie player.

A DVD drive by itself (without the decoder card) is essentially a faster CD-ROM drive that can also read DVDs. This configuration is a good option for computer owners who want to be able to read the next-generation discs for games and multimedia but who don't feel the urge to watch movies on their computer.

The Dolby Digital sound standard is also referred to by audiophiles as *AC-3* technology, so you may see AC-3 listed in the description of a DVD drive that includes a decoder card.

One more stumbling block stands in the way of your Dolby Digital listening pleasure: Even if your DVD drive kit includes a decoder, you need a stereo amplifier or a stereo receiver that supports Dolby Digital input as well as the proper speaker system. And don't forget that you have to run wires from your computer to your stereo.

What You Need to Know about CD Recorders

CD recording is just plain neat. With CD-R technology (short for *compact disc-recordable*), you can record your own commercial-quality audio CDs with as much as 74 minutes of music or save as much as 700MB of computer data. Plus, you can play these discs on any standard CD-ROM drive (although older DVD drives can't read them).

How long does a recorded CD last? Although companies cite many different figures, the average shelf life of a recorded CD is usually somewhere around ten years.

Until the past three years or so, CD recorders were so expensive and hard to use that most computer owners simply thought that they were out of reach. The good news is that this technology (the CD recorders, blank discs, and related software) has really dropped in price. Blank discs are now available for 50 cents each through the mail, and recorders that used to sell for more than $1,000 have dropped to $250 for a complete kit that includes the SCSI adapter card and recording software.

CD recording software has also become easier to use. In fact, programs such as DirectCD, from Adaptec, enable you to write data directly to a CD recorder under Windows 98, just as though the recorder were a huge floppy drive.

In case you're wondering, when you aren't using a CD recorder to create CDs, it doubles as a standard CD-ROM read-only drive, so you need to buy only one drive.

Remember that copyright restrictions determine what you can legally record! Unless you're sure that you can copy the material, I strongly advise you to contact the copyright owner for permission.

Any PC with an Intel Pentium processor of at least 233 MHz and a hard drive with an access time of 12 milliseconds or fewer can record CDs at 2x; faster recorders, however, require a faster processor — make sure that you check the system requirements for a drive before you buy it. I recommend that you dedicate at least one gigabyte of hard drive space to recording. (You need that space to hold all the data you intend to record.) If you select a SCSI recorder, you need a SCSI adapter as well. Windows 98 and Windows NT are currently the best operating systems for CD recording on the PC.

Why record my own CDs?

A number of computer applications can benefit from a CD recorder — in fact, they'd sit up and beg for one if only they could speak. If your primary application appears on this list or you're interested in any of the following applications, you should consider a CD recorder rather than a simple read-only CD-ROM drive:

✔ **Creating audio CDs:** If you're an audiophile with a ton of hard-to-find vinyl albums (or a stack of irreplaceable cassettes or tape reels gathering dust in a corner of your home), you can transfer those musical treasures to compact disc. Today's higher-end recording programs enable you to rearrange tracks in any order you like, print a cover for the CD jewel box with a list of the track names, and even remove some of the crackle, pop, and hiss associated with older media.

If you're buying a CD recorder primarily for recording audio, make sure that it supports a recording format called *disc-at-once;* this format enables you to create discs without irritating clicks between each of the tracks.

✔ **Archival storage:** How would you like to remove those 3-year-old tax records, spreadsheets, and word-processing documents from your hard drive and free up all that space — without losing a single byte of that data in case you need it in the future? Although you could back up that data to tape, you'd have to restore it to your hard drive in order to use it, and magnetic tape has a limited shelf life. If you use CD-R discs to archive your data, however, you can be assured that those old files will be available for years to come and can be read on any CD-ROM drive. Plus, you can run programs and read data files directly from the disc, so you don't have to restore anything.

✔ **Moving data:** Do you have a presentation or slide show to perform on a business trip? A recorded disc is a perfect way to carry as much as 700MB of data with you wherever you go, without worrying about magnetism or X-rays in airports (two dreaded enemies of exposed film in cameras and magnetic media, like floppies and backup tapes). With the universal acceptance of CD-ROM, it's now a safe bet that the computer at your destination will be able to read your disc.

✔ **Digital photo albums:** If you have a CD recorder and a digital camera (or a scanner that can digitize regular photographs), you have everything you need to create your own custom photo albums on a disc. You can display these photo albums on any computer with a CD-ROM drive and an SVGA color monitor.

You can even include on your CD-R a shareware graphics program like Paint Shop Pro (www.jasc.com) so that family members who don't have a graphics viewer can install one right from your disc. Paint Shop Pro is not only shareware, but it also has an excellent slide show feature that can display your pictures automatically.

✔ **Small business:** A CD recorder is practically a requirement these days for distributing beta copies of most software, or even distributing the finished product if you don't want the expense of duplicating a large number of CDs at a commercial replicating plant. A good example is a new-employee CD-ROM that contains all the templates, clip art, and documents for a new employee hired by your company. Having everything on one recorded CD-ROM beats scurrying around and looking for the company logo clip art.

If you have a large number of people who will be accessing the same data on a network, Web site, or bulletin board system, consider recording a disc with the data instead of storing it on a hard drive. You can save time because you don't have to back up the data if it's stored on a disc and everyone can access the data from a CD-ROM drive on the server.

What's the deal with rewritable CDs?

Most CD recorders today are CD-RW drives, which stands for *compact disc-rewritable.* Unlike an older CD-R blank disc, which can be recorded only once, you can reuse and re-record a CD-RW disc.

A rewritable CD sounds like the ideal choice, until I mention the downside: CD-RW discs can be read only on drives that support CD-RW, which means that virtually no older CD-ROM drives or audio CD players can read CD-RW discs. Although many new CD-ROM drives can read both (check out the MultiRead feature I mention earlier in this chapter), check closely the specifications of a drive (or call the manufacturer's technical support) to make sure that a specific drive can read CD-RW discs. When it comes to compatibility, CD-R is clearly the winner: A standard CD-R disc can be read on the standard CD-ROM drives and audio CD players that have been around for years.

Prices for CD-RW hardware, software, and blank discs are only slightly higher than standard CD-R prices, so the decision is a simple one: If you need to record discs that everyone can read, stick with CD-R. If you're recording discs for use on your own computer, and the convenience and savings of using rewritable discs appeal to you, go with the CD-RW.

 If you want comprehensive information and expert advice on recording your own audio and data discs under Windows 98 and Windows NT, I recommend the *Hewlett-Packard Official Recordable CD Handbook,* written by Mark L. Chambers and published by IDG Books Worldwide, Inc.

Caring for Your CDs

Contrary to popular opinion, compact discs are not indestructible. Although CD-ROMs aren't affected by magnetic fields (as are floppy disks or backup tapes), they have their own preferences for care and feeding. Even if your new CD-ROM drive isn't your first foray into the world of compact discs, pay close attention to this section and you'll never lose a byte of data (or a single musical note).

Don't even consider doing these things

Here's a quick checklist of the most common archenemies of any compact disc — avoid all of them! (Unless, of course, you just plain enjoy throwing round things into your trash can.)

✔ **Heat:** Keep those CDs cool! The same hot car seat that claimed your favorite cassettes (or those videos from the rental store) can melt your discs or render them unreadable.

✔ **Dust:** Like any audio CD player, a single speck of dust can cause a CD-ROM drive to skip to skip to skip (you get the idea).

✔ **Liquids:** Anything from water to grape juice to prussic acid can mess up a CD. If you're lucky, you may be able to remove a liquid stain with a little isopropyl alcohol, although it's better to keep your discs dry and away from all liquids.

✔ **Fingers:** Oily fingerprints can lead to dirty discs, and your drive will occasionally refuse to read them. Handle your CDs by the edges or use your finger as a spindle by sticking it through the hole in the center of the disc.

✔ **Sharp objects:** A surface scratch on the reflective side of a CD-ROM can deflect the laser light, which leads to lost data. If you're handling a recordable CD-R disc, make certain that you don't scratch the gold layer on the top side of the disc. Stay away from ballpoint pens when labeling your discs — use a felt-tip pen to label your CDs.

Check your CD-ROM drive manual to see whether the drive cleans the laser lens automatically. If not, you may want to invest in a CD-ROM drive laser lens cleaner, which you can pick up at any computer or electronics store. Do *not* use a laser lens cleaner with a CD recorder, however — CD recorders have more than one laser and a more complex lens system, and most don't require cleaning.

All you ever need to know about cleaning CDs

If you already have an expensive, hi-tech compact disc cleaning apparatus, you can use it on your computer CD-ROMs as well. However, I really don't think that these James Bond contrivances are necessary. Compact discs were designed to be easy to clean. I recommend a lint-free *photographer's lens cloth* for dusting the bottom of your CDs. Figure 8-4 illustrates how you should wipe the bottom surface of a CD (from the center spindle hole straight toward the outside of the disc).

Never wipe a compact disc in a circular motion, which can scratch the surface and result in lost data.

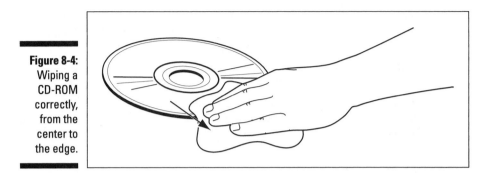

Figure 8-4:
Wiping a
CD-ROM
correctly,
from the
center to
the edge.

Installing Your IDE CD-ROM or DVD Drive

If you installed an EIDE hard drive (I show you how in Chapter 7), you may need to unplug some connections; your IDE CD-ROM or DVD drive uses the same controller and cable as your EIDE hard drive. If you like, take a permanent marker and mark the cables in their current position so that you can restore the existing connections quickly after you have the CD-ROM drive in place.

If your computer uses a single EIDE hard drive configured as *single drive, master unit* (which is the default hard drive installation I describe in Chapter 7), you need to change the jumper settings on your hard drive so that it's set for *multiple drive, master unit.* Until you complete this task, your computer can't correctly recognize the CD-ROM drive. Just follow these steps:

1. **Now that you've taken off that heavy wool sweater, touch a metal surface before you handle your drive; this step discharges any static electricity your body may be carrying.**

2. **If your computer chassis is plugged in, unplug it and remove the cover.**

3. **Check the jumper settings on your CD-ROM drive to make sure that it's set for *multiple drive, slave unit.***

   Multiple drive, slave unit is the default factory setting for most CD-ROM drives, although it never hurts to be sure. If the jumpers aren't set correctly, move them to the correct position. (Your CD-ROM manual shows where the jumpers are located on your drive and how to set them.)

4. **Select an open drive bay for your CD-ROM drive.**

   A CD-ROM drive requires a 5¼-inch half-height bay. External CD-ROM drives, of course, have their own case and don't need an internal drive bay.

5. **From the front of the computer case, slide the drive into the drive bay.**

   The end of the drive with the connectors should go in first. Usually, a label or some kind of writing on the front of your drive indicates which end is up.

6. **Attach the drive to the side of the bay.**

   Slide the drive back and forth until the screw holes in the side of the bay line up with those on the side of the drive. Secure the drive with the screws that came with the drive.

7. **Connect one of the power cables from your power supply to the power connector on the drive.**

   Note that the power connector fits only one way.

8. **Connect the ribbon cable coming from the controller card (or your motherboard, if it has a built-in controller) to the back of the CD-ROM drive.**

   A second connector should be on the ribbon cable connecting your hard drive to your controller — that's the connector for your second IDE device, which in this instance is your CD-ROM drive. The wire with the markings is on the side with Pin 1. If you're unsure which pin on the CD-ROM drive's connector is Pin 1, check your drive's manual. The connector should fit snugly, so press it all the way on after you correctly align it.

If you're installing a DVD drive with an MPEG-2 decoder card, you should also install the decoder card at this time. Check your DVD kit manual for any cable connections you need to make between the decoder card and the DVD drive.

Hooking Up an External SCSI CD-ROM Drive or CD Recorder

Installing an external SCSI CD-ROM drive or CD recorder requires an existing SCSI port on the outside of your computer, so if you haven't installed a SCSI adapter card inside your computer yet, go ahead and do so first. (You can make a quick jump to Chapter 11 for all the information on SCSI.)

Follow these steps to connect an external SCSI CD-ROM drive or CD recorder:

1. **Locate the external SCSI port on the back of your case.**

   The SCSI port is a flat, thick connector with a large number of pins, as shown in Figure 8-5.

Figure 8-5:
A standard
SCSI
external
port in all its
glory.

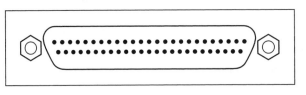

2. **Align the connector on the end of your SCSI cable with the SCSI port.**

   The angled edges on the connector are designed to make sure that it goes on only the right way.

3. **After you correctly align the connector, push it in firmly.**

4. **If you like, you can tighten the connector by snapping the wire clips toward the center of the cable, as shown in Figure 8-6.**

   If you feel that the connector is in firmly, you can leave it as is.

5. **Connect the power cord from your CD-ROM drive to the wall socket.**

Figure 8-6:
SCSI
connectors
typically use
wire clips to
ensure that
the cable
stays on.

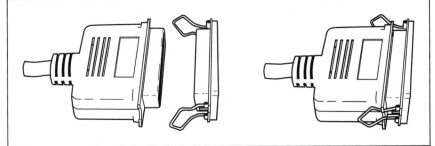

Loading Drivers and Testing Everything

Before your system can recognize its new CD-ROM drive, you need to install a DOS driver, and then you can test your installation. You'll find this process much easier than installing the CD-ROM drive itself: Stick in a disk, run a program, and the rest is automatic!

Are you installing a scavenged CD-ROM drive from another computer? If so, you *must* use the original installation software. No choice on this one — using the original installation software is absolutely mandatory because every CD-ROM manufacturer uses a different proprietary driver under DOS and

Windows 3.*x*. If you can't find the software, check the manufacturer's Web site for a copy of the driver or contact the manufacturer's technical support department.

Windows 98 and Windows NT usually don't require a separate CD-ROM driver — and, depending on the BIOS you're using, you may be able to boot and install Windows from the Windows CD-ROM. If you're using an older motherboard, though, you have to install Windows from DOS, using a CD-ROM! Kind of a *Catch-22,* isn't it? Therefore, with an older BIOS, you typically must install DOS, install the CD-ROM driver, and then install your new operating system. For this reason, you should always keep a backup copy of your CD-ROM DOS installation software, even if you plan to immediately install another operating system; that way, you can always start over from scratch if necessary.

Follow these steps to install your CD-ROM driver and test your drive:

1. **If you've unplugged your computer, plug it back in now.**

2. **Connect the monitor and push the power switch on your monitor.**

3. **Connect the keyboard.**

4. **Push the power switch on the front or back of your computer case.**

   Most CD-ROM drives have a power indicator or an activity light. If your drive is correctly connected to a power cable, you should see the power indicator light up on the front of your CD-ROM drive. If everything looks dead and the tray (or caddy) doesn't open when you press the eject button, your drive probably isn't receiving power. Check the power cable connection on the back of the drive.

5. **Allow your computer to boot.**

   The DOS prompt should eventually appear on your screen.

6. **Run the CD-ROM installation software.**

   Insert the installation disk into your floppy drive and follow the instructions in your CD-ROM drive manual to install the driver.

7. **After you install the driver, reboot your computer.**

8. **Load a computer game or application CD-ROM into your drive and display the directory of the CD.**

   Your new CD-ROM drive has a separate drive letter, just like your hard drive. If you've installed a single hard drive, for example, your computer will probably assign drive D: to your CD-ROM drive.

   To display the directory of drive D:, type **DIR D:** at the DOS prompt.

   If your CD-ROM drive has been assigned another letter, substitute that letter for the D: in the DIR command. Don't forget to press Enter after you type the command. If your drive is working and you've loaded a computer data CD-ROM, your computer should display a listing of all the files and directories stored on the CD-ROM.

If your drive doesn't seem to be working, make sure that it's receiving power: Is the drive's power indicator lit? If not, check the power connection to the drive.

If the drive is receiving power but doesn't seem to be able to read a CD-ROM, you may have the cable upside-down. Reverse the IDE cable connected to the back of the CD-ROM drive by flipping it over and reconnecting it.

This procedure completes your CD-ROM installation! In the next chapter, you add a sound card and enjoy digital audio and music.

Chapter 9

Let Your PC Rock!

*L*et's face it — the days of the computer as a big, silent monolith have passed. A perfect example is how computers are portrayed by Hollywood: These days, multimedia computers in movies sound more like video games. More than anything else, this change in perception is because of the audio revolution that started with the Macintosh many years ago, which has culminated in home and office PCs that speak, sing, scream, and even sob! (What, you've never heard a computer sob? Try running Quicken on my computer; it must be hard to balance my financial mess.)

In this chapter, you add real, honest-to-goodness high-quality stereo sound to your PC — you can make your games (and even your serious word processor) come alive. I discuss the speakers and subwoofer that will satisfy even the most demanding computer audiophile. No more silly "beeps" from that archaic internal PC speaker — you're going to add a multimedia sound system, and your new PC will suddenly sing like a bird.

Sorting Out Sound Card Basics

Remember the last time you went shopping for a new cassette deck or receiver for your stereo system or your car? Despite all the fancy jargon and the pretty brushed chrome, some of the equipment just didn't sound good enough. And, if you're like me, you may have found that the most expensive models often didn't sound much better than the less expensive ones.

As you probably already know, the best way to select audio equipment is to listen with your own ears — so how do you choose a sound card from a mail-order catalog? The secret is to know which of the computer audio buzzwords actually *improves* the sound you hear. Luckily, teaching yourself the lingo of computer audio is actually pretty easy. If you're an audiophile, you want to make a good choice when shopping for your sound card because it is the most important component in your computer that contributes to sound quality. Choosing the right sound card is akin to buying the best receiver you can for your stereo because the receiver is the heart of a good stereo system.

Recognizing common breeds of sound cards

Three common types of sound cards are available today: the 8-bit card, the 16-bit card, and the 32-bit card. *Bit* refers to the type of adapter card slot required for the card and the processing capability of the card, although it also has much to do with the overall quality of the sound you get:

- ✔ **32-bit:** The 32-bit card is today's state-of-the-art sound card. A good 32-bit card can deliver spectacular stereo sound effects for your games and can record in stereo with CD quality at 44 KHz; in other words, the audio you hear from one of these cards can reach the clarity and low noise level you enjoy with audio CDs. The sound card you select for your PC should also have an onboard amplifier and a game port for your joystick.

  Virtually all 32-bit sound adapter cards now on the market are *Plug and Play.* This type of adapter card doesn't use jumpers or DIP switches. Instead, Plug and Play adapter cards configure themselves automatically (which, in this case, means that your new sound card won't fight tooth and nail with other parts, such as your tape backup). The advanced 32-bit 3D sound cards available these days use a PCI slot.

  Figure 9-1 shows the 32-bit Sound Blaster Live! sound card.

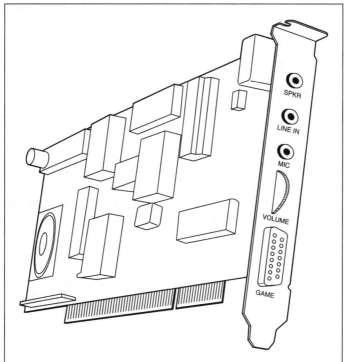

Figure 9-1:
The basic
standard for
today's
audio cards:
The Sound
Blaster 16
PnP.

SPKR

LINE IN

MIC

VOLUME

GAME

✔ **16-bit:** Once the latest in technology, the 16-bit sound card is no longer top-of-the-line, although it's still a good choice for a PC dedicated to casual gaming, office applications, and Internet fun. You get stereo recording and playback with CD quality, but you aren't likely to get bells and whistles, like 3D spatial sound or MP3 hardware compression (buzz-words that I explain later in this chapter). Again, a good 16-bit sound card has an amplifier and a game port. A 16-bit sound card needs (you guessed it) a 16-bit ISA slot, and they're often Plug and Play too.

✔ **8-bit:** These cards are sometimes called *original Sound Blaster-compatible* cards. Typically, 8-bit cards don't support true stereo recording or stereo effects, they don't have an amplifier, and they're usually the cheapest sound cards you can find. Unless you found one of these in an Egyptian tomb and you're not interested at all in the quality of the audio produced by your PC, steer clear of these cards. As the name suggests, these cards fit in an 8-bit slot.

If you happen upon an older 8-bit AdLib music card, promptly run over it with your car — repeatedly. Eight-bit cards are bad enough, but AdLib cards were some of the first audio cards available for the PC, and they're practically worthless these days. They don't produce audio effects (like the sound of a bullet or a baby crying), and they're strictly mono. You can tell an 8-bit AdLib card by the name AdLib on the card.

Surfing the sounds of the Web

You may encounter many types of sound and music files in the multimedia world, especially if you spend lots of time on the Internet and the Web. If you have the right software or browser plug-in, your sound card should be able to play these other files, too:

✔ The WAV format is the Microsoft standard for recording, storing, and playing digital sound (and it's a popular format on the Web). Both Netscape Navigator and Internet Explorer can recognize and play WAV files automatically. The sound quality of WAV files can range from compact disc quality to mono sound files of telephone quality. (The lower the sound quality, the smaller the file size — and the less time it takes to transfer over the Web.) Windows 95, Windows 98, and Windows Me (as well as Windows NT and Windows 2000) include simple sound-editing tools, and any sound-editing program worth installing can save and play WAV files. You'll find a hard drive's worth of WAV files at my favorite audio site, The Daily .WAV (www.dailywav.com).

✔ You often encounter AU sound files on the Web. This sound format was developed by Sun Microsystems, and AU files are popular in the Unix and Linux worlds. Because AU files are compressed, they require less time to download. Although most sound-editing programs can play AU files, it's more important that your Web browser support them so that you can hear them directly while surfing. For example, if you connect to a Web site featuring sound files and click on one of the recordings, you can hear voices speak within your browser. If you're using Netscape Navigator or Internet Explorer, AU support is built-in.

✔ The AIFF format is a popular sound standard for Macintosh computers — most sound-editing programs can import AIFF files, so you can play them if you download them to your hard drive. As in the Windows WAV format, AIF files are CD quality, but they're usually not compressed like WAV files. Therefore, they're not all that popular on the Web because of their size.

✔ MP3 format music files have recently taken the Internet by storm. They're CD-quality and very small as compared to the same music in WAV format. An entire underground of Web sites has developed to distribute dance, pop, and alternative singles in MP3 format — illegally, I might add, because these songs are, of course, copyrighted. You can create MP3 files on your PC, and some companies have even introduced pocket MP3 players that resemble portable cassette players.

✔ Like MIDI files (which I tell you about in the upcoming "Do I need MIDI ports?" section), MOD files are actually music files, but they can also include digital sound effects as "instruments." In fact, MOD files sound great even on older sound cards without wavetable technology. Although the format dates back to the Commodore Amiga, it's not generally recognized by most sound-editing programs — you probably need a program that plays MOD files, like MOD4Win (www.mod4win.com).

Don't forget the software part!

Make sure that the sound card you choose is both Sound Blaster-compatible (a standard of sorts) and well supported with software and drivers written for the operating system you're using.

If you scavenge a used sound card and you don't get any software along with it, check the company's Web site (if possible) to find out whether you can download the latest drivers. If you can't connect to the Internet, call the manufacturer's technical-support line to get the software. One online resource for drivers that I use is The Driver Zone, at www.driverzone.com.

If you're buying a new 32 or 16-bit card, it should include not only the drivers you need but also a number of nifty software toys. These programs often include an on-screen "stereo deck" that lets you play digital sound files in Windows WAV format, MP3 files, or MIDI music. (See the upcoming section "Do I need MIDI ports?") Figure 9-2 shows an audio mixer that came with my sound card. You may even get a voice-recognition program or a text-to-speech program that lets your computer talk to you and "read" text files aloud.

Figure 9-2: Hey, that looks like my stereo, man — can your new computer play my Metallica CD?

Riding the wavetable

Most sound cards around today offer what's called *wavetable* technology. Exactly what is this voodoo?

Rather than get bogged down with a discussion of waveforms and analog/digital processing, here are the real facts on wavetable: It is indeed worth adding to your system. Most older 16-bit sound cards used a technique called *frequency modulation* (FM) — the sound card creates the closest possible imitation of a sound. For example, if your PC should sound like a grand piano, an FM sound card produces the closest possible sound. It would probably be a fairly close imitation, but you will still be able to tell that the sound is computer generated.

On the other hand, a wavetable card actually stores the *real sound* of a grand piano in digitized form (within a certain chip on the card itself) and plays that instead — a big improvement! Whether you're playing a game with background music or listening to MIDI music, a wavetable card definitely sounds better (which is why musicians and audiophiles who own computers usually invest in a wavetable card). Most wavetable sound cards can also be upgraded with additional onboard RAM, which enables them to offer more than one sound for the same instrument.

However, wavetable technology means nothing when it comes to digitally recorded music or digital sound effects in WAV format (which are actual sounds recorded as data on your hard drive or a CD-ROM). Wavetable support only improves computer-generated music, and it doesn't make an audio CD played on your computer's CD-ROM drive sound any better; keep that in mind while deciding on your card.

"Why do I need 3D for my ears?"

Another feature offered by many advanced sound cards is — get ready for a real mouthful here — *3D spatial imaging.* This type of sound has three applications:

- ✔ Playing audio CDs
- ✔ Playing digital WAV audio files
- ✔ Playing sound effects within games

Sound cards with 3D spatial imaging provide an "auditorium" or "concert hall" effect — the music sounds as though the speakers are separated farther apart than they actually are.

Computer game players are the ones who can really take advantage of 3D imaging. If you're playing a game that supports one of these 3D cards, a laser bolt streaking past the right side of your ship actually comes from the right speaker. If you hear the deep, guttural growl of a dragon to your left, it would behoove you to turn your character to the left quickly (and with sword drawn)!

If you're a game player, I definitely recommend that you spend a few extra dollars for a card that supports 3D spatial imaging. On the other hand, if you're not an audiophile and you're not into computer games, this feature may not be important to you.

The software in many game programs provides a less effective form of 3D spatial imaging that plays on standard sound cards. However, you always get better sound effects with a sound card that has hardware which supports 3D imaging.

"Send help — I'm surrounded by sound!"

Take 3D spatial imaging one step further — including both sound effects *and* music — and you have *surround sound,* just like the super-realistic audio you've experienced in movie theaters and with the best home stereo systems. DVD players usually offer Dolby Digital surround sound built-in. You can join in the fun with your PC, however, if you add both a DVD drive and an MPEG decoder adapter card to your computer. You can play games and watch commercial movies, and some audio discs are recorded in surround sound as well. (For more information on DVD drives and MPEG decoding, refer to Chapter 8.)

Only the most expensive, high-end PC sound cards can deliver surround sound — and, don't forget that you need five speakers and a game, movie, or audio CD that's encoded for surround sound. As the line between your PC and your traditional stereo system continues to blur, however, you'll be seeing more of surround sound, and it'll be less expensive to add to your existing PC.

MP3 fanatics, pay attention!

Do you have a collection of hundreds of songs in MP3 format taking up hundreds of megabytes of hard drive space? You can enjoy these CD-quality sound files through your computer's sound system, or you can even record them directly to an audio CD if you have a CD-RW drive. MP3 files are all the rage on the Internet, and many companies are now offering personal MP3 players (similar to personal cassette players). I've even seen one or two MP3 car audio decks that have appeared recently!

If you're already an MP3 fanatic and you're shopping for a sound card, I can't stress this enough: *Buy a card with built-in MP3 hardware encoding and digital effects!* Because these features are built-in to the card rather than added through software, one of these cards is well worth the extra investment when you create your own MP3 files or listen to your collection. For example, my SoundBlaster Live! MP3+ card allows me to add environmental effects to a recording to simulate a concert hall or stadium, and I can record the highest-quality MP3 files from a number of different audio sources (including analog and digital CD audio, of course).

If you're using an older computer with a slower hard drive and processor, you may have noticed that MP3 audio tends to drag and stutter — or even stop entirely — when you're running other programs. With a sound card that features MP3 processing in hardware, your MP3 songs sound great no matter how many other applications you're using. The card takes care of the MP3 processing so that your computer's CPU can concentrate on its other tasks.

"Do I need MIDI ports?"

All right, it's time to come face-to-face with *MIDI* (a rather cute acronym for Musical Instrument Digital Interface), an international standard shared by computers, synthesizers, and many types of specialized musical instruments (like drums and keyboards). MIDI music is shared in the form of data files, which enable most computers to play the same music, and MIDI files enable musicians to record and play music by using computers. MIDI files are often found on the World Wide Web; in fact, one HTML command enables your Web page to play a MIDI song as background music. Most sound cards can play MIDI music files without any extra hardware or software, and a wavetable card can really sound great while playing MIDI.

However, most sound cards do *not* provide the MIDI interface connectors that enable you to hook up a synthesizer or other musical instrument that supports MIDI directly to your computer. These connectors are usually offered as an upgrade that you can buy and install later, or they come with the card for a higher price. Naturally, musicians get a big kick out of connecting a musical instrument to their computers. If you're running music-editing software with MIDI support, you can play notes on the instrument and create MIDI music directly, or you can instruct your computer to "play" the instrument automatically.

Do you need MIDI interface connectors (sometimes referred to as a MIDI *daughterboard*)? If you're not a musician, I recommend against spending extra money on a sound card with these connectors. If you're a musician and you want to experiment with computers in your music, these connectors are worth every penny! (If you're a professional musician, chances are that you're already an expert on MIDI and you've long since skipped to the next section.)

Uhh . . . Is This Mike On?

Your ears are not the only lucky body parts to benefit from a sound card — your mouth also gets to enjoy itself. With a microphone attached to your sound card, you can take advantage of computer applications like these:

- ✔ **Voice recording:** The simplest application for a microphone is to let you record your voice and other sounds. You can create digital WAV files of sounds and "attach" them to specific actions within Windows (so that actions like pulling down a menu, running a program, or closing a window are accompanied by their own sound effects). You can also edit your recordings with a sound editor to add special effects, add these sound files to your Web page for Web surfers to enjoy, or just have a little fun with your dog.

✔ **Voice command and dictation:** Imagine talking to your computer through a microphone to run programs, open and close windows, and even dictate into your word processor with a program like ViaVoice Gold, from IBM Corporation — the idea has sort of a Buck Rogers or Luke Skywalker feel, doesn't it? You can even control some computer games these days with spoken commands. Thanks to the popularity of the PC sound card, these applications are available right now. But you typically have to "train" your computer to recognize your verbal patterns, and these applications are nowhere near 100 percent accurate. However, this kind of technology is constantly improving, and it's a great help to disabled computer owners and computer owners who may not feel comfortable with the keyboard.

✔ **Voice e-mail:** If you have an Internet e-mail client application that allows attachments, you can record your own voice as a digital WAV file and send it along with the text. Because of the large size of digital audio, voice e-mail applications record your voice at less than CD quality. Even so, attaching a human voice to an e-mail message still has considerable impact (especially when you haven't heard that certain voice in several weeks).

✔ **Internet telephone:** No doubt about it, Internet telephone programs are just plain neat — if you call someone at long distance or international rates often, you can save a ton of money! An Internet telephone program turns your microphone and sound card into a telephone — but rather than talk over standard telephone lines, your voices are transmitted over the Internet as data. Therefore, the only cost you incur is the online time from your Internet Service Provider; the person on the other end of the conversation must also have a computer, an Internet connection, and a copy of the same Internet telephone program you're using. Some of these programs are so sophisticated that they have call screening and Internet telephone answering machines, too.

If you decide that an Internet telephone program is a good idea, look for one that supports *full duplex* operation. With a 32- or 16-bit sound card on both sides of the conversation, full duplex enables both of you to speak at the same time. If you're restricted to half duplex, you can only talk in turns, much like a CB radio.

You can find three basic types of computer microphones: the clip-on/stick-on model shown in Figure 9-3, the fancier boom microphone shown in Figure 9-4, and the headset microphone. The clip-on microphone is designed to clip onto your lapel or collar, and it's naturally better for capturing your voice. When not in use, this microphone fits into some sort of holder that sticks to the front of your computer case. The boom mike sits on your desk or on top of your computer case. Boom mikes tend to pick up a little more background sound from around your computer. Headset microphones (which you've typically seen used by telephone operators) enable you to use both hands while you talk, and they're the microphone of choice if you're using a voice command or voice dictation system. A headset microphone may come with or without stereo headphones.

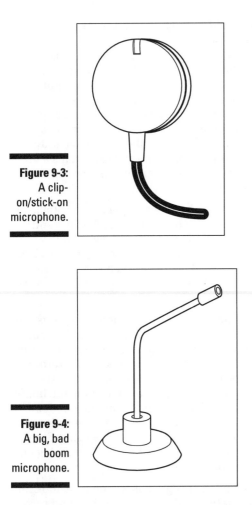

Figure 9-3:
A clip-
on/stick-on
microphone.

Figure 9-4:
A big, bad
boom
microphone.

Do you already have a microphone with a standard jack you use with a cassette recorder? This type of microphone should work just fine with your sound card; just make sure that it has some sort of stand to hold it upright.

Speaking of Speakers

Computer speakers are another part of your system that may vary widely with your personal preferences. For example, some computer owners are happy with a set of headphones, which helps all family members maintain their sanity (especially if the computer room is located right next to the baby's room). In fact, if you have a portable stereo cassette player or FM stereo radio, you can use the headphones that came with it with your new sound card.

On the other end of the spectrum, some computer owners are as demanding on their computer speakers as they are on their stereo speakers. For these audiophiles, only the very best audio reproduction is acceptable, especially when they're battling slobbering purple dragons from Medieval Dimension X. Your preferences in audio quality determine whether you spend $10 or $200 (or even more) on your computer's speaker system.

Speakers are connected to your system in one of two ways:

✔ **A traditional Line Out jack and plug:** Every sound card has a Line Out or Speaker jack — in fact, your speakers connect to your PC exactly like the headphones on your personal CD or cassette player.

✔ **A USB connector:** If you've invested in a set of digital speakers, you'll use one of your USB ports. These speakers often don't require an AC adapter because they draw electricity directly through the USB port. Because these speakers require USB support, you should be using Windows 98, Windows Millennium Edition, or Windows 2000.

Unless you have a definite reason why you prefer using headphones, I strongly recommend a set of speakers especially designed to be used on a computer. Computer speakers come in all shapes and sizes — some are even integrated into your computer monitor — but a multimedia monitor is typically much more expensive than a regular monitor and a separate set of speakers. Speakers are best placed on either side of the monitor, about a foot away from your ears.

While you shop for a set of speakers, look for these features:

✔ **Amplified power:** Today's 32-bit sound cards have a built-in amplifier, although some models provide only about 6 to 8 watts of punch. If you're looking for a little more power and better sound, select a speaker set that has its own built-in amplifier. The downside is that the built-in amp needs power — depending on the size of your speakers, you need to provide C or D cell batteries. If your speaker set comes with its own AC wall adapter, you don't need batteries.

✔ **Magnetic shielding:** Your monitor is highly susceptible to distortion from magnetic sources. Because larger speakers use larger magnets, the more powerful the speaker set you choose, the greater the chance that they can interfere with your monitor. To guard against this interference, most computer speakers are magnetically shielded so that you can place them next to a monitor without causing problems.

✔ **Speaker controls:** If your sound card has a volume control (and you can control the volume of your speakers from within Windows 98), why do you need separate bass, treble, and volume controls on your speakers? If your sound card has a separate volume control, it'll be at the back of your computer and hard to reach easily. I prefer speaker controls because they're much more convenient; if you need to adjust the volume for a particular game or a Web site with audio, you can do so without opening another window, launching another program, or having to reach around to the back of your computer.

✔ **Flat-panel design:** Some people feel that flat-panel speakers are a little funny looking — they're not much thicker than a CD case — and other technotypes consider them cool. Flat-panel speakers produce the same quality of sound as a standard speaker; although they can save space on your computer desk, they're typically a little more expensive than traditional computer speakers.

The Subwoofer: Big Dog of Computer Speakers

If you enjoy your computer games — I mean *really* enjoy your computer games — I should mention one other speaker enhancement. A computer subwoofer provides the deep subsonic bass punch that adds realism, whether you're flying a jet or playing an old arcade classic like Asteroids. You'll feel every explosion! Figure 9-5 shows a standard subwoofer.

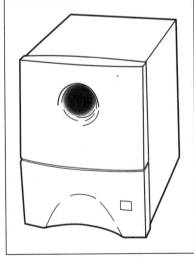

Figure 9-5: A subwoofer can deliver an extra measure of realism to games.

You can buy a subwoofer separately or shop for a speaker system that includes one. (Most high-performance sound systems sold for home theaters include a subwoofer, which produces the same effect.)

Unlike the rest of a computer speaker system, a subwoofer is best placed on the floor to cut down on vibration — unless, of course, the idea of your computer desk rattling like a tin roof in a hailstorm appeals to you.

Installing Your Sound Card

So you're holding your sound card and you're ready to delve into the world of digital audio? Keep your sound card's manual handy because you may have to perform a little "jumper surgery" during the testing phase. Follow these steps:

1. **If your computer chassis is plugged in, unplug it.**

2. **Remove the cover from your case.**

3. **Finished dusting your antiques? You had better touch a metal surface before you install your card. By doing so, you discharge any static electricity you may have picked up before it can damage a computer component.**

4. **Select an open 32- or 16-bit adapter card slot for your sound card.**

   In almost every case, your sound card will be a 32-bit PCI card; however, if you've scavenged an older 16-bit sound card, it works in a 16-bit ISA slot. (For more information on PCI cards and PCI bus slots, see Chapter 4.)

5. **Remove the screw and the metal slot cover adjacent to the selected slot.**

   Don't forget to stick the screw and slot cover into your parts box — you know, that shoe box or coffee can that holds all the small computer parts. You can't be a technowizard without a parts box.

6. **Line up the connector on the sound card with the slot on the motherboard.**

   The card's metal bracket should align with the open space that remains when you removed the slot cover.

7. **Apply even pressure to the top of the card and push it down into the slot.**

   If the card is all the way in, the bracket should be resting tightly against the case.

8. **Add the screw and tighten down the bracket.**

If you install a CD-ROM drive in your computer, you should also connect a special audio cable from the back of your CD-ROM drive to your sound card. This setup enables your computer to play audio CDs directly through the sound card and speakers, without using the headphone jack on the front of your CD-ROM drive. This cable should be included with your CD-ROM drive (some sound cards include one); refer to your sound card and CD-ROM drive manuals for information on how to connect this cable. (Chapter 8 explains more about CD-ROM drives.)

Connecting Your Speakers

Before you can test the operation of your sound card, you need to connect your speakers. Follow these steps and refer to Figure 9-6, which illustrates the business end of a typical sound card:

1. **Locate the speaker jack on the sound card.**

   Usually the speaker jack is labeled Speakers or Spkr, although some cards also use the stereo term Line Out. If you need help in identifying which jack to use, check your sound card manual.

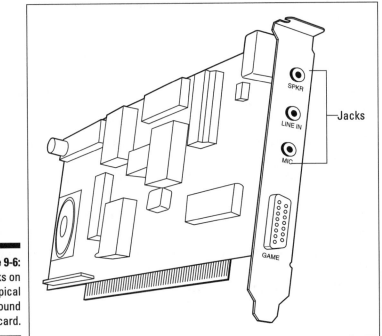

Figure 9-6:
The jacks on a typical 16-bit sound card.

2. **Insert the audio cable plug from your speakers into the sound card's speaker jack.**

3. **If your speakers are amplified, add the required batteries.**

   If your speaker set uses an AC adapter, plug it into a nearby wall socket and plug the connector into the DC power connector on one of the speakers.

4. **Set the volume controls on all parts.**

   Many sound cards have their own onboard volume control (generally a thumbwheel next to the speaker jack). If your speakers are amplified, they probably have their own separate volume control. To avoid waking the neighbors and avoid permanent hearing loss, make sure that all volume controls are set at less than the halfway point.

5. **If your speakers are amplified, turn them on.**

Configuring Software and Testing Your Sound Card

Time to install the software required by your sound card, configure it, and test your new audio hardware.

Most of the programs that are bundled with today's 16-bit sound cards are written for Windows 95/Windows 98 or Windows NT. If you plan to use one of these programs, wait to install the software until you have installed your Windows operating system. You read all about different operating systems and their pros and cons in Appendix A.

Follow these steps:

1. **If you've unplugged your computer, plug it back in now.**

2. **Connect the monitor and keyboard (if you haven't already done so) and push the power switch on your monitor.**

3. **Push the power switch on the front or back of your case and allow your computer to boot.**

   The DOS prompt should eventually appear on your screen.

4. **Run the sound card installation software.**

   Insert the installation software into your CD-ROM or floppy drive and follow the instructions on-screen (or in your sound card manual) to install the driver. The installation program will probably make changes to your system files.

You may need to change jumper settings on your sound card if the default DMA (short for *Direct Memory Address,* sometimes called *base address*) and *IRQ* are already used by other parts within your computer; if this happens, your computer could lock up when it attempts to use the sound card, you may hear a buzzing noise, or the card may not produce any sound. The installation software for your sound card provides you with possible settings for the base address and IRQ values, and, luckily, most hardware manufacturers are finally starting to use the same default address and IRQ for most sound cards. (If you've written down the values you used with components you've installed earlier, you have a list of the addresses and IRQ values you should avoid.) Usually, fixing this problem is a matter of removing the card, setting the new values, reinstalling the card, and testing it. After you've hit on a combination of values that work, jot them down in your sound card manual for future reference and proceed to Step 5.

If your sound card is a Plug and Play model, you shouldn't need to make any DMA and IRQ adjustments.

5. **After the software is installed, reboot your computer.**

6. **Run the diagnostics software supplied with your sound card.**

Your sound card should come with a diagnostics program that lets you test its operation; if you can't find the diagnostics software, try installing a game that has support for your sound card to see whether the card is working correctly. Typically, these diagnostics programs play digital audio effects and MIDI music from both speakers, individually and together. For example, you may be asked whether you hear a sound effect from the left speaker, from the right speaker, and then from the "center" channel.

If you've scavenged a sound card but didn't get any of the bundled software, don't despair! Digital audio players, MP3 players, sound editors, and text-to-speech conversion programs are available for just about every platform. Try connecting with the manufacturer's Web site or searching the Internet for programs that work.

Adding a Microphone

Follow these steps only after you've tested your installation and your sound card is working properly. If you need to remove your sound card to change some jumper settings, you only have to disconnect your speakers:

1. **Locate the microphone jack on the sound card.**

On most cards, the microphone jack is labeled Microphone or Mic, although some cards also use the stereo term Line In. If you need help in identifying which jack to use, check your sound card manual.

2. **Insert the audio cable plug from your microphone into the sound card's microphone jack.**

3. **If your microphone has an ON/OFF switch, turn it on.**

4. **Adjust (or affix) your microphone.**

   If you're using a clip-on/stick-on microphone, remove the paper backing and stick the holder on your case. Make sure that the microphone and its cable don't obscure or block any switches, lights, or openings on the front of your computer. If you're using a boom microphone, place it on top of your case or to one side of your monitor.

For best operation, your microphone should be no more than one or two feet away from your chair. Of course, clip-on microphones work best attached to your person, and headset microphones will work correctly only when worn.

Installing a Subwoofer

Follow this procedure only after you've tested your installation and your sound card is working properly.

Unless your subwoofer is part of a speaker set, you have to disconnect your speakers. The subwoofer plugs directly into your sound card, and the speakers then plug into the subwoofer.

1. **Find the speaker jack on the sound card.**

   Usually the speaker jack is labeled Speakers or Spkr, but some cards also use the stereo term Line Out. If you need help in identifying which jack to use, check your sound card manual.

2. **Insert the audio cable plug from your subwoofer into the sound card's speaker jack and connect your two speakers to the subwoofer.**

3. **Plug the power cord for your subwoofer into the wall socket.**

4. **Set the subwoofer's volume control at less than the halfway point.**

5. **Turn your subwoofer on.**

Chapter 10

Modems and the Call
of the Internet

· ·

· ·

*M*ore than any other computer part, the modem has become a true household word — it's the major star of the Internet show. For most of us, the modem is your ticket to the Web — if you want to venture into the online world, you get the most performance for your money by adding a fast modem. Just four or five years ago (before the Internet became a media sensation), modems were second-class computer citizens. But because "getting online" is the reason that many people get a computer in the first place, the modem has arrived at center stage.

Would you like to join the online crowd? In this chapter, I show you how to select a modem with the features you need and then install it (either inside or outside your computer case). In fact, you may even want to celebrate your new modem by sending a few faxes to your friends and coworkers — without ever touching a fax machine!

A Modem Primer for Real People

Exactly what is a modem? I could give you the lengthy technonerd explanation — or I can give you the explanation favored by those who'd rather do something else with the next 30 minutes of their lives. Here's the abridged version: A *modem* is a device that translates, or *modulates,* the digital language of computers (zeros and ones) into an analog signal (variable waves, like a human voice), which can travel over a telephone line. This analog signal doesn't sound anything like a human voice, but it can carry data. The receiving modem then translates, or *demodulates,* the incoming signal from analog back to digital, which the receiving computer can then use. Figure 10-1 gives you an idea of what's happening.

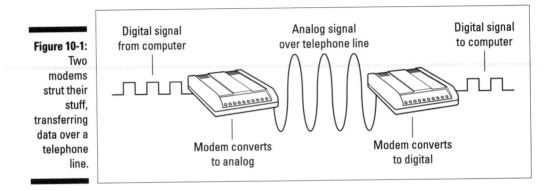

Figure 10-1: Two modems strut their stuff, transferring data over a telephone line.

Digital signal from computer — Analog signal over telephone line — Digital signal to computer

Modem converts to analog — Modem converts to digital

In fact, the word *modem* is actually one big monster acronym. It's short for *mo*dulate-*dem*odulate, the terms usually used for the digital-to-analog and analog-to-digital conversion process. Over the years, the capitalization of the acronym was dropped, and it has become an honest-to-goodness word (as even Noah Webster himself would agree).

Modems are *serial* devices, meaning that they send data one bit at a time over the same wire (in this case, your telephone line). As you may have guessed, a serial device usually connects to the serial port — and it can connect to a USB port as well. Or, if you select an internal modem adapter card, that card comes with its own serial port. If all this talk of internal cards and ports is Greek to you, don't worry; I cover the different types of modems in detail later in this chapter. (Curious about serial and USB ports? Chapter 5 covers the installation of all types of ports.)

A bit of quaint modem history

Although you may not have heard of modems until recently, they've been available for well over 20 years now. During that time, an "online world" of some type has always existed.

In the beginning, *cyberspace* (a fancy term that refers to the online community as a whole) consisted of a number of individual computer technowizards who connected with each other over telephone lines to transfer programs and chat, much like ham radio operators. Mainframe computer centers also used modems to connect outside businesses and offices to the central computer.

The arrival in the early 1980s of the automated computer bulletin-board system (or *BBS,* one of the older acronyms in this book) provided the first true *online service,* where callers in the same town could leave messages, play games, share files, chat with each other, and even participate in woldwide conferences through the *Fidonet* message network system. Most bulletin boards are free, and most are ready for calls 24 hours a day. Although bulletin-board systems have lost much of their popularity because of the Internet, they'll always be around. Many thousands of bulletin boards are still in operation around the world — they offer a local online community that you don't find on the Internet.

Most of of the online world is now centered around the global network called the Internet (especially the portion of the Internet called the Web, short for *World Wide Web*). Originally, the Internet served as a military and scientific information system, and people used it to search for information and files. The Internet is still a tremendous tool for researching almost any topic, although it has become increasingly commercial in past couple of years and now is considered by many to be one heck of an entertainment value. If you want all the details on every angle of the Internet, I suggest the most recent edition of the fine book *The Internet For Dummies,* by Margaret Levine Young, John Levine, Jordan Young, and Carol Baroudi (published by IDG Books Worldwide, Inc.).

The whole speed thing explained

In days of old, you practically had to have a degree in advanced quantified thakamology to buy a modem — you had to consider modem standards, whether you needed fax technology, actual throughput, and so on. As more and more people jumped on the online bandwagon, however, shopping for a modem has become much easier. Today you need to concentrate only on the modem's speed and the standards the modem supports. (So much for that Ph.D. in advanced quantified thakamology.)

You usually see speed advertised as *bps,* which is short for *bits per second.* (A *bit* is the smallest "subparticle" of computer data; it's either a zero or a one. Different combinations of ones and zeros represent letters, numerals, and other characters that make up words, numbers, and even entire computer programs.) When you transfer data across a telephone line with a modem, you're actually sending a long stream of bits between the two computers.

When speeds differ

You may be wondering what happens if you have a 33.6 Kbps modem and your friend has a 14.4 Kbps modem. For example, if the two modems are transferring data at different speeds, how do they communicate? The answer is that the faster modem in a connection always *falls back* automatically to match the best speed of the slower modem. This process is called *handshaking,* and each modem connection you make begins this way: Both modems compare top speeds and standards and automatically pick the fastest possible speed and standard supported by *both* modems.

The first modems generally available to the public sent 300 bps. This speed was fine for simply reading text from a bulletin board (the characters would appear on your monitor at about the rate of a fast typist). As programs became larger and people wanted to do more online (with less waiting), modems moved through a number of speeds: from 300 to 1,200 bps, and then to 2,400 bps, and then 9,600 bps, 14,400 bps, 28,800 bps, 33,600 bps, and even faster.

Speeds in the tens of thousands are typically abbreviated. For example, 28,800 bps is usually expressed as 28.8 Kbps (kilobits per second).

What modem speeds are "acceptable" for the Internet and the Web? Keep in mind that the Web and FTP file transfers are the parts of the Internet that really require a fast modem connection; if you're only sending and receiving e-mail, you can easily get by with a slower modem. As a simple answer, I recommend that you buy the fastest modem you can afford. If I had to draw the line, I would say that you should find a modem with a minimum speed of 14.4 Kbps — but that's *only* if you've been given one or you've scavenged one at a garage sale, and you'll be able to read half your daily newspaper waiting for a single page to load! *Remember:* A 28.8 Kbps modem with a good connection can download the same Web page or shareware program in half the time of a 14.4 Kbps modem. The fastest possible telephone modem available today can *theoretically* reach speeds of 56 Kbps, which would cut the time you wait in half yet again! You can see why buying the fastest possible modem is important.

Remember to check with your *Internet Service Provider* (ISP) to determine its top modem speed (and what modem standards it supports) before you buy or scavenge a modem. Also, if you can afford a high-speed ISDN, DSL, or cable connection to the Internet, you'll experience the Web without the Wait; if you're going to spend two or three hours a night on the Net, I strongly recommend that you invest the money in high speed! (Find out more about ISDN, DSL, and cable Internet connections in Chapter 13.)

Behind-the-scenes stuff: Modem standards

All modems sold in the past three to four years include a form of *error control,* which makes sure that none of the data is lost or changed by noise on your telephone line. Modems also use some form of *data compression,* which lets the modem send more data in a shorter time. These features are specified by international standards — every modem around the world that supports the same standard as your modem can automatically transfer data at the fastest possible speed.

You don't really need to remember what standards your modem supports in order to use it, although you should consider modem standards while shopping. The following standards determine the maximum speed at which your modem can connect to your Aunt Mildred's system in Wassaugh Falls, for example. Other factors that influence modem speed include the clarity of the telephone connection, the top speed of both modems, the overall performance of both computers — even the type of data you're transferring.

Here's a quick list of the standards you'll encounter while shopping for a modem:

- **v.90:** The international standard approved in 1998, which can provide transfer speeds as fast as 56 Kbps. Virtually all modems now sold support the v.90 standard.

- **56K x2:** One of two 56 Kbps *pseudostandards* that emerged before the v.90 standard was finalized. These modems connect at up to 56 Kbps, but only with other modems that support the same x2 standard. If the other modem doesn't support the proprietary x2 standard, the modems fall back to 33.6 Kbps. The x2 standard was developed by U.S. Robotics.

- **56K Kflex:** The other 56 Kbps pseudostandard that appeared while v.90 was in development. These modems connect at as much as 56 Kbps, but only with other modems that support the same Kflex standard. If the other modem doesn't support the proprietary Kflex standard, the modems fall back to 33.6 Kbps. Lucent Technologies and Rockwell developed the Kflex standard.

- **v.34 extended:** An improved version of the v.34 standard. The v.34 extended standard allows for transfer speeds as fast as 33.6 Kbps.

- **v.34:** The most common modem standard for the past couple of years; provides transfer speeds as fast as 28.8 Kbps.

- **v.32bis:** Delivers a maximum speed of 14.4 Kbps.

- **v.42/v.42bis:** The original error control/data compression combination (and probably the oldest standard you'll encounter in a modem). These modems usually transfer data at a maximum of 9,600 bps.

A bit of clarification is necessary for the 56 Kbps modem specifications:

- ✔ Do you have an older, proprietary 56 Kbps modem? Unless it's *upgradable,* you won't be able to connect at the highest speed with a standard v.90 modem. If you buy one of these proprietary 56 Kbps modems, check with the manufacturer to determine whether it can be upgraded.

- ✔ You're more likely to encounter an African wildebeest wearing a hula skirt in your living room than to connect at a full 56 Kbps with any telephone modem, no matter what the specification. Your telephone line has to be crystal-clear, and conditions must be perfect. In fact, I have *never* actually received a full 56 Kbps. And, coincidentally, I've never seen a wildebeest, either.

In essence, 56 Kbps is the fastest modem speed available, but the most you can squeeze from a standard telephone line is a respectable 49.3 Kbps connection. Part of this restriction is due to the conversion process between digital and analog that the modem must perform, and part is due to the less-than-perfect conditions provided by an analog telephone line.

This speed limit doesn't apply to *ISDN, DSL, or cable Internet,* which are true digital connections. A digital Internet connection couldn't care less about your analog modem, which it considers strictly "horse and buggy." If you're a speed racer, you're not afraid to spend money, and you want all the facts on a *really* fast connection, zip directly to Chapter 13.

If you're shopping for a modem (no matter what the speed), buying an upgradable model is worth the extra money. These modems can be "reprogrammed" with the latest standards. Look for models advertising *flash ROM* or *upgradable firmware* (fancy terms for upgrading your modem). For Windows 98, Windows 2000, and Windows NT users, the manufacturer should supply a file called a *modem information file* (or .INF) so that Windows can control your specific brand of modem. Your modem support should be installed automatically when you run your modem installation software for your particular operating system; if not, follow the directions provided in your modem's manual for your operating system.

Plug and Play modems are also becoming very popular, and for good reason: These modems handle most of the necessary configuration automatically. Windows 98, Windows 2000, and Windows NT can change the settings on your Plug and Play components and devices so that they all work together instead of fighting. For more information on Plug and Play, steer a course to Chapter 3.

If you've chosen a well-known modem brand that's been on the market for a year or so, it's very likely that Windows already has the correct information on your modem. If so, Windows automatically recognizes your modem when you install it. Your manual should tell you whether you need to install a new control file.

"Do I Need a High-Speed Serial Port?"

Today's superfast modems transfer data at an incredible rate — in fact, the original designers of the IBM PC would have fallen out of their squeaky office chairs with laughter if you had suggested that a modem could ever reach speeds like 56 Kbps. Now that modems are living life in the fast lane, your computer needs a high-speed serial port with the right type of chips to keep up.

Unfortunately, older serial port adapter cards just weren't designed to handle these high speeds; because of this limitation, they're basically worthless with a modern modem.

How can you be sure that you have the right serial port for the job? Buying an *internal modem adapter card* is the easiest way. Because these cards fit inside your computer and aren't connected to it through cables, internal modems have their own built-in serial ports. This way, you're *guaranteed* to have the hardware you need. (Any modem manufacturer who produces a high-speed internal modem without a high-speed serial port onboard should be locked in a basement with an angry skunk.)

If you scavenge an external modem that's faster than 14.4 Kbps, you should make sure that your serial adapter card has 16550-class high-speed UART chips. Any PC components manufactured within the past four years or so are practically guaranteed to have high-speed chips. However, if you've scavenged older parts and you have MS-DOS 6.22 on your computer, you can run the Microsoft Diagnostics utility (MSD.EXE), which displays information about your computer; this is an easy way to find out whether you have the right serial adapter card.

To run the Microsoft Diagnostics utility, follow these steps:

1. **At the DOS prompt, type** MSD **and then press Enter.**

   The main MSD screen appears, as shown in Figure 10-2.

2. **Press C to select COM Ports.**

   The program displays the screen shown in Figure 10-3. If you have a high-speed serial adapter, at least two of the columns next to the heading UART Chip Used begin with the numbers 16550.

3. **To exit the COM Ports screen, press Enter; then press F3 to exit the MSD utility.**

If your computer is using different UART chips that don't begin with 16550, it's time to start shopping for a new serial adapter card if you're planning on using an external modem that's faster than 14.4 Kbps.

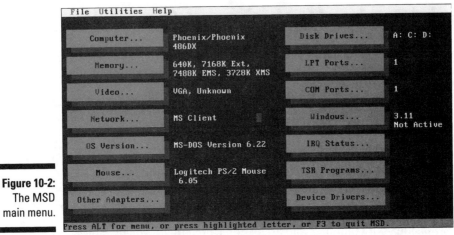

Figure 10-2:
The MSD
main menu.

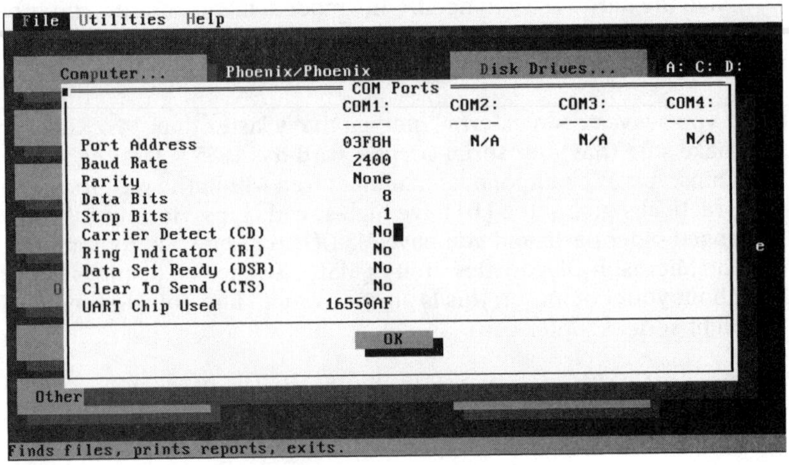

Figure 10-3:
Checking
the speed of
your serial
ports.

Will That Be a Card or a Case?

You can uncover plenty of pros and cons for both internal and external modems, so determining which type is right for you is generally pretty easy. Here's a list of the clouds and their accompanying silver linings:

✔ **Cost:** Internal modems don't need their own case and separate power supply, so they're generally 20 to 30 percent cheaper than their external brethren.

✔ **Status lights:** As you can see by the example shown in Figure 10-4, external modems have lights that let you monitor how your call is proceeding; if you know something about what the lights mean, they can be a valuable tool in figuring out whether your modem and computer are cooperating (or if your modem has sprung a leak). Internal modems have no lights and live inside your computer's case, so it's hard to tell exactly what they're doing.

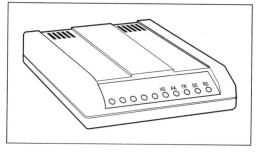

Figure 10-4:
A typical external modem, complete with light show.

✔ **Portability:** If you have more than one computer (or if you need to carry your modem between work and home), an external modem is worth the extra cost. An internal modem, on the other hand, isn't very portable — it's buried deep inside your computer case, and you have to open the case if you want to move the modem to another computer.

✔ **Security:** It's harder for an internal modem to "walk off" in an office environment.

✔ **Less clutter:** If you have limited desk space, an internal modem means one less box cluttering up your computer desk.

✔ **Built-in serial port:** An internal modem comes with its own built-in serial port, so you don't need to worry about whether your serial ports are fast enough for your modem. Also, if both the serial ports on the back of your computer are already in use, an internal modem is a good choice. (For everything you always wanted to know about ports, see Chapter 5.)

✔ **Overcrowding:** If you've already filled all the slots in your computer with various goodies, like a SCSI adapter and a sound card, you don't have room for an internal modem. This is another reason that many technoids have external modems.

✔ **Easy to install:** Installing an external modem is generally easier because it doesn't argue with other parts (like a serial mouse) over a COM port — and, naturally, a USB modem doesn't suffer from hardware conflicts, either. Find out more about this subject in the installation section, later in this chapter.

If you choose an external modem with a serial connection, make sure that you also pick up the proper modem serial cable while you're shopping. Most modem cables use a 9-pin connector on the computer side and a 25-pin connector on the modem end. But many serial adapter cards with two ports have one 9-pin and one 25-pin serial connector. If your mouse is connected to your 9-pin serial port, you have to connect your modem to the second serial port.

While shopping for your modem cable, avoid buying a *null modem* cable. These special cables are designed to hook together two computers with a direct serial connection. A null modem cable will *not* work with your modem.

Time to Face the Fax

Back when a 2,400 bps modem was considered a speed demon, you could choose a modem with or without fax technology. Due to improvements in technology and chip manufacturing, however, all new modems sold today have built-in fax support, for the same price.

The good and the bad on fax modems

Just what exactly can you do with a fax modem? Actually, just about anything you can do with a real fax machine, and a whole lot more to boot! Naturally, you can use a fax modem to send and receive faxes from other fax machines or other computers. You can also build a telephone directory, automatically send faxes at night, allow other fax machines to *poll* your computer for new documents, send *broadcast* faxes to multiple destinations, and design your own cover sheets, just like you can with an expensive fax machine. With a fax modem, you can even send programs and data files to other computers with fax modems.

Before you decide to spend your life savings on an expensive fax modem, however, I must tell you about two drawbacks to faxing with a computer:

- ✔ You can send only documents you've created on your computer, which includes just about any word-processing document, spreadsheet, image, or whatever you could normally print. However, you can't fax a photograph from today's newspaper, nor a recipe from Aunt Bertha's Hometown Hash Handbook. Anything existing on paper is called *hard copy* by both the press and computer tech types — the only way you can send hard copy with a fax modem is to first scan it into your computer. If you're interested in scanners and how you can capture digital images of hard copy, flip your hard copy of this book to Chapter 14.

- ✔ Your computer must be on 24 hours a day if you're serious about using it as a fax. Leaving your computer on enables your modem to answer fax calls while you're away and send faxes at the times you specify. If you leave your fax program running under Windows, you can still take care of your work while your fax modem silently lurks in the background, ready to pounce like a fierce jungle cat on any incoming call.

✔ Leaving your computer turned on isn't as bad as it sounds: Your computer actually uses less power than you may think. Your monitor is the real power hog in your computer system, and most people who run their computers constantly simply turn off the monitor unless they need to use the machine.

If you decide to use your new computer as a part of a home office, I strongly suggest that you have a second telephone line installed especially for your computer — otherwise, anyone trying to send you a fax while you're on the phone ordering pizza is going to get an irritating busy signal. You can also use a separate telephone line for voice mail, as you can see in the section "Let Your Modem Speak," a little later in this chapter.

Can't add a second telephone line? Then you should consider adding *distinctive ring* service to your existing line. This neat feature from the telephone company lets more than one telephone number "use" the same physical telephone line to your home. The telephone rings differently for each number, so you can tell which calls are for you and which are for the computer. As a matter of fact, most modern fax modems and fax software can distinguish calls and can be configured to answer only a certain ring pattern. If you want to use this feature, make sure that your modem supports both distinctive ring and *adaptive answer* (which enables the modem to automatically switch to fax mode when necessary).

More good fax facts

"Okay, Mark, that's all well and good, but what can I really *do* with a fax I've received?" That's part of the magic of a fax modem. If you want, you can simply save the faxed document as a file on your computer and then view it on-screen whenever you need it (complete with rotation and zoom). If you want to get fancy, though, try these features on for size:

✔ You can print a fax on your system printer (no more of that flimsy thermal stuff that turns yellow — we're talking *real* paper here).

✔ If friends or co-workers have the same fax software, you can attach the document in an Internet e-mail message to them and they can load it just as though they had received it over the phone. This is an easy way to "send" a fax anywhere on the Internet.

✔ If your fax software includes OCR (a short acronym for a real whopper of a term, *optical character recognition*), your computer can actually "read" the words on the fax and insert them as text into your favorite word processor. Although this recognition isn't 100 percent accurate, it's good enough to save you lots of time that you would have spent retyping the document.

✔ You can *annotate* the fax and send it back — most fax programs enable you to add your own text or even draw on the original fax and then resend it. This function is great for correcting errors or making suggestions during the development of a document.

If you're shopping for a fax modem, it's usually hard to tell what features are supported by the bundled software that's included with your modem. If the fax software you get doesn't support these features, invest in a full-featured fax or communications program like WinFax PRO or Procomm Plus.

Let Your Modem Speak!

Have you ever called a business and tried to contact someone who was out of the office? You likely encountered *voice mail,* with which you can leave a verbal message for a specific person. If you think that this kind of technology is too expensive for your home office, think again: With today's voice modems, callers are presented with a professional telephone "answering service" for your business, and usually for only $50 to $100 more than a regular fax modem.

Voice modems provide a number of individual, personal voice mailboxes (the number of mailboxes and the features available for each mailbox vary with the modem and the software that comes with it). A caller can store a voice message for you by pressing keys on the telephone, which sends numeric commands to your computer, and most voice modems allow you to pick up your voice mail from a remote telephone, so you don't even need to be at your computer to check your messages.

Most voice modems also provide other amenities — for example:

✔ One of my favorite voice modem features is the speakerphone, where you can dial the phone and talk to someone through your PC's microphone and speakers — no telephone handset necessary! (You can read more about microphones and speakers in Chapter 9.)

✔ If you have more than one message mailbox, your voice modem should enable you to store an individual voice greeting for each mailbox.

✔ If you're curious about the origin of a call, make sure that you get a voice modem with Caller ID support, including an on-screen display of the caller's telephone number. (You also need to sign up for Caller ID service through your telephone company.)

✔ The best voice modems enable you to transmit both voice and data in the same connection — simultaneously. For example, you can talk to other players during multiplayer online games, or talk to someone while sending that person a spreadsheet file.

> ✔ Some voice modems can even dial your pager to tell you when you've received voice mail (personally, I don't ever want to be *that* tightly wired to my computer).

You can choose a combination voice, fax, and data modem — or if the voice features aren't attractive, just a fax and data modem. The choice you make depends on how you plan to use your computer and the price you're willing to pay for a modem. Although voice technology is neat, it's certainly not a requirement when connecting to the Internet or sending a fax.

Installing an Internal Modem

Installing an internal modem has been compared favorably to wrestling an enraged tiger with your bare hands — but often this observation has more to do with trying to shoehorn an internal modem into an existing computer, where several devices have already claimed serial ports.

You may need to change jumper settings on your internal modem if the default COM port (another term for *serial port*) is already being used by another component in your computer. For example, if your mouse is using a serial port, it's likely connected to COM1, so you need to configure your modem as COM2. The installation software for your modem provides you with possible settings for the COM port.

Follow these instructions step by step in order to install an internal modem — and you should come out unscathed on the other side:

1. **Did you just brush the family dog? You'd better touch a metal surface before you install your card!**

   By touching a metal surface before you touch any components, you release any static electricity you may have picked up.

2. **If your computer chassis is plugged in, unplug it and remove the cover from your case.**

3. **Select an open 16-bit adapter card slot for your modem.**

   Modem adapter cards are almost universally 16-bit, but if you've scavenged an older 8-bit modem, it should still fit in a 16-bit slot.

4. **Remove the screw and the metal slot cover adjacent to the selected slot.**

   Don't forget to stick both these parts in your parts box.

5. **Line up the connector on the card with the slot on the motherboard.**

   The card's metal bracket should align with the open space created when you removed the slot cover.

6. **Apply even pressure to the top of the card and push it down into the slot.**

   If the card is all the way in, the bracket should rest tightly against the case.

7. **Add the screw and tighten down the bracket.**

8. **Plug the telephone line from the wall into the proper jack on the back of your computer.**

   Do you have two jacks on the back of your modem? If you have two jacks, your modem accepts both the telephone line and a standard external telephone, so you can call others using the telephone when the modem isn't using the line. Check your modem manual to see which jack should receive the telephone line from the wall; it's typically marked Line or has a picture of a wall telephone jack next to it. If you want to use a separate telephone, connect the cord from the telephone to the other jack (usually marked Phone).

Connecting an External Serial Modem

Have you decided on an external serial modem? If you have an open serial port on your computer and a modem cable with the right connectors, you're ready to go. Follow these steps:

1. **Locate the 9-pin serial port on the back of your case.**

   The serial port is a small connector, as shown in Figure 10-5.

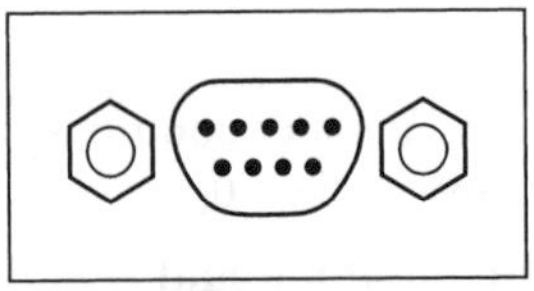

Figure 10-5:
A 9-pin
serial
connector.

If your 9-pin serial port is already being used by your mouse, don't panic. Simply connect your modem to your second serial port, which is usually set as COM2. You will, however, need a cable that matches the connector for your second serial port, and these are typically 25-pin ports. Most computer stores sell little converter things that can turn a 9-pin connector on the end of a cable into a 25-pin connector.

2. **Align the connector on the end of your modem cable with the serial port.**

   The angled edges on the connector are designed to make sure that it goes on only the right way.

3. **After the connector is correctly aligned, push it in firmly.**

4. **If you want, you can tighten the connector by turning the knobs on the connector clockwise.**

   If the connector uses screws instead, you need a small screwdriver. If the connector is already tight enough, you can leave it as is.

5. **Connect the power cord from your modem to the wall socket.**

6. **Plug the telephone line from the wall into the proper jack on the back of your computer.**

   Most external modems have two jacks, which means that you can also plug in a standard telephone and use it when the modem isn't using the line. Your modem manual should tell you which jack should receive the telephone line from the wall; it's usually marked Line or has a picture of a wall telephone jack next to it. If you want to use a separate telephone, connect the cord from the telephone to the other jack (typically marked Phone).

7. **Turn your modem on.**

Connecting an External USB Modem

Follow these steps to install a USB modem:

1. **Locate one of your computer's USB ports.**

2. **If necessary, connect the USB cable to your modem (some modems have USB cables that are permanently connected).**

3. **Connect the power cord from your modem to the wall socket.**

4. **Plug the telephone line from the wall into the proper jack on the back of your computer.**

   Most external modems have two jacks, which means that you can also plug in a standard telephone and use it when the modem isn't using the line. Your modem manual should tell you which jack should receive the telephone line from the wall; it's usually marked Line or has a picture of a wall telephone jack next to it. To use a separate telephone, connect the cord from the telephone to the other jack (typically marked Phone).

5. **Turn your modem on.**

6. **Align the connector on the end of the modem's USB cable with the USB port.**

   The USB connector goes on only the right way.

7. **After the connector is correctly aligned, push it in firmly.**

Installing modem software

The following generic tips give you some idea of what you can expect while installing your modem. However, always follow your modem manual and any on-screen instructions!

1. The installation program displays the COM ports now in use on your computer and asks you to select an unused COM port. (For most internal modems, the default is COM2.)

2. After you've selected your settings, the installation program tests your modem with a diagnostics program to see whether the modem resonds properly. This test typically involves the diagnostics program's sending the modem a series of AT commands, which

the modem responds to if it has been properly installed. If a conflict exists with the COM port you selected, you have to select another COM port. If you're using an external modem, make sure that you turn the modem on before you start the test.

3. When the modem is working properly, the installation program makes changes to your DOS or Windows system files. It may also copy additional bundled communications software.

4. Typically, you must reboot to complete the installation.

Windows automatically recognizes that you've added a USB modem, and you'll probably be prompted to load the CD-ROM from the modem manufacturer so that Windows can install the modem's drivers. After the software is loaded, you're ready to go — and you can connect or remove your modem from your PC at any time without rebooting because Windows 98, Windows Me, and Windows 2000 all support the USB hot-swap feature. *That's* convenient (and it's one of the reasons that USB devices are so doggone popular these days)!

Installing Software and Testing Your Modem

To configure and test your internal or external modem, you must install the software and communications program that came with it. Follow these steps:

1. **If you've unplugged your computer, plug it back in.**

2. **Connect the monitor and keyboard and push the power switch on your monitor.**

3. **Push the power switch on the front or back of your case.**

   Allow your computer to boot.

4. Run the modem installation software.

Insert the installation software into your CD-ROM or floppy drive and follow the instructions (on-screen or in your modem manual) to install the diagnostics software (and any communications software that may be bundled with your modem).

If you've scavenged a modem and you don't have any communications software, I would recommend a commercial program suitable for your operating system (such as Procomm Plus).

PCs have four separate standard COM port values (COM1 through COM4). If your modem doesn't seem to recognize commands on COM1, try the other three values. Most internal modems are configured at the factory as COM2, while external modems really don't care which COM port they use.

An internal modem will not work if it's trying to use a COM port that's already claimed by another component. If you're using an internal modem card with jumpers, fixing this problem is a matter of removing the card, setting the new values provided by the software, reinstalling the card, and then testing it. If you're using a Plug and Play or a "jumperless" internal modem, you should be able to choose another COM port by running the configuration utility that came with your modem. After you've found a combination of values that work, jot them down in your modem manual for future reference.

If your modem is a Plug and Play model, you should be able to make all COM port adjustments by running the modem's configuration program.

5. Run the diagnostics program.

Because of a limitation in the design of the original IBM computers, you can't use COM1 and COM3 at the same time — nor can you use COM2 and COM4 at the same time. Unfortunately, this standard simply hasn't been fixed yet; the COM port restrictions are a legacy from the Dark Ages (luckily, the only serial devices still in common use today are modems and mice). Just grin and bear it, or do like I do: Hang a picture of the original IBM PC on the wall and throw darts at it. I never miss.

Today's communications programs are written for Windows 98, Windows NT, or Windows 2000. If you plan to use one of these programs, wait to install the communications software until you have installed your new operating system. You can read all about different operating systems and their pros and cons in Appendix A.

Part IV
Adding the
Advanced Stuff

The 5th Wave   By Rich Tennant

Software Obsolescence Syndrome - The need to own only the latest version of any program.

In this part . . .

1 describe the "power user" peripherals often found on high-performance computers. You find out more about speeding up your PC with SCSI, building a simple network, using a digital scanner or digital still camera, and adding high-speed Internet connections like ISDN, cable, or DSL to your computer. The advanced (and sometimes expensive) technology you find in this part isn't a requirement for your average home or small office PC, although these chapters serve as an introduction to the world of power-user computing.

Chapter 11

Attack of the SCSI Monster

● ●

In This Chapter

▶ Understanding SCSI technology

▶ Assigning ID numbers to SCSI devices

▶ Terminating the SCSI chain

▶ Installing your SCSI card

▶ Adding SCSI devices

▶ Installing software and testing your work

▶ Troubleshooting your SCSI components

● ●

*T*here's no avoiding SCSI (which, by the way, is pronounced "scuzzy" and stands for Small Computer Systems Interface). Perhaps you first hear of it in casual conversation at your computer user group. Maybe a friend of yours who's a computer guru recommends it. Or your friendly salesperson at the computer store sidles up to you and says something like "You know, you could *really* speed up that PC of yours with a SCSI card."

Oh, you're not being flim-flammed because the salesperson is telling you the truth. A SCSI component like a hard drive can transfer data at a phenomenal rate compared to standard IDE drives. If you crave raw speed, SCSI is indeed the answer to your dreams. SCSI can also support seven devices on a single adapter card, including neat stuff like scanners, CD recorders, tape backup drives, and removable cartridge drives.

However, as the old adage says, "You can't get something for nothing" — and when it comes to adding SCSI support to your computer, the process is definitely more difficult than adding an EIDE hard drive (as covered in Chapter 7). I doubt that you'll need a bottle of your favorite headache medication, and you probably won't turn antisocial during the installation process — but make sure that you read in their entirety both this chapter and the manuals that accompany your SCSI hardware.

In this chapter, I show you how to properly install and configure your SCSI adapter card and SCSI devices.

"Do I Really Need SCSI?"

Before you decide to add SCSI, you need to take a hard look at your computer and its applications. SCSI is *definitely* not a requirement for the average Pentium II- or III-series computer, and there's no reason to add it to your system without a darn good reason. With that in mind, here are the darn good reasons:

- ✔ **Speed:** The most common SCSI devices, SCSI hard drives, are the current king of the racetrack. For example, a properly configured SCSI hard drive can typically transfer data at least twice as fast as a standard EIDE hard drive. A SCSI adapter card provides the fastest possible data-transfer rates, but you need to buy SCSI components to take advantage of that speed. In fact, some peripherals that you wouldn't consider speedy (like digital scanners) work faster and more efficiently on a SCSI system. The most common SCSI adapter cards can transfer data at around 5MB per second, and more advanced variants of SCSI (like UltraSCSI) can achieve a phenomenal transfer rate of anywhere from 40MB to 80MB per second. Figures like that, ladies and gentlemen, make a technowizard sit up and take notice. Blazing transfer rates also make network and Web site administrators take notice, which is why SCSI hardware is typically used on server computers that handle Internet traffic.

  For many power users, this speed increase is reason enough to jump on the SCSI bandwagon — however, if you want to save money or you really aren't worried about squeezing that extra speed from your PC, a standard EIDE system is fine.

- ✔ **Expansion:** If you plan on hanging every peripheral except the kitchen sink on your computer, a SCSI adapter card is a natural choice. When everything is configured correctly, a single SCSI adapter card can take care of 7 devices. (The UltraWide SCSI variety can even handle 15!) An EIDE controller card, on the other hand, can support a maximum of only four devices (two on the primary connector, and two on the secondary EIDE connector). Your SCSI card automatically routes data to and from these devices, so you can even use them simultaneously.

  You may be asking, "Why not use USB rather than SCSI?" That's the popular trend these days — USB peripherals are a cinch to add to your system. However, USB peripherals are all external — aha! — *there's* the rub. So you won't find an internal hard drive, CD recorder, or tape backup unit that works with USB.

- ✔ **Compatibility:** Some parts that require fast transfer rates use only a SCSI interface. For example, many CD recorders and most DAT backup drives use the SCSI standard and require a SCSI adapter because these peripherals need the fastest possible data transfer.

  SCSI is also recognized by a wide range of operating systems, including DOS, Unix, Linux, all versions of Windows, and OS/2.

SCSI is also available as a built-in feature on many Pentium II- and III-series motherboards. If you're sure that your PC will include SCSI peripherals, you may want to pay the extra cash for one of these advanced motherboards. You can save the card slot that would otherwise be occupied by a SCSI adapter.

SCSI adapter cards and devices are typically more expensive than their IDE cousins. If you decide to walk the SCSI road, expect to pay the higher toll. On average, SCSI controller cards and peripherals cost about 20 to 25 percent more than a similar piece of IDE hardware.

Figuring Out SCSI (Or, "It Sounds So Simple!")

In theory, the internal workings of a SCSI card and the various parts attached to it sound no more difficult than pouring a bowl of cereal. Most SCSI adapter cards enable you to connect as many as seven devices, so you can attach all sorts of neat toys, such as scanners, superfast hard drives, Jaz drives, Zip drives, and CD recorders. Internal peripherals fit on one nice cable, and external peripherals connect directly to the external SCSI port on the adapter card. It couldn't be simpler: Your SCSI adapter card identifies each device attached to it by a unique number, called a *SCSI ID*. Pass the milk, right?

Wrong — you must take care of a couple of other requirements before everything will work:

- Your SCSI adapter *must* be properly configured so that it doesn't argue with the other SCSI parts in your computer. You must assign a *unique ID number* to each of your SCSI devices. For example, if you assign the same SCSI ID to your SCSI hard drive and your SCSI CD-ROM drive, these components argue and fight over who gets the ID number, and neither drive works.

- Each SCSI device connected to your SCSI card forms a link in a chain (made from cables rather than from metal), and the two ends of that chain *must* be correctly *terminated* to indicate that no more devices are left for the SCSI adapter to access. The combination of a SCSI adapter card and at least one SCSI component is often called a *chain*. If your SCSI components (including the SCSI adapter itself) aren't properly terminated, your computer will be unable to recognize them.

Whenever possible, make sure that your SCSI peripherals all conform to the same SCSI standard. (The most popular is SCSI-2, although it's not the fastest.) Before you buy a SCSI device, it's a good idea to check with your SCSI card's manufacturer to make certain that there are no known compatibility problems unique to that model. (Check the manufacturer's Web site or call its technical support number.)

Multiple SCSI cards for the technowizard

I know that many of you are sticking up your hand with a question, and I'll bet that question is "Can I install more than one SCSI card in my computer?" Yes, you can install more than one SCSI adapter card in your system, but unless you use Plug and Play SCSI adapter cards, you'll be facing a serious round of configuration before everything works. Unless you know a technowizard with an extremely powerful computer,

you'll find that a PC with multiple SCSI cards is about as rare as a white tiger.

Virtually all SCSI installations involve a single SCSI card by itself, or perhaps add a single SCSI card to an existing computer that's already using EIDE hard drives and devices. Enhanced IDE and SCSI actually coexist pretty well in the same machine.

If you keep these important requirements in mind when you install your SCSI card and devices, your SCSI chain will be easier to configure.

More about SCSI ID numbers

Each SCSI device on your SCSI chain (the adapter card as well as the SCSI peripherals) must have a unique SCSI ID number that identifies it to your computer. SCSI-2 cards use a range of ID numbers from 0 to 7, with ID number 7 typically reserved for the adapter card itself (which leaves seven ID numbers for your SCSI components). If you're unsure which default ID number your SCSI controller card uses, check your manual.

Suppose that you've decided to add a SCSI hard drive and a SCSI internal CD recorder to your computer so that you can record your own audio CDs and computer CD-ROMs. That's a total of three ID numbers. If your SCSI card reserves ID number 7 for itself, you could assign the SCSI hard drive ID number 1 and the CD recorder ID number 3. Figure 11-1 illustrates a simple SCSI chain.

Figure 11-1:
A simple SCSI device chain, showing the unique ID for each component.

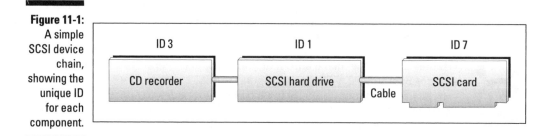

This scenario is all fine and dandy if those ID values happen to be unique *and* they're the defaults for each part — in fact, this is sometimes the case if you're adding just a SCSI adapter card and one or two devices. Once again, check the manuals for your SCSI components to determine what number the various devices use for ID number defaults.

If you're really lucky, the controller card and peripherals will have ID numbers that are already unique. If so, you can joyfully jump to the following section, "More about SCSI terminators." Otherwise, grumble to yourself about Murphy's law and change the matching SCSI ID numbers until each of them is unique.

You can use one of these three methods to set SCSI ID numbers on SCSI adapter cards and devices:

 ✔ **Spin the wheel:** Your device may have a thumbwheel on the bottom, which you can use to change the ID number. To change the ID number (which appears in a little window, as shown in Figure 11-2), turn the thumbwheel until a unique number (that's not already assigned to another SCSI peripheral or the SCSI adapter card) appears.

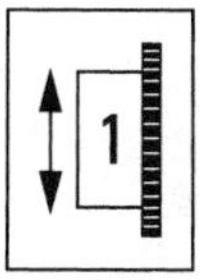

Figure 11-2:
A SCSI ID
thumbwheel.

 ✔ **Set the jumper:** Your SCSI adapter card or device may have a series of jumpers, which you move to set the correct ID. Figure 11-3 shows a typical *jumper* (a plastic-and-metal crossover you can move to connect different sets of pins). To change the ID number on a device that uses jumpers, pull the jumper off the pins and move the jumper to the correct pin; for example, you may have to move a jumper that connects pins 1 and 2 to pins 3 and 4. Check the part's manual for information about configuring the jumper. A pair of needlenose pliers or tweezers make a good tool for moving jumpers.

Figure 11-3:
A SCSI ID
jumper
block.

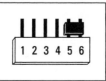

✔ **Let the device set its own ID number:** That's right — some components set their own SCSI device IDs automatically. These devices require a SCSI adapter card that supports SCAM (a tacky acronym that stands for SCSI Configured Automatically). All devices on the SCSI chain must also be SCAM compliant.

More about SCSI terminators

The other requirement for a successful SCSI installation is the proper configuration of terminators. If you're thinking of Arnold as a big walking robot with a bad temper and a bazooka, forget it — in the SCSI world, a *terminator* is a "stop sign" for your SCSI adapter card. All SCSI hardware (including SCSI adapter cards) can be terminated.

The terminator tells your SCSI adapter card that the SCSI chain has ended and that no other SCSI devices are remaining on the chain. Without a terminator, your SCSI card continues to look for devices farther down the SCSI cable. On the other hand, if you terminate the chain too early and another SCSI peripheral is connected farther along the cable, that part will never be recognized by your SCSI adapter card. Either way, it's no picnic.

Suppose that you want to add a SCSI adapter card and a SCSI digital scanner to your PC. You need only two SCSI ID numbers, but you must also indicate to your SCSI adapter card that there is one (and one only one) SCSI peripheral on the chain. This SCSI configuration is the easiest type to figure out — because both these components mark an end of the SCSI chain, both need to be terminated. Figure 11-4 illustrates a simple SCSI chain.

Figure 11-4:
A simple SCSI device chain, showing the proper termination.

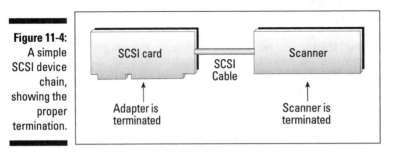

However, when you introduce another SCSI peripheral, things get trickier. To illustrate, suppose that you have a SCSI adapter card with a SCSI hard drive and an internal CD recorder. Figure 11-5 shows a properly terminated chain, and Figure 11-6 illustrates what happens when the SCSI adapter card is improperly terminated: Your adapter card doesn't recognize your CD recorder, and you can't use it.

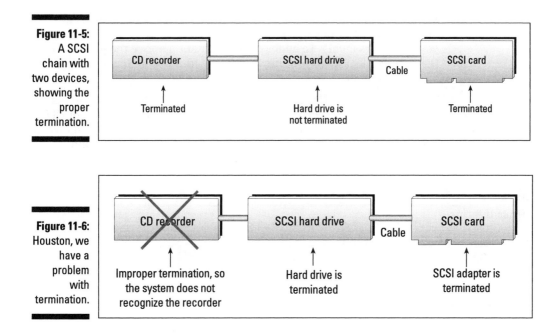

Figure 11-5:
A SCSI chain with two devices, showing the proper termination.

Figure 11-6:
Houston, we have a problem with termination.

Because the effects of improper termination are easy to spot, it's usually pretty simple to fix this problem: If your computer doesn't show a device after installation (like a SCSI hard drive or CD recorder) or you can't operate the peripheral, the termination is probably the first thing you should check. Your SCSI adapter card should include a SCSI diagnostics program; running this program may help you determine what's wrong.

You can use one of three methods to set termination on SCSI adapter cards and peripherals:

✔ **Insert the resistor pack:** As you can see in Figure 11-7, a resistor pack is an electronic plug that typically looks something like a silicon caterpillar. To terminate a SCSI device with a resistor pack, simply plug in the resistor. Your device manual should show you where the socket is located.

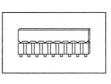

Figure 11-7:
A SCSI terminator of the resistor pack variety.

✔ **Set the jumper:** Your SCSI device may have a jumper, which you can move to enable or disable termination (according to the instructions in your device manual). To change the termination, move the jumper to the correct pin. Check your device manual for information about configuring the jumper.

✔ **Set the DIP switch:** Use a pointed object to slide the tiny switches, as specified in your device manual. The switches can be either ON or OFF (generally the ON direction is noted on the DIP switch itself, as shown in Figure 11-8). One series of ON and OFF will equal termination, and another will disable termination (as specified in your manual).

Figure 11-8:
A SCSI terminator of the DIP switch variety.

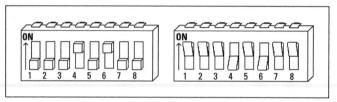

External SCSI (or, putting it out in the open)

If you're using an external SCSI device on your SCSI adapter card (like a Jaz or Zip drive), that component still needs a unique ID and the proper termination. Your SCSI adapter should provide an external connector, which is usually on the back of the card. Because it has 50 pins, your SCSI port is typically easy to locate. Figure 11-9 illustrates a common external SCSI port.

Figure 11-9:
The exotic curves of an external SCSI-2 port.

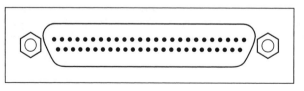

Unfortunately, you can find a number of variations on the cable connectors for a SCSI external device, so it's a good idea to buy the cable after you've both installed your card and bought the device. You can attach multiple external SCSI devices to your PC, such as a digital scanner and an external

SCSI tape backup — a process that old, burned-out hackers that date back to the days of the Atari and Commodore 64 (like myself) call *daisy chaining.* When two external SCSI devices are daisy chained, you connect the two peripherals with a short *SCSI cable* — in effect, continuing the chain through the devices.

If you're connecting an external SCSI peripheral to a SCSI card that's already connected to internal SCSI devices, remember that your SCSI adapter card should no longer be terminated. In effect, the SCSI card is now in the middle of the SCSI chain, with devices on either side.

If you do install multiple external SCSI devices, you need to terminate only the *last* external peripheral in the daisy chain. For example, Figure 11-10 shows a typical external chain — adding an external CD-ROM drive to your PC.

Figure 11-10:
A properly terminated SCSI chain with an external device.

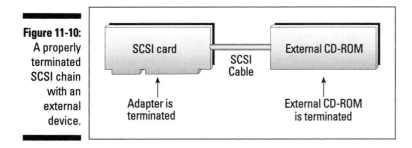

As you can see in Figure 11-11, the improper termination of your SCSI adapter card (when it shouldn't be terminated) will prevent other SCSI devices from being recognized.

Figure 11-11:
Better take that terminator off the adapter card!

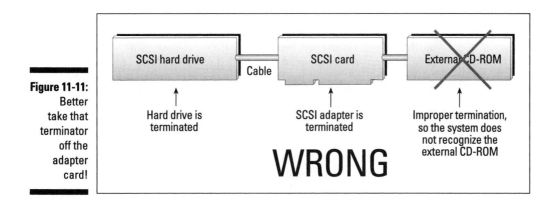

Your SCSI Shopping List

If you've decided to add SCSI support to your computer, be prepared to spend anywhere from $75 to $250 for your SCSI adapter card. With such wide price ranges, it makes sense to weigh the advantages of one card against another. While you're comparing SCSI adapter cards, keep these advanced features in mind:

✔ **PCI or bust:** If top transfer rates for your SCSI hard drive, CD-ROM, and Jaz drives are your goal, buy a *PCI SCSI adapter card* (or buy a motherboard with built-in SCSI support). Of course, you can use a cheaper 16-bit ISA SCSI adapter card, but they're cheaper for a reason — a 16-bit ISA SCSI card can't match the speed of a 32-bit PCI SCSI card.

Not everyone is a speed demon! If you're installing SCSI simply to add a digital scanner, or if you've scavenged a 16-bit SCSI card and you don't covet the fastest possible SCSI transfer rates, a 16-bit adapter card is wonderful. (Heck, I probably have one or two in my parts box.)

✔ **Plug and Play:** As with other adapter cards, if your motherboard supports *Plug and Play,* you save a great deal of time and trouble if you buy a Plug and Play SCSI adapter card. Plug and Play enables your computer to automatically configure your SCSI adapter card.

✔ **Bus mastering:** *Bus mastering* is a data transfer protocol that greatly increases the efficiency of multitasking operating systems like Windows and Linux. When you reduce the technology to terms that mere mortals can understand, bus mastering enables your SCSI card to move different files smoothly to different places at the same time. Generally, bus mastering SCSI cards fall at the high end of the price scale.

✔ **Upgradable firmware:** Your SCSI adapter card actually has its own BIOS, so it really doesn't need the help of the BIOS on your motherboard to recognize SCSI peripherals and hard drives. (If the acronym *BIOS* makes your head hurt, jump to Chapter 3, where I talk about the BIOS on your motherboard.) However, just like the BIOS on your motherboard, your SCSI BIOS should be upgradable; a card with this type of BIOS can be "reprogrammed" with bug fixes, new features, and support for new devices. Some SCSI cards may call this feature *flash ROM.*

✔ **Cache memory:** SCSI adapter cards with onboard cache memory are typically used whenever your SCSI hard drive (or drives) must transfer data at the fastest possible speed, or when your computer will be accessing a large number of files simultaneously (for example, a network or a Web server). These SCSI cards have their own RAM onboard, which holds data that the CPU accesses frequently, so your SCSI drive doesn't have to actually reread that data over and over. Some cards can even "anticipate" the data your computer will need. For example, SCSI cards with cache memory can load the entire contents of a file that's several megabytes long into RAM, where the drive can access it faster later on. The larger the RAM cache, the better (and usually the more expensive the SCSI adapter card).

Installing Your SCSI Card

The typical SCSI installation will have to share your computer with an existing EIDE hard drive, so this section mentions your IDE parts from time to time. However, you can install SCSI by itself and ignore the IDE world — if you've decided on a SCSI-only system, simply ignore any mention of IDE that follows. (Oh, and don't forget to strut your SCSI stuff at the next technoid get-together!)

1. **You've just been kidnapped by aliens and returned, and you want to install a SCSI adapter card? In case you picked up any static electricity, you'd better touch a metal surface before you install your card.**

2. **If your computer chassis is plugged in, unplug it.**

3. **Remove the cover from your case.**

4. **Select an open PCI adapter card slot for your SCSI card.**

   If you've scavenged an older 16-bit ISA SCSI card, you need a 16-bit card slot instead.

5. **Remove the screw and the metal slot cover adjacent to the selected slot.**

   Don't forget to stick both these parts in your parts box.

6. **Check your SCSI adapter for proper termination.**

   If your SCSI card needs to be terminated (because it's at one end of the SCSI chain), you'll find that setting a jumper or adding a resistor pack is much easier *now* than after you've installed the card. Your SCSI adapter will need to be terminated if you have only internal SCSI components to add, with no external peripherals (and vice versa). Because you're installing your SCSI adapter card first, the default SCSI ID number is okay.

7. **Line up the connector on the card with the slot on the motherboard.**

   The card's metal bracket should align with the open space that's left when you removed the slot cover.

8. **Apply even pressure to the top of the card and push it down into the slot.**

   If the card is all the way in, the bracket should be resting tightly against the case.

9. **Add the screw and tighten down the bracket.**

10. **Attach the SCSI ribbon cable to the proper connector on the card.**

    Your adapter card manual can help you locate the SCSI cable connector.

For any ribbon cable, Pin 1 on the male connector must always match the hole for Pin 1 on the female connector. In almost every case, Pin 1 on the male connector is the pin in the upper-left corner of the connector on the device. Every ribbon cable has one wire that's painted red, or somehow marked; that wire is Wire 1, and it should always connect to Pin 1.

Adding an Internal SCSI Device

After you install a SCSI adapter, you can then add internal SCSI components, such as a CD-ROM drive, a CD recorder, a hard drive, or a Jaz drive. If you're adding a new internal SCSI peripheral to an existing SCSI chain, remember that this installation usually involves a change to your current termination configuration. You may have to change the termination on either end of the SCSI chain. If you forget to set the proper termination, your SCSI adapter card may not recognize your new peripheral. Even worse, an existing SCSI part that's been working flawlessly for months will suddenly stop working, too.

To install an internal device, follow these steps:

1. **If your computer chassis is plugged in, unplug it and remove the cover.**

2. **You've been rubbing a birthday balloon on your head, and now you want to install a SCSI component? Don't forget to touch a metal surface to discharge any static electricity.**

3. **Check the termination and SCSI ID number on your new device and configure these settings properly.**

   If your new part will be connected closer to the end of your SCSI cable than any existing SCSI components on the chain, the new device should be terminated. For more information on terminating your SCSI hardware, see the section "More about SCSI terminators," earlier in this chapter; for details on setting the SCSI ID number, see the section "More about SCSI ID numbers," earlier in this chapter.

   If you've forgotten the SCSI ID numbers for other SCSI components you've previously installed, you can use the SCSI diagnostics or utility program that came with your SCSI adapter to determine the ID numbers without disassembling your computer.

4. **Select an open drive bay for your new component.**

5. **From the front of the case, slide the device into the bay and attach it to the side of the bay.**

   Slide the component back and forth until the screw holes in the side of the bay line up with those on the side of the device, and secure the part with the screws that came with it.

6. **Connect one of the power cables from your power supply to the power connector on the device.**

   Note that the connector fits only one way.

7. **Connect the ribbon cable coming from your SCSI adapter card (or your motherboard if it has a built-in SCSI adapter) to the back of the device.**

   If you're installing the first internal SCSI peripheral on your SCSI chain, use the first open device connector on the cable. If you're installing an internal SCSI peripheral on an existing SCSI device chain, use the next open connector on the cable. On the ribbon cable, the wire with the markings is on the side with Pin 1 — if you're unsure which pin on the device's connector is Pin 1, check your manual. The connector should fit snugly, so press it all the way on after you align it correctly.

Connecting an External SCSI Device

If you're adding a new device to an existing SCSI chain, you'll probably have to change your current termination configuration; you may need to change the termination on either end of the SCSI chain. If you forget to set the proper termination, your SCSI adapter card may not recognize your new part.

To install an external device, follow these steps:

1. **Set the correct termination and SCSI ID number for your external peripheral.**

   For more information on termination, see the section "More about SCSI terminators," earlier in this chapter; for details on setting a SCSI ID number for your new external peripheral, see the section "More about SCSI ID numbers," earlier in this chapter.

2. **Locate the external SCSI port on the back of your case.**

   The SCSI port is a flat, thick connector with 50 pins, as shown in Figure 11-9.

   If you're installing a new external SCSI peripheral on an existing external daisy chain, plug the cable from the new device into the secondary SCSI port on the external device that's now last on the chain.

3. **Align the connector on the end of your SCSI cable with the SCSI port and push the connector in firmly.**

   The angled edges on the connector are designed to make sure that it goes on only the right way.

4. **Tighten the connector by snapping the wire clips toward the center of the cable, as shown in Figure 11-12.**

5. **Connect the power cord from your external device to the wall socket.**

Figure 11-12:
External
SCSI
connectors
typically use
wire clips to
ensure that
the cable
stays on.

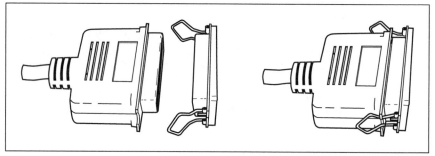

Installing Software and Testing Your SCSI Adapter

To install the software required by your SCSI card and to test your new SCSI chain, follow these steps:

1. **If you've unplugged your computer, plug it back in now.**

2. **Connect the keyboard and the monitor (if you haven't already done so) and turn the monitor on.**

3. **Push the power switch on your computer case and allow your computer to boot.**

4. **Run the SCSI card installation software.**

   Insert the installation software into your CD-ROM or floppy drive and follow the instructions on-screen (or the instructions in your SCSI card manual) to configure your SCSI management software.

5. **After the software is installed, the installation program may prompt you to reboot your computer.**

6. **Run the diagnostics software supplied with your SCSI card.**

   Your SCSI card should come with a diagnostics program that lets you test its operation. Typically, these diagnostics programs also enable you to check for proper recognition of devices on the SCSI chain.

Troubleshooting Your SCSI Devices

So you've installed a SCSI device and — nothing. Your computer doesn't recognize your new peripheral. Brothers and sisters, I've been there, and I feel your pain. Believe me, this situation is the definition of the word *hassle*. Before you take a chain saw to your computer, here's a quick checklist of possible causes for the problem:

- ✔ **Are your ribbon cable connections correct?** Pin 1 on the male connector must match Hole 1 on the female connector — this applies to both the adapter card and the device. (External SCSI peripherals don't have this problem.)

- ✔ **Termination, termination, termination!** This is the classic problem when adding a new SCSI component: The last device on the internal SCSI cable should be terminated. If you have one (or more) external SCSI peripherals, the last of those peripherals should be terminated. If you don't have any external components, your SCSI adapter should be terminated.

- ✔ **Does the device have a unique SCSI ID?** Without a unique ID, two SCSI peripherals will fight to a standstill (like drenched cats), and neither of them will work.

- ✔ **Is your SCSI device receiving power?** Don't forget to plug in an external SCSI peripheral. Internal SCSI components should be connected to one of the power cords leading from your computer's power supply.

- ✔ **Do you need to install a device driver?** Although your SCSI card may recognize your new SCSI component, don't forget to install any manufacturer-specific software drivers that may be required for the peripheral.

- ✔ **Is the device conflicting with existing SCSI components in your PC?** Run the SCSI diagnostics program that came with your adapter card to determine whether your new peripheral is recognized by your computer; if it is, the problem is probably not caused by a SCSI device conflict. If the new part isn't recognized (and both termination and SCSI ID numbers are okay), it's probably time to call the manufacturer's technical support hotline.

Chapter 12

So You Want to Add a LAN?

*A*mong the many so-called revolutionary concepts that have rocked PC design for more than two decades, the most important has proven to be the desktop *computer network.* On a *Local Area Network* (or LAN, for short), your desktop PC can share programs and data with other computers in your office or run programs that reside on a central *server* computer. In fact, with network software called *groupware,* you can participate with others in officewide projects, where everyone works and communicates together. Networks can be as small or as large as you like — they can link desktop computers in an entire building or an office with ten computers, or you can simply connect two or three PCs to share the same printer and exchange e-mail.

Gamers, don't feel left out because the business types get to have all the fun. Networks also enable several players to compete in the same game, with each player using a different PC. These first-person graphic multiplayer battles began with Doom, the classic shoot-'em-up. But now just about every game that arrives on the store shelf features network play. You can race cars, build empires, pilot star fighters, or deliver a cyber karate chop to your boss. (If you're a real gladiator, you can even set up a network at home just for gaming.)

Of course, adding network support isn't for everyone; if you have access to only one computer or you have no pressing reason to add your computer to an existing network, you can stop reading here and jump to the next chapter.

Feel like connecting? Then read on!

Adding the Network Advantage

If you use several PCs in a small business or if your home has more than one computer, you may want to connect them through a network. By doing so, you can share data between your computers — everything from a business proposal to your kid's artwork. In addition, with a network you can also look forward to benefits like the *Four Cs:*

✔ **Convenience:** Imagine being able to load a document into your word processing application directly from someone else's hard drive — no running back and forth with a floppy disk. (Most technotypes call the floppy disk method a *SneakerNet.*) If your PC is connected to a network, you can transfer files, run programs, and access data on the other networked computers — just as though those programs and files resided on your *local* hard drive (the drive that's physically in your own PC).

The convenience of a network doesn't stop with just data, though — you can also share peripherals across a network. For example, on a network, you can share a printer, a CD-ROM jukebox, a fax/modem, or a CD recorder, which is a great way to cut expenses for a small business that has just a handful of employees. Rather than buy a printer for each PC, everyone can share the same printer.

With software like Procomm Plus (from Symantec, at `www.symantec.com`), you can even access your network from a remote site by using a modem connection. For example, you can use the modem on your home computer to connect to a *modem server* on your office network. After you successfully *log on* (enter your username and the correct password), you can retrieve files or answer e-mail.

✔ **Communication:** One of the primary uses for a small office network is interoffice electronic mail. E-mail software is built into Windows 98, Windows NT, and OS/2, although you can find e-mail *clients* (applications that let you read e-mail) for DOS and Linux as well. E-mail can contain more than mere text messages; you can include attachments like data files, voice and video clips, or even entire programs.

Unfortunately, you can also share a virus with the outside world through a LAN connection or e-mail attachments. I can't stress this enough: *Get yourself a good antivirus program, like Norton Antivirus (*`www.symantec.com`* again), install it, and keep it updated!* With an antivirus program running while you're using your computer, you're protected — just in case.

Advanced NetWare networks with fast transfer rates can support videoconferencing between computers on the network. Because everyone involved needs a fast multimedia PC and a video camera, videoconferencing isn't widespread yet, although it could eventually replace the telephone in your average "wired" office.

✔ **Cooperation:** For businesses of every size, the answer to office cooperation is a *groupware system*. A typical groupware system like Lotus Notes (www.lotus.com) includes e-mail and an electronic public message base (where you can leave messages of general interest, like announcements), along with a common word processor, spreadsheet, and database program that everyone uses. Each of these common applications shares the same documents, so anyone can use and update those documents. Groupware enables users to discuss, change, and revise data on a project, often simultaneously. For example, in a small office, Bill can add a note to a proposal for a new product while Jane makes a change to the product's dimensions.

Using groupware also enables you to coordinate numerous schedules when you want to organize a meeting or office event. By using a *shared calendar,* for example, employees can specify when they're available during any given week, allowing anyone who's planning a meeting to use this data to determine the best time to get together.

✔ **Contact:** In this case, contact with the Internet. If your computer has access to an existing office network, that network may already have a fast, dedicated connection to the Internet. With a network connection on your office PC, your file transfers and Web surfing will be many times faster than they would be over a modem connection.

Do you need to connect to a network in order to access the Internet? Definitely not! Most home computer owners connect to the Internet through a *dial-up connection* (Chapter 10 tells you all about using a modem), or one of the three types of high-speed connections: ISDN, DSL, or cable modem (as described in Chapter 13). Although the Internet is actually a huge network of smaller networks, you do *not* need your own network to use it.

Deciding Which Network Architecture Is Best for You

This section explains the basic terms you need to know when discussing networks. I show you the fundamentals of network *architecture* (the structure in which you string the computers together). Read on to find out how to construct a basic network with the smallest investment in time and money.

Of course, you could go full-bore and network all the PCs in your entire neighborhood, but that's not what this book is about. For you home users and small-business owners, this section gives you the very basics on constructing a small network of two to five computers, called *nodes* in network terms. For more-detailed information on building a network, I suggest that you check out *Networking For Dummies,* by Doug Lowe (IDG Books Worldwide, Inc.).

Comparing client-server and peer-to-peer networks

Desktop networks fall into one of two mysterious categories; you continually hear them mentioned if you hang around a networking technonerd. Rather than force any well-adjusted human being into hanging around such a nerd, let me explain these terms up front:

- **Client-server:** This term is one of the more popular buzzwords in use by the computer elite these days. Luckily, *client-server* turns out to be quite simple. On a network, a *client* is simply a computer that uses the network's resources. Usually, a client computer is the computer on your desk.

  The other half of the name, the *server,* refers to a computer that is dedicated to providing some sort of resource for the client computers on the network. For example, a *file server* provides the other computers on the network with the fastest access possible to a set of files (which reside on the server rather than on the individual client computers). Other servers, such as dedicated CD-ROM servers, printer servers, and modem servers, allow everyone on the network to use the same hardware and access the same data.

  A *client-server network* is simply a network that includes one or more server computers, no matter what the function of the server. Although file servers and printer servers are the most common shared resources, any server transforms your network into a client-server network.

- **Peer-to-peer:** For once, the name means what it says. A *peer-to-peer* network has no servers — all computers are connected to each other (in fact, every computer is as good as its peers). Of course, you save the cost of an expensive server computer, but it's harder for computers to share the same information. A peer-to-peer network is best for the home user or for an office in which everyone simply wants to exchange e-mail and files or use a common printer. Windows 98, Windows Me, and Windows 2000 all include simple peer-to-peer networking built-in, which is suitable for file and printer sharing.

Comparing network configurations

Wait — don't breathe yet! Now that you understand the difference between *client-server* and *peer-to-peer,* you should know something about the three popular configurations of desktop computer networks:

- **Ethernet:** *Ethernet* was the first widespread network topology used with PCs (*topology* is a 50-cent word that means "network structure"). Ethernet is still the most popular network topology by far, and it works equally well as client-server or peer-to-peer. Although Ethernet transfers data more slowly and less efficiently than token-ring networks (which I describe in the following bullet), Ethernet uses the least expensive *network interface card* (a fancy phrase for a network adapter card). Ethernet is also the least expensive cable network, so it's the cheapest to install.

On an Ethernet network, packets of data are broadcast across the entire network with an identifying electronic "name." The computer that matches the name collects the packet and processes it, and computers that don't match the packet ignore it. If two computers attempt to broadcast packets at the same time, the entire network is basically placed "on hold" until the conflict passes. This on-hold delay accounts for the relative inefficiency of an Ethernet network. Figure 12-1 illustrates an Ethernet network.

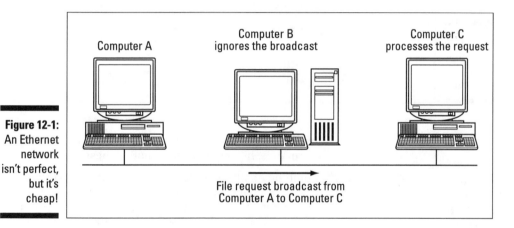

Figure 12-1:
An Ethernet network isn't perfect, but it's cheap!

Computer A

Computer B ignores the broadcast

Computer C processes the request

File request broadcast from Computer A to Computer C

✔ **Token-ring:** *Token-ring* is a more advanced networking topology that features faster transfer rates and more efficient operation. However, the cost of the equipment is higher than Ethernet.

A token-ring network is essentially a giant circuit loop, similar to a giant electronic doughnut. All the nodes on the network are connected to this loop (that's the *ring* part). An electric signal (or *token*) is continually repeated so that it constantly moves through the loop. When a data packet is generated by a node, it changes the token to indicate that the circuit is in use. The computer that matches the packet's identifier collects the packet and processes it, and computers that don't match a packet ignore it. After the packet is processed, the token is again reset to indicate that the network can send another packet. Figure 12-2 illustrates a token-ring network.

Unlike an Ethernet network, no conflicts occur between computers attempting to send packets on a token-ring network (because only one computer is sending packets at one time over the circuit).

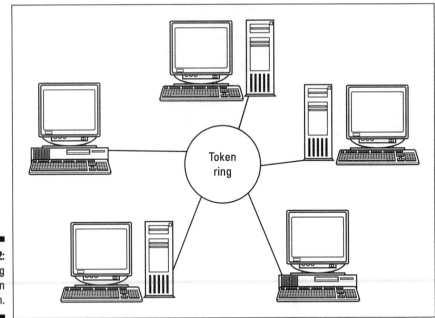

✔ **Star:** The *star* network topology is the king of the hill in PC networking, with the best performance, highest efficiency, and highest cost.

A star network is built much like a modern railroad switching station: Each computer sends data packets to a central switch, which routes the data to the proper receiving node. Because each node is separately connected to the switch, a star network enables each computer to send data packets at the same time, and no conflicts arise that might reduce the efficiency of the network. The switch simply keeps up with each packet and suspends those it can't send immediately (rather like an airport control tower placing an airplane in a holding pattern). When the receiving node is ready to accept the data, the switch gives the packet "clearance to land" and the packet is allowed through the switch. Figure 12-3 illustrates a star network.

Most home- and small-business owners who want to install a network should stick with the *Ethernet* topology in a *peer-to-peer* environment. Hey, you're now a network technogenius — you understood the buzzwords! Better go look in the mirror and see whether you've grown a beard or suddenly sprouted a pocket protector full of old ballpoint pens. (Suspenders are a dead giveaway, too.)

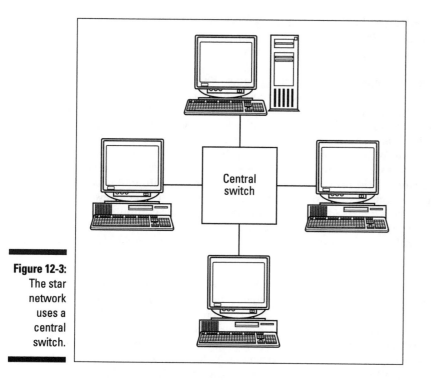

Figure 12-3:
The star
network
uses a
central
switch.

Anyway, peer-to-peer Ethernet best fits the requirements of "quick, easy, and cheap." In fact, many Ethernet networking do-it-yourself packages are now available, like the following:

- ✔ LANtastic, from Artisoft, Inc. — my personal favorite
- ✔ The 3Com Starter Kit (which is also available with a hub for client-server operation)
- ✔ PC MACLAN, from Miramar Systems, Inc., which even enables your PC to share printers and drives with a Macintosh, of all things

These packages include most of the required hardware and software, and they can be installed by mere mortals (or a brand-new technowiz like you). Note that most of these packages still require you to buy your own cable and connectors.

Selecting a network operating system

By far, the most popular of these small network packages is LANtastic. It's compatible with Windows 98 and Windows NT but also works with older computers running DOS and Windows 3.1. If you need to share a modem on your network, LANtastic features built-in modem sharing and multiple Internet sessions through one modem. LANtastic also provides CD-ROM and printer sharing for any node on the network without requiring a server.

If you're familiar with networking under Windows 98, you may be asking "Why not use the built-in peer-to-peer support offered in Windows 98?" Actually, you can — but unlike the LANtastic "everything's included" approach, you need to provide your own network interface cards and cabling. Also, you miss out on many network functions that Microsoft didn't include in Windows, and it's much harder for a networking novice to set up and configure a Windows peer-to-peer network. LANtastic handles many of these installation and configuration steps for you automatically, and you can upgrade your system to add new functionality each time a new version of LANtastic is released. Finally, if you have any older computers in your home or office running Windows 3.1 or DOS, you need additional network software anyway because these older operating systems don't include all the software you need to run a peer-to-peer network.

Although LANtastic offers everything you need for a typical peer-to-peer network, Windows NT (and its new sibling, Windows 2000) has become the operating system of choice for larger networks that use a server. Windows NT is available in both a comprehensive server package (which includes better security and faster, more efficient operation) and a workstation version (which works well in a peer-to-peer environment). However, even the stripped-down Windows NT workstation is more expensive than LANtastic. For peer-to-peer networking, LANtastic is also a better pick than Unix and Linux; Unix and its progeny work best as servers, and Unix is more difficult to learn than LANtastic.

Collecting What You Need for a LANtastic Network

A typical LANtastic package comes with a number of network interface cards, a length of cable, connectors, and the actual LANtastic software you need to run the network. That's the nice thing about spending extra on a full package. However, if you're setting up your own Windows 98 peer-to-peer network, buying your network supplies from different places, or you've scavenged an adapter card or two, you need to make sure that you have the proper hardware. Here's a quick checklist of what you need:

- ✔ **Network interface cards:** You need a *network interface card* for each computer you plan to connect to your network. I discuss these cards in the next section.

- ✔ **Cabling:** The cabling you choose depends on whether your network uses an extra piece of equipment called a *hub* (which acts as a central connection point):

• **Coaxial cable:** If you choose the traditional Ethernet installation without the extra expense of a hub, you need standard network *coaxial cable* to connect all the computers in your network. (Coax is the same type of cable used on your cable TV, so you've probably seen it before.) Each end of your coax cable must have a *terminator* to end the network circuit. Figure 12-4 illustrates a coax cable and connector. Figure 12-5 shows a typical coax Ethernet configuration.

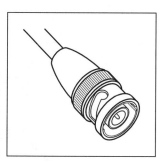

Figure 12-4:
A coax cable and connector.

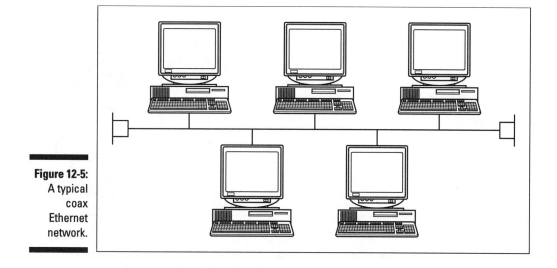

Figure 12-5:
A typical coax Ethernet network.

• **Twisted pair cable:** If you do use a hub, you can use *twisted pair cable,* which resembles telephone wire — this option is usually chosen for a home network. Twisted pair cable has a connector (called an RJ-45) very much like a telephone wire, as you can see in Figure 12-6. With twisted pair cabling, each computer is connected to the hub. Figure 12-7 shows a typical twisted pair Ethernet configuration.

Figure 12-6:
A twisted pair cable and connector, ready to rock.

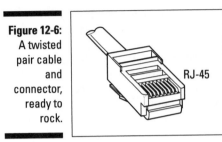

RJ-45

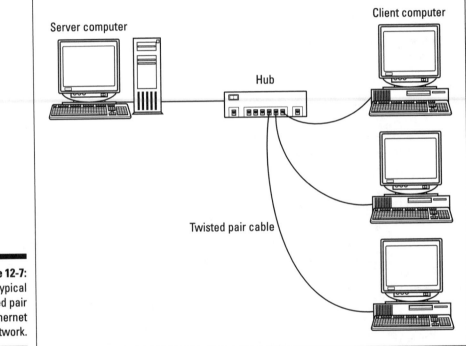

Server computer

Client computer

Hub

Twisted pair cable

Figure 12-7:
A typical twisted pair Ethernet network.

Your network interface cards must support the type of cable you're using. If you use coax, make sure that your cards have *BNC connectors*. If you use twisted pair cable, your cards should have *RJ-45 connectors* instead. Many Ethernet cards carry both types of connectors, just in case.

You *can* connect two computers using twisted pair cable without using a hub, but three or more computers on a twisted pair network require a hub. If you're connecting just two computers for multiplayer games or printer sharing, ask your local computer store for a *twisted pair crossover cable*.

✔ **Connectors:** If you choose a coax network, you also need to pick up a set of *coax connectors*. These metal gizmos enable you to attach and detach cables, to other cables and to network adapter cards. Figure 12-8 shows a pair of typical coaxial connectors. Connectors are easy to lose, so make sure that they're safely stowed in a bag or in your parts box.

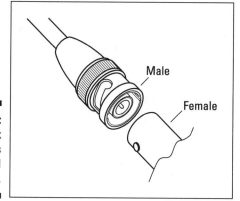

Figure 12-8:
Coax
connectors
are cute and
shiny.

Male

Female

✔ **Software:** LANtastic comes in single-user and 10-user packs (each PC on your network counts as a user). Whenever you need to add additional computers to your network, you can add as many users (singly or in groups of 10) as is necessary. Although LANtastic is self-contained and includes all the support software you need, you can find entire mail-order catalogs chock-full of expensive network software utilities and applications. As the old saying goes, "Spend as much as you want, we'll code more."

✔ **Hub:** Most small peer-to-peer networks don't require a hub, but a hub does make the maintenance and upgrading of your network much easier. It's a choice of convenience versus money. If you spend the extra money on a hub, you can use twisted pair cable and all your network computers are connected to a single box (which is much more convenient).

More stuff about network interface cards

The most expensive part of a coax-based Ethernet network is the network interface card required for each computer. A typical network card uses either a 16-bit slot or a PCI slot. However, unlike a SCSI or IDE adapter card, it's not necessary to spend extra on a PCI network card for the simple Ethernet network I'm discussing. A 16-bit ISA card is fast enough to handle a simple LANtastic or Windows 98 peer-to-peer network — these ISA cards are cheaper, too.

Like every other adapter and part you can stick in your PC, some cards cost more than others. The following checklist tells you what important features are offered by a good network card:

- ✔ **Dual connectors:** Better network cards have multiple connectors for different types of cable, so you don't have to replace all your adapter cards if you upgrade from a network using coax to a network using twisted pair cabling.

- ✔ **Plug and Play:** If your computer's motherboard supports Plug and Play, I recommend a Plug and Play network adapter card to match. A Plug and Play card is automatically configured (without changing any jumper settings) when you boot your computer.

- ✔ **LED status lights:** The status lights on a network adapter card help determine what's gone wrong if you experience problems. For example, a red light usually indicates that the adapter isn't receiving a broadcast signal from the cable.

- ✔ **Certified:** How can you tell whether the network interface card you've picked will work with LANtastic? Look for interface cards carrying manufacturer's certification that the card works with your chosen network software. The certification process involves testing by both the software manufacturer and the card manufacturer, ensuring that the card performs without problems. Most certified network cards advertise their compatibility, but if you need reassurance, you can always check with the card manufacturer.

- ✔ **Automatic or software configuration:** No one in his right mind wants to bother with setting jumpers to configure a network card. The best network cards automatically configure themselves after you've connected them to your network.

- ✔ **Full driver support:** Check the manufacturer's Web site or technical support department to make sure that the card comes with the necessary drivers for your network software. Those drivers should also be available for multiple operating systems because you never know when you might have to hook a computer running DOS or Windows 3.1 to your network.

More stuff about cables and connections

Installing the cables and connecting everything is the most time-consuming chore involved in setting up an Ethernet network. Keep these guidelines in mind as you shop for cables and connectors (and also as you crawl around under desks):

- ✔ **Making cables is no picnic:** I can't stress this enough — unless you've created your own network cables before, buy them ready-made. Building your own cables from scratch is roughly akin to crafting a grand piano from a bowl of jelly — with a pair of chopsticks. I'm not going to discuss how to create cables in this chapter: Coaxial cable is tough stuff, and a number of different varieties are available (each of which uses a different technique to attach a connector). It's much easier to walk into your computer store or call your favorite mail-order outlet and ask for a pre-made network cable (sometimes called a patch cable). Ready-made cables come in several different standard lengths and already have the connectors on both ends, too. You don't waste time or money trying to learn how to cut cable, and you can be sure that the cable works.

✔ **Always buy extra cable, connectors, and terminators:** No matter how well you plan your network and how closely you measure the distance between your computers, something's going to come up that demands more cable or more connectors. (If you're using coax, spare terminators don't hurt, either.) Buy cables at least a foot longer than you think you need.

✔ **Get help:** Enlist the aid of someone to hand you things, prepare cable, and listen to your epithets.

✔ **Just Say No to exposed cable:** Running cable behind a desk or along the baseboards works, but avoid exposed cable whenever possible. You'd be amazed at how clumsy people can be (even if you've taped your cable under a rug).

If your cable has to cross a hallway or corridor and your building uses a suspended ceiling, you may try routing the cable above the ceiling tiles. For a solid ceiling, the molding used by electricians to cover exposed cables works well.

There Are Always Exceptions!

Now that you're familiar with the virtues and requirements of a traditional Ethernet network using coax or twisted-pair cable, guess what? You can toss all that to the four winds! What if I told you that I can install a network without running a single piece of Ethernet cable or a pesky network interface card?

It's true: Thanks to the arrival of three different alternative network technologies, you're no longer tied down to your grandfather's LAN, and these technologies work with any network software that uses a standard Ethernet connection. All three are compatible with Windows 98, too.

However (isn't there always a "however" whenever it comes to computers?), these new networks also have their own limitations, so let's take a look at all three. After you've finished this section, you can decide whether to stick with the tried-and-true twisted-pair cable network or whether to strike out on your own with a new breed of home network.

Use your telephone wiring

Alexander Graham Bell would have never conceived that his invention could carry network packets, too — of course, he had very little training in computer hardware. With a home phoneline network (HomePNA for short, at www.homepna.org), your Ethernet hardware uses existing telephone wiring in your home or office to transmit network data packets. To connect a new PC to the network, you install a special network interface card, locate the nearest telephone jack, and (snap!) plug in a cable. The jack can be located anywhere within your home.

Unlike a dial-up connection to the Internet through your modem — which rudely claims your telephone line and presents a busy signal to the world — a HomePNA network allows you to use your telephone normally for answering and dialing voice calls.

On the downside, a HomePNA network is slower than a standard cabled Ethernet connection (although it should be quite fast enough for multiplayer gaming and sharing an Internet connection). Also, the hardware is a bit more expensive than a typical Ethernet kit, running approximately $150 for a two-PC HomePNA kit from Diamond Multimedia (www.diamondmm.com). You should also consider how many telephone jacks are spread throughout your house — most homes have only a handful, so you're somewhat limited with this option.

Use your AC wiring

Come to think of it, there's another "network" of wiring within the typical house — but can AC current and computer data co-exist? You bet! Intelogis (www.intelogis.com) offers a home/office AC networking system, and it doesn't even require a network interface card (so you don't have to open the case on that brand-new PC you just built). You simply plug the powerline adapter plug into any AC wall socket in your home and connect the other end of the cable to your computer's parallel port. Naturally, you probably have an AC outlet in just about every room of your home, so this system is a little more adaptable than a HomePNA network.

If you're networking to share a printer, this powerline kit has another advantage: It includes a printer module that allows your printer to run on the network *without* a connection to a PC! Suddenly, you have the same convenience offered by an expensive printer with a "built-in" network adapter, so you can locate your printer by any convenient AC outlet!

As you may expect, that convenient parallel port connection really slows down the powerline network; it's even slower than a home phoneline system, and it's still much more expensive than a basic twisted-pair Ethernet kit. I'd recommend this option for those who want basic file and printer sharing because it's not really fast enough for multiplayer gaming or for sharing a DSL or cable Internet connection.

Use your USB port

Finally, if you don't mind actually cabling things together, the USB port — the jack-of-all-trades of the PC world — can act as a network portal for your computers. Like a powerline network, this option doesn't require network cards, and you don't have to remove the case on your computer. The cables connect to the USB port on each PC in your network, and they're connected in turn to a black box that both connects the cables and acts as a hub.

A USB network is about the same price as a standard Ethernet network kit, so it's cheaper than a home phoneline or powerline network. It's also almost as fast as an average 10MB-per-second twisted-pair network.

Unfortunately, the downside for a USB network is tied to the length of the cable. There can be only a maximum of 10 meters between computers on a USB network (which, coincidentally, is also the maximum length of a standard USB cable). Anything longer and your network signal fades between computers. Of course, this isn't a problem if all your computers are in the same room, but I don't think that the Brady Bunch will be using a USB network.

Installing Your Network Interface Card

Ready to install your first network interface adapter? If you've decided on PCI cards, make sure that every computer on your network has at least one PCI slot open. Follow these steps:

1. **Just finished polishing the silverware? Touch a metal surface before you install your card to discharge any static electricity on your body.**

2. **If your computer chassis is plugged in, unplug it.**

3. **Remove the cover from your case.**

4. **Select an open card slot for your network card; then remove the screw and the metal slot cover adjacent to the selected slot.**

5. **Line up the connector on the card with the slot on the motherboard.**

   The card's metal bracket should align with the open space left when you removed the slot cover.

6. **Apply even pressure to the top of the card and push it into the slot.**

   The bracket should be resting tightly against the case.

7. **Add the screw and tighten down the bracket. Connect the network cable to the corresponding port on the card.**

Your adapter card manual can help you locate the network cable connector on your card.

8. **Install the network adapter card driver software.**

Check your card's manual for information on how to load the driver software for your particular operating system.

Connecting a Coaxial Cable

Coaxial network connectors normally come in one of two flavors — a single connection (*cable-to-cable* or *cable-to-network card*) or a T-connection (*cable-to-cable-to-cable*). Connect cables to both varieties by following these steps:

1. **Push the female connector onto the male connector.**

The locking pins on the female connector should align with the grooves cut into the male connector, as shown in Figure 12-9. Push the two connectors together until the locking pins rest against the angle in the groove (they're spring-loaded, so you have to push firmly).

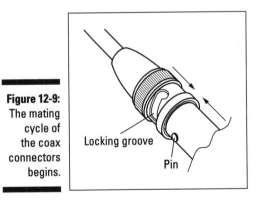

Figure 12-9: The mating cycle of the coax connectors begins.

Locking groove

Pin

2. **Push the connectors together and twist the collar on the male connector.**

Figure 12-10 illustrates the twist. The locking pins should end up at the circular area at the end of the groove, and the connector should maintain a bit of pressure.

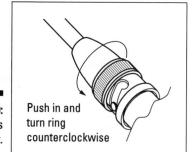

Figure 12-10:
The twist is
the secret.

Push in and
turn ring
counterclockwise

Connecting a Twisted Pair Cable

If you've ever plugged a telephone cord into a wall or a modem, you've probably performed this action before:

1. **Push the male connector into the female connector until it clicks.**

   The connectors fit only one way. Figure 12-11 illustrates the connection.
   The connection is the same for both cable-to-hub and cable-to-network
   cards.

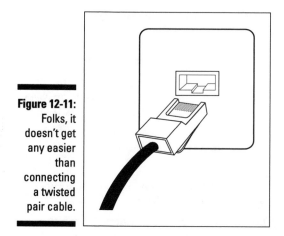

Figure 12-11:
Folks, it
doesn't get
any easier
than
connecting
a twisted
pair cable.

2. **There is no step two.**

Installing LANtastic

After you install the network adapter cards in all your computers, install the adapter card driver software, and connect your cables, all that remains to get things running is for you to install LANtastic software on each computer.

The exact steps and the order they follow in the LANtastic installation process vary according to the version of the software, the operating system on the computer, and the options you select. Therefore, the steps in this section may not match what you see on-screen. Luckily, each screen in the installation process displays complete instructions on what you're doing, so you should always follow the on-screen directions when things vary. To install the software, follow these steps:

1. **If you've unplugged your computer, plug it back in now.**

2. **Connect the keyboard and monitor (if you haven't already done so) and push the power switch on your monitor.**

3. **Turn on your computer by pushing the power switch and allow your computer to boot.**

4. **Run the LANtastic installation software.**

   Insert the install software into your CD-ROM or floppy drive and follow the on-screen instructions.

5. **Enter an identifying name for this computer on your network.**

6. **Select the Typical Install.**

7. **Select the brand and model of adapter card you've installed.**

   The installation program recognizes most popular cards automatically, but if your adapter brand and model isn't included, try the generic NDIS Supported Adapter setting. You may have to supply a driver disk that should be included with your card.

8. **Select any drive or printer connections you want to make to other computers.**

   After you select the default options for your system, the installation program copies the required files to your hard drive.

9. **Allow the installation program to reboot your computer. Watch the network startup messages and write down any error messages that appear on-screen.**

   These error messages and possible solutions are listed in your LANtastic manual set.

Chapter 13

Life in the Fast Lane — with ISDN

*I*SDN. Great — another acronym. This particular set of letters, however, represents a dream come true for telecommuters and Internet junkies, and it's taken a long, long time to come true. Imagine transferring data over existing telephone lines with throughput up to 256 Kbps. Think about smooth, real-time videoconferencing that doesn't look like a bad silent movie from the 1920s. Picture an Internet connection that lets you receive a Web page and talk to someone on the telephone, simultaneously. Huzzah! You've just *got* to have ISDN, right?

As my favorite Western star, John Wayne, used to drawl, "Hold on there, pardner." Yes, you can do all that with ISDN, and this chapter covers all the advantages of an ISDN connection. But ISDN definitely isn't for everyone, although many technonerds and ISDN "cheerleaders" on the Internet want you to believe that. (After all, if ISDN were *that* essential, everyone would already have it, like a toothbrush or a pair of cheap sunglasses.) Plus, there are other even faster methods of making a high-speed Internet connection these days, like cable and DSL, and they may be easier (and probably cheaper) for you to use.

This chapter *also* covers all the disadvantages to ISDN, such as its expensive hardware. In fact, ISDN is still not available in some areas of the United States, and the rate your telephone company charges for ISDN access may be outrageous. Unlike an Internet connection, voice and fax connections don't make use of the high-speed ISDN link. It's far cheaper in the long run if you stick with a standard-combination fax and telephone unit on a separate analog line.

In this chapter, I present you with a fair and honest picture of your high-speed Internet options — you can decide for yourself whether "you've just got to have ISDN."

Figuring Out Whether You Need ISDN

Before you go any farther in this chapter, you should decide whether you need a broadband (another technoterm for "high-speed") connection to the Internet. *Remember:* That connection may not automatically mean ISDN service. For example, there's no reason to even consider the expenses involved in ISDN, cable, or DSL if all you do is connect to the Internet for a few minutes a day to check your e-mail. Of course, you don't have to meet any certain criteria to add a broadband Internet to your system, but it really isn't cost-effective to use it for only a few minutes a day.

Choosing ISDN, cable, or DSL may be a winning proposition if you fit one of these descriptions:

- **Internet junkie:** I'm talking heavy-duty Web surfing here — at least three or four hours a day of Internet access. If your primary activities on the Internet are file transfers via FTP or Web surfing, a broadband connection will be great for you. If you use the Internet for only an hour a day (or if your primary Internet applications are e-mail, newsgroups, telnet, Gopher, or Archie), I recommend sticking with a 56 Kbps analog modem (see Chapter 10 for more about modems).

- **Telecommuter:** If you need high-speed access to your office network from your home, ISDN is a very good choice. You can call an ISDN line connected to the network at your office and log on normally, just as though you were sitting at a computer at work.

- **Conferencing wizard:** A broadband connection is practically a requirement for high-quality videoconferencing (over a Local Area Network connection or over the Internet). If you've tried conferencing over an analog modem, you'll be amazed — broadband provides the fast data-transfer rates for audio and a larger screen, as well.

How does ISDN work, anyway?

ISDN stands for Integrated Services Digital Network (there's a name chock-full of healthy buzzwords) — but the really important piece of the name is the "digital" part. (For those of us who have been running bulletin-board systems and using the Internet long before it became fashionable, the acronym has subtly changed. If you've been waiting for The Arrival of digital networks for several years now, like I have, ISDN used to mean It Still Does Nothing.)

Although an ISDN connection uses the same physical telephone line as a traditional analog connection, ISDN can carry digital data, which opens up an entire suitcase full of possibilities — digital video, CD-quality audio, Web pages, multiplayer game data, and even good old-fashioned text, and at speeds higher than any traditional analog modem. (For a complete discussion of computer modems and all their eccentricities, jump to Chapter 10.) In fact, the modem is no longer necessary because digital data doesn't have to be converted into an analog signal and back again. Figure 13-1 illustrates an analog signal from a traditional analog telephone connection.

Figure 13-1:
A slow, tired analog signal.

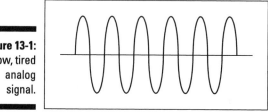

Figure 13-2 shows a digital signal. Basically, a digital signal is simply a long string of zeros and ones, or ON and OFF states (the same digital vocabulary spoken by your computer and your audio CD player).

Figure 13-2:
A spunky digital signal ready for the new millennium, full of vim and vigor.

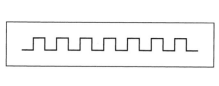

This digital wonderland is static-free, too. Unlike the noise and static you've probably heard on an analog line, an ISDN line is (for all intents and purposes) a perfect connection. Static plays havoc with a regular analog modem connection, resulting either in a long delay while the modems get back in sync or even hanging up the connection altogether. With an ISDN line, the connection is perfect.

The only limitation to this perfection and speed is that you must be calling another ISDN line. You can make an ordinary voice call to an analog telephone number, although you won't notice a bit of improvement over a plain-old analog telephone; it will sound the same.

You may be wondering whether you have to spend a fortune to get new wiring installed that supports ISDN. Luckily, ISDN works over your current telephone line. And, much like the SCSI chain allows you to add seven peripherals to your computer, an ISDN line allows you to connect as many as eight telecommunications devices on one line (devices such as computers, fax machines, and telephones). Each device can have a separate telephone number. Neat stuff!

Not every ISDN line can call every other ISDN line; some compatibility problems still exist (mostly due to hardware problems). Although telephone companies and hardware manufacturers have done much in the past few years to standardize ISDN hardware and connection protocols, the connection is still not universal. It's a good idea to check with your telephone company for any recommendations it may have before buying any ISDN hardware.

I thought BRI was a kind of cheese!

In the ISDN world, *BRI* (short for Basic Rate Interface) is the technoterm for the configuration of an ISDN line. BRI service is usually the least expensive ISDN connection to a home or office, so it's the typical choice for almost all ISDN service. A BRI line has three *channels* (or separate data pathways) within the same physical wire. Two of these, called the B channels, can carry data at approximately 64 Kbps. Figure 13-3 shows one of the neat side effects of having two B channels: One channel carries an FTP file transfer from an Internet server, and the other is simultaneously receiving a Web page from the Internet. Your ISDN hardware can separate these signals and route them to the correct devices.

Figure 13-3: A BRI ISDN line carrying two different types of data simultaneously.

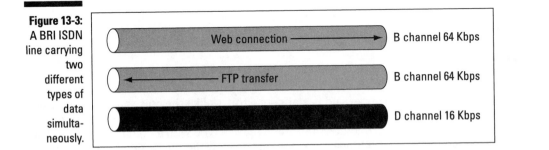

Web connection ——————————→ B channel 64 Kbps

←—————— FTP transfer B channel 64 Kbps

D channel 16 Kbps

The two B channels in a BRI ISDN line can also be merged for higher bandwidth at about 128 Kbps (or, in English, approximately twice the data speed of a single BRI channel), as shown in Figure 13-4. This trick is called *bonding*. Similar bonding technology is just now appearing for analog modems as well, enabling speeds as fast as 112 Kbps over two bonded analog telephone lines (both carrying data for a single connection); however, like the 56 Kbps technology I discuss in Chapter 10, you're not likely to see that top speed because of the connection quality of traditional analog telephone lines.

Figure 13-4:
Merging the data channels in a BRI line really speeds things up.

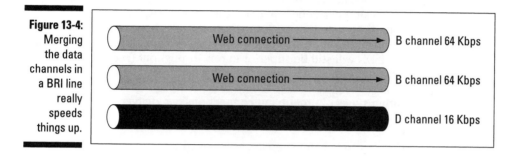

The third channel, the *D channel,* moves at a much slower 16 Kbps. The D channel carries control signals and assorted stuff required by your ISDN hardware, freeing the other two channels to carry nothing but data.

PRI is short for pricey

Although BRI lines make up the vast majority of ISDN connections, a step-up is available. If you have the money, you can add a PRI (short for Primary Rate Interface) ISDN line. A *PRI* line is really suitable only for larger businesses and schools because it provides 23 data channels, each moving at 64 Kbps. That's way too much bandwidth for mere mortals like you and me who own home and small office PCs. So while you're investigating the cost of an ISDN line and talking to your local telephone company, make doggone sure that you ask for prices for ISDN BRI service.

Comparing ISDN to Other Communications Technology

For many years, people wondered whether 28.8 Kbps was the fastest transfer rate that could be squeezed out of an analog modem over a typical telephone connection. (Notice that I said "typical" there — because a crystal-clear analog modem connection is a very rare jewel indeed, it pays to remember that analog lines are probably only 85 percent noisefree.) Modem manufacturers then squeezed a little harder, and — lo and behold — suddenly the top possible transfer rate was 33.6 Kbps. Everyone shook their heads with finality and said, "Surely that must be the fastest possible speed!"

Nope. Modem manufacturers have again proven the technotypes wrong. The v.90 international standard now provides a top data-transfer rate of 56 Kbps (with compression), and suddenly the notion of an ISDN line is a little less impressive — will this new technology spell the eventual doom of broadband?

The answer is "Definitely not!" The advantages still far outweigh the money you save with a simple analog modem connection. First, you'll never be able to make multiple connections on a single analog telephone line, as you can with an ISDN line. The nearly perfect quality of the digital ISDN line means no interference. ISDN will still be superior in raw throughput (remember that an ISDN line provides either 64 Kbps or 128 Kbps *before* compression, and with compression those figures can reach up to a whopping 256 Kbps transfer rate), and other types of broadband connections can deliver data at an even faster rate.

Analog technology just can't keep up. You'll need a nearly perfect analog connection to get anywhere near the top throughput of 56 Kbps on an analog modem, and that just doesn't happen very often in the real world (you'll more likely end up with anywhere between 36 Kbps and 43.2 Kbps throughput). Your throughput will vary from call to call. (For more information on high-speed modems and their mating habits, jump to Chapter 10. I'll wait for you here.)

However, a 56 Kbps analog modem connection will certainly have an effect on the popularity of ISDN. The high cost of an ISDN connection, higher ISP subscription prices, and the extra hassle involved with setting up ISDN will keep millions of people satisfied with a high-speed analog modem.

What other choices does a small office or a home have for a high-speed Internet connection? I'm glad you asked!

- ✔ **Cable modems:** With a cable modem and an enhanced cable network (which must be capable of two-way communications), your cable company suddenly becomes an ISP and can supply you with a digital Internet connection of 500 Kbps or faster. Cable modem service is now available to most cable subscribers; with the nearly universal access of cable, this type of broadband connection may well turn out to be the long-awaited high-speed connection for the common person. (Unfortunately, a cable modem connection forces you to share bandwidth with all the other cable Internet subscribers in your area. Therefore, your top speed depends on the time of day and the current number of connections to your cable provider.)

  Cable service has other advantages: A high-speed cable modem connection doesn't interfere with your cable TV service, and if your house is already wired for cable TV, it's a cinch to expand that service to a cable modem. Your telephone suddenly reverts to the job it had originally: handling voice (and sometimes fax) calls, blissfully free of busy signals and modem noise! Your cable Internet service is "always on." Unlike with an ISDN link, you don't have to connect to your ISP (in a fashion very similar to an analog modem) before you start surfing or transferring files.

Most cable Internet providers include a cable modem as part of their service. This "black box" actually looks like a regular analog modem, but it connects to your cable coax on one end and connects to a network card installed in your computer on the other. If your computer doesn't have a network interface card installed already, your cable company will probably provide one and install it as well.

✔ **DSL:** That's short for Digital Subscriber Line. Like cable modems, DSL was once yet another "could be big in just a year or so" technology — like cable Internet access, it was about as available as sunshine in Carlsbad Caverns. Recently, however, DSL is starting to catch on as local telephone companies expand and improve their DSL coverage, with top speeds around 4 to 8 Mbps for received data (depending on the flavor of DSL being installed) and as much as 1 Mbps for transmitted data. Those are fast speeds indeed, reaching up to 70 times faster than 128 Kbps BRI ISDN.

Like ISDN, DSL uses a digital signal, and it works over the standard copper telephone line in your home, so all you need is — you guessed it — a DSL modem, which is usually supplied by your local phone company, and a network interface card for your computer. (Depending on the service you receive, you may also need a splitter to separate the regular phone signal from the higher-frequency DSL signal.) Like a cable modem connection, DSL is always on, so you don't have to dial your ISP, and you can use your voice telephone and place regular calls at the same time you're connected to the Internet!

✔ **Bonded analog modems:** A bonded analog connection using two telephone lines and a special modem can deliver data at up to 112 Kbps. Diamond Multimedia Systems and 3Com are both offering "doubling" modems. As I mention earlier in this chapter, a bonded analog connection uses standard telephone lines (which are nowhere near perfect), so don't expect 112 Kbps with every connection. Windows 98 and Windows Me provide support for these types of connections, which it calls *multilink* connections. I wouldn't recommend a bonded analog connection unless you simply can't get faster Internet access in some other way (including ISDN); the hassle of two telephone lines for a relatively small increase in speed just doesn't compare with cable or DSL.

✔ **Satellite Internet connections:** Chapter 15 discusses satellite Internet connections in detail. They're fast, but they require you to continue to use your analog modem connection — and most Internet junkies don't want anything to do with those "antique" 56K analog modems anymore.

Determining What Hardware You Need

Even though you won't require new telephone wiring to add an ISDN line, don't think that you're getting away scot-free! Because your old analog modem isn't suitable for a digital network, you definitely need new hardware to take advantage of the full speed of an ISDN connection. Any Pentium-class computer is fast enough to use ISDN. As for operating systems, Windows 98 and Windows NT offer the best support for ISDN connections.

What other hardware do you need for an ISDN connection? Here's a quick tour:

- **ISDN "modem":** I know, I know — I said that *modems* aren't necessary with an ISDN line. But doggone it, that's what many people (and even many hardware manufacturers) like to call a stand-alone ISDN *black box* (others call it a *converter*). After all, an ISDN converter does connect to your PC's serial port (or fits inside like an internal modem), and it does connect to the ISDN wall jack, much like an analog modem. However, an ISDN converter is totally digital and performs no analog conversion. Popular external ISDN modems that use your serial port include the BitSURFR Pro EZ, from Motorola, Inc. (about $200), and the 3ComImpact IQ ISDN modem, from 3Com, Inc. (about $175).

- **High-speed serial card:** If you do buy an external ISDN modem that connects to your serial port, make sure that your computer is using a serial card with 16550-series UARTs. (What's a 16550-series UART? Good question — go to Chapter 10, where I discuss high-speed serial cards.) Figure 13-5 illustrates the back end of a typical external ISDN modem.

What do I need for videoconferencing?

A typical ISDN-based videoconferencing system includes a special card that plugs into your ISDN NT1 adapter, a videocamera, speakers, a microphone, and the necessary software. The videoconferencing card handles both video and audio, but it typically plugs into your existing sound card. You can connect directly by dialing another computer on your ISDN line, or you can use the ISDN line to connect to the Internet and then use an Internet-based videoconferencing system like CU-SeeMe. I recommend a PCI-based video card with 4MB worth of onboard RAM for best results with a videoconferencing sytem.

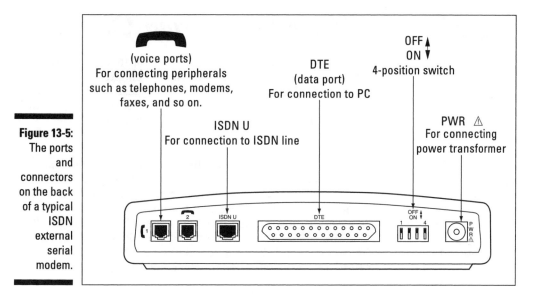

Figure 13-5:
The ports and connectors on the back of a typical ISDN external serial modem.

✔ **An NT1 device:** Every ISDN line needs an NT1 device. NT1 stands for *Network Termination 1,* and it's somewhat similar in function to the terminators necessary for a SCSI chain or an Ethernet network. An NT1 device effectively ends the ISDN line and provides power for the line. ISDN adapters typically have NT1 built-in, so an ISDN adapter is the only piece of hardware you really need to connect to the Internet. Check with the manufacturer of your ISDN adapter to see whether it includes NT1.

Repeat after me: "I promise not to buy a 16-bit ISA ISDN adapter. I promise to buy only a PCI ISDN adapter." If you're spending the money on an internal ISDN adapter, make sure that you're going to get the speed you need. Stick with a 32-bit PCI card.

Do you want a WAN?

If you've installed an Ethernet network, you can connect your network to an ISDN line and create a WAN (a ridiculous-sounding acronym that stands for Wide Area Network). This procedure is one method of tying together more than one network — you connect the two networks via an ISDN line. Creating a WAN is no easy matter, and there are security concerns (such as hackers trying to access your network over the same ISDN line), so it's best to seek professional help in tying your network to an ISDN line.

Figuring Out Those Connection Charges

The hardware you need for an ISDN connection — or, for that matter, any type of broadband connection I mention earlier in this chapter — will cost much more than a standard analog modem, but the biggest expense to add ISDN to your PC isn't the hardware you add to your computer; it's the installation charges and monthly access fees levied by your local telephone company.

Installation charges for a broadband connection differ widely across the globe, and every local telephone and cable company has a different pricing plan. Some telephone companies are working to make it as easy to install an ISDN line as a standard analog line. They offer telephone ordering for ISDN service, Web sites with helpful instructions, and some will even charge a flat monthly rate. Other telephone companies offer no presale help for ISDN users (forget the Web site) and charge a per-minute rate that will leave you pounding your head against a wall when the bill comes in. It all depends on where you're living.

The important thing to remember is that you need full support from your telephone company before you begin your broadband quest. Installing an ISDN, DSL line, or cable modem is not a "fun project" you can do yourself.

Whether you can obtain ISDN service also depends on your distance from the telephone switch. In most areas, your home or office can't be farther than 18,000 feet from a switch or local cable loop that supports ISDN (so it's nigh impossible to obtain ISDN service in your mountain cabin).

What's an average rate for ISDN service? Installation costs an average of $75 to $100. Monthly line charges typically range from $40 to $100, usually with some sort of metering for your total usage tacked on. Some companies offer a package deal with a number of free hours every month (followed by metering by the minute), and other companies charge by the connection on a per-minute basis. For a good example of an online site offering ISDN information, check out the AT&T Digital Long Distance page (www.att.com/home64/).

Locating an Internet Service Provider

Even if you have a working ISDN line, you're not connected to the Internet yet. You have another bridge to cross: You need to find an *Internet Service Provider* (or *ISP,* for short) that offers ISDN service. (From this angle, ISDN callers are no different from callers using analog modems — you still must have an ISP to link you to the Internet). Figure 13-6 illustrates the elements in a successful ISDN connection to the Internet.

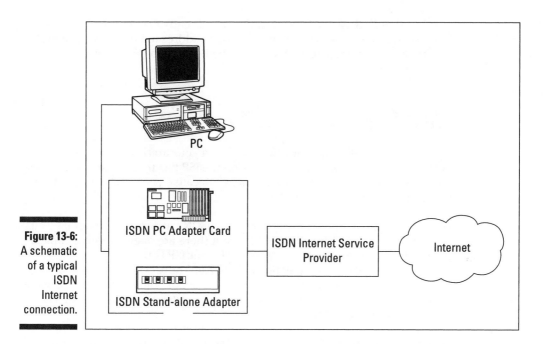

Figure 13-6:
A schematic
of a typical
ISDN
Internet
connection.

If you're looking for a connection to the Internet for your brand-new ISDN setup, you quickly learn a very irritating fact: Internet Service Providers make their profit from subscribers using analog modems, *not* from ISDN subscribers. Many ISPs are not prepared for ISDN subscribers because they don't have an ISDN line of their own, and it's up to you to do the detective work to find one. It's always better to find a local ISP with ISDN support than to have to hunt for a long-distance provider.

Also, check to make sure that your potential ISP can offer compression on its ISDN line. If so, you can at least double the transfer rate of a simple 64 Kbps BRI connection.

Need help finding an Internet Service Provider in your area? Here's a quick checklist of possible sources for local ISP information:

- ✔ **Your telephone book:** Like any other business, the Yellow Pages likely lists the ISPs in your area.

- ✔ **Friends, relatives, and neighbors:** Ask those around you for the name of their ISP. You can also find out whether they're satisfied with the quality of service they receive from their ISP.

- ✔ **Local computer stores:** Computer stores are always a good source of information.

- ✔ **Computer club or user groups:** You'll get a chorus of possibilities from club members.

✔ **Local bulletin-board systems:** If you're already calling a local bulletin-board system (or BBS), leave a message addressed to everyone about their ISP recommendations, or ask the BBS sysop (short for *system operator*).

How busy is your ISP?

If you locate an ISP that offers ISDN access in your area, the next step is to determine just what kind of a connection the ISP has to the Internet, and how many subscribers the ISP is serving. Why? Because your ISDN data transfer rate depends directly on your ISP.

For example, the connection between your ISDN hardware and your ISP will probably be a full 64 Kbps or 128 Kbps, but there are many possible connections between your ISP and the Internet. If your ISP is trying to divide up a relatively slow Internet connection among 5,000 subscribers through 32 analog telephone lines at the same time, you're not going to get the full speed of your connection. Instead, the ISP acts as a bottleneck, not as a pipeline between you and the Internet.

To avoid such a bottleneck, ask your potential ISP whether it can guarantee that you'll receive the full throughput of your ISDN line *at all times* of the day and night. If the ISP doesn't back up its claims, I recommend that you look for another ISP possibility.

Do I need a dedicated Internet connection?

If you're installing an ISDN link, your ISP may ask whether you need a *dedicated* Internet connection — an Internet connection that's active 24 hours a day. (As I mention earlier in this chapter, those using cable or DSL connections to the Internet need not read this section because these connections are "always on" and active.) This idea has its advantages:

✔ You can set up your own Web server on your own computer with as much hard drive storage as you need (most Web servers on the Internet allow you between 5MB and 50MB of storage space).

✔ You can run an online service using a shareware or commercial bulletin-board system. Your callers can use telnet to connect to your service from anywhere on the Internet.

✔ With a dedicated line, it's easier for you to arrange for your own domain name (the part of your Internet e-mail address after the @), like hford@modelt.com or michelangelo@ceilings.com. Your ISP can usually help you obtain your own domain name.

TIP

Use the Net to find an ISP

Do you already have Internet access (perhaps at work)? If so, check out The List, at thelist.internet.com or ISPs.com at (you guessed it) www.isps.com. These Web sites have information and links to thousands of ISPs in the United States, Canada, and around the world (so that even you readers in Djibouti or Liechtenstein can find an ISP easily). Use these resources to find out which ISPs in your area offer ISDN, what type of 56K modem standard they suypport (refer to Chapter 10), and what the ISP charges for ISDN installation and monthly access.

Is a dedicated line more expensive? Oh yes, it always is, but if you need a constant, 24-hour Internet connection over an ISDN line, you may be able to arrange a flat monthly fee with your ISP that will end up making more financial sense. If you decide against a dedicated connection, your computer must dial out and establish a connection each time you want to access the Internet over ISDN. (If you've set up an Internet connection, this process is automatic within Windows 98 and Windows NT; if you haven't, see the section "Creating an Internet Connection in Windows 98" at the end of this chapter.)

Installing Your Internal ISDN Adapter Card

In this section, you install an internal ISDN adapter card with a built-in NT1 function. Before you begin, consult your adapter card manual to see what information you'll need from your telephone company and ISP. Typically, you need at least a *service profile identifier number, switch type,* and *directory number,* which your telephone company can give you, as well as the ISDN line number from your ISP. Follow these steps:

1. **Thought you'd try on that old polyester leisure suit from your disco years? Touch a metal surface before you install your card, to discharge that funky static electricity before it can harm your computer's components!**

2. **If your computer chassis is currently in, unplug it.**

3. **Remove the cover from your case.**

4. **Select an open card slot for your ISDN adapter card.**

5. **Remove the screw and the metal slot cover adjacent to the selected slot.**

6. **Check your ISDN adapter card manual for any necessary configuration.**

   Check your manual to see whether you have to change any settings before you install the card. If a jumper must be adjusted, use a pair of needlenose pliers or tweezers to move it to the proper pins. If a DIP switch must be adjusted, use a ballpoint pen or a screwdriver to set the switches in the specified order.

7. **Line up the connector on the card with the slot on the motherboard.**

   The card's metal bracket should align with the open space left when you removed the slot cover.

8. **Apply even pressure to the top of the card and push it down into the slot.**

   If the card is all the way in, the bracket should be resting tightly against the case.

9. **Add the screw and tighten down the bracket.**

10. **Connect the telephone cable from your ISDN wall jack to the corresponding port on the card.**

    Your adapter card manual will help you locate the cable connector on your card. Push the connector into the port until it clicks into place.

Creating an Internet Connection in Windows 98

Need to set up a new Internet connection within Windows 98 for your ISDN modem (or even a boring, old-fashioned analog modem)? Then go ahead and invoke the mystic powers of the Internet Connection Wizard!

It's important to note that this procedure should be used **only** for ISDN connections to the Internet, since DSL and cable Internet subscribers are effectively connecting through a local area network — they don't dial to connect to the ISP.

Follow these steps, and marvel at the handiwork of The Gates himself:

1. **Start the Internet Connection Wizard.**

   Click the Start button and then choose Programs⇨Accessories⇨ Communications⇨Internet Connection Wizard. On the Internet Connection Wizard's opening screen, select I Want to Set Up My Internet Connection Manually and click Next to continue.

2. Select your connection method.

Because you're not connecting to the Internet through a Local Area Network, click I Connect Through a Phone Line and a Modem and then click Next.

3. Enter the telephone number provided by your ISP.

Your computer dials this number to access your ISP. Don't forget the area code if your ISP is a long-distance call. Unless your ISP gives you specific instructions, leave the Advanced button alone. Click Next to continue.

4. Enter your username and password.

Your ISP should provide you with your username and password. Click Next to continue.

5. Enter the name of your Internet Service Provider.

This name is used to identify the connection profile. After you enter the name, click Next to continue.

6. Specify whether you need to set up an Internet mail account.

If you need to set up Internet mail, click Yes — otherwise, click No and then click Next to continue. (If you don't need to set up Internet mail, skip to Step 12.)

7. Select your Internet mail preference.

If you want to use Windows Messaging, Exchange, or Outlook for your Internet e-mail — which I recommend — select Create a New Internet Mail Account and click Next to continue.

8. Enter your display name.

9. Enter your e-mail address.

Again, your ISP owes you this data. Click Next to continue.

10. Specify your POP3 and SMTP server information.

You need to enter more information that should be provided by your ISP (all this data is unique for each ISP). Click Next to continue.

11. Specify your Internet mail logon name and password.

Note that this logon and password may be different from the logon name and password you gave earlier — once again, your ISP must furnish this information. If you're setting up an account for home use, where security is usually less of a problem, make things easy on yourself and enable the Remember Password check box. Click Next to continue.

12. All done! Click Next and then Finish to complete the process.

If you'd like to immediately connect to the Internet, enable the To Connect to the Internet Immediately check box before you click Finish.

Windows 98 creates a new icon for your connection in your Dial-Up Networking folder, which you can display by double-clicking the My Computer icon and double-clicking the Dial-Up Networking icon. From this point on, each time you double-click the connection icon, your computer automatically dials your ISP and establishes an Internet connection.

Chapter 14

Input and Output: Scanners, Cameras, Video Capture, and Printers

*I*f you have lots of artistic talent, your computer can be a wonderfully creative tool — just ask anyone who makes a living as a computer desktop publisher, graphics designer, or 3D rendering wizard. With the help of today's powerful software, you can use a computer to produce a convincing image of an oil painting, build a complete cartoon without ever drawing a single frame of animation, or even create a fleet of 3D spaceships so real that you'd swear they really exist.

But what if you're like me? I learned long ago that I failed finger painting in first grade for a good reason — I can't even draw a stick figure. Thanks to today's scanners and video capture devices, though, anyone can convert a kid's drawing, a photo of a ball team, or a small business logo into a digital image. You can even use a digital camera to snap your own original digital images.

This chapter also explains how you can print your own work on paper with an inkjet or laser printer. Which type of printer is more expensive? Which one prints in color? You'll find all the answers here.

The Wide, Wonderful World of Scanners

Are you looking for images to add to your desktop publishing projects or your personal Web page? If you're searching for graphics and you're not having much luck, cheer up — you're probably sitting in the middle of a gold mine. With the help of a *scanner,* which converts a printed page to a digital image, you can digitize graphics from books, magazines, cereal boxes, CD covers, your children's doodlings, and even the daily newspaper. Anything you can legally copy (and lay flat) is fair game for scanning. I discuss more about copyrights in the sidebar "The lazy person's guide to copyrights," later in this chapter.

A few years ago, a top-quality high-resolution color scanner would set you back at least $1,000 — but today, thanks to the wonders of modern manufacturing, good clean living, and the worldwide popularity of digital scanning, that same color scanner will cost you less than $300. In this section, I discuss the various types of scanners on the market and what you should look for while shopping.

Recognizing scanners in the wild

Scanners come in four flavors these days:

✔ **Flatbed scanner:** "Yessir, this here's your Cad-ee-lac of scanners. Ain't she a beaut?" In fact, the flatbed scanner looks more like a copy machine than a luxury car. But now that flatbed models have dropped so dramatically in price, they're the clear choice for most shoppers. The large scanning area of a flatbed enables you to spread out an entire magazine or book. Flatbed scanners typically offer higher resolutions and better color depth than a sheetfed scanner (which I discuss in the following bullet), and you don't have to tear a page out of your favorite book or magazine to scan it. In other words, images scanned on a flatbed scanner offer greater detail and more true-to-life colors. The Hewlett-Packard ScanJet and the Microtek ScanMaker series are two well-respected models of flatbed scanners.

Older flatbed scanners typically use a SCSI interface, which provides the fastest possible scanning speed. Most late-model flatbed scanners now use either a parallel port connection (where the scanner plugs into your parallel port and your printer plugs into the back of the scanner) or a USB connection. The parallel port configuration is slower than SCSI, but you don't need to install a SCSI adapter card to use a parallel port scanner. If your PC has USB connectors, a USB scanner is *definitely* the easiest route for connecting a scanner. As a general rule, the flatbed scanner is your best choice! Figure 14-1 shows a typical flatbed scanner.

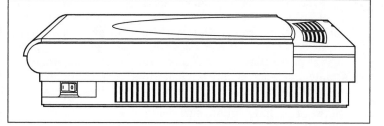

Figure 14-1:
All hail the
flatbed, the
king of
scanners.

✔ **Sheetfed scanner:** A typical sheetfed scanner looks similar to a fax machine and takes up less space on your desk (as shown in Figure 14-2).

With a sheetfed scanner, you feed in letter- or legal-size sheets of paper, which the scanner draws in automatically. Unfortunately, this process limits sheetfed scanners to source material no larger than a sheet of paper. Unlike with a flatbed scanner, you have to tear a page out of a book or magazine (or photocopy the page first) in order to scan it. Also, if your source image is smaller than a page, you may need to tape the image to a sheet of paper in order for the sheet feeder to pull the image in. (You can also use a clear plastic sleeve to hold smaller items for scanning.)

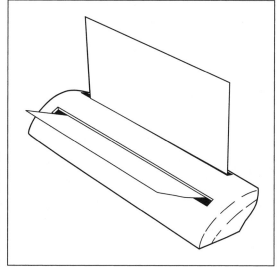

Figure 14-2:
A sheetfed
scanner
looks much
like a fax
machine.

✔ **Photo scanner:** Photo scanners are a relatively new breed of image scanner. They're internal IDE devices that are meant to fit inside your computer, and they scan individual pictures (or even small printed items, like business cards or a driver's license). Most people use photo scanners to digitize prints they've taken with a regular film camera. Because a photo scanner can't accept any original wider than a photograph, the size of the material you can scan with one of these devices is very limited.

On the other hand, photo scanners are automatic and fun to use — just feed the picture in and the scanner slowly spits the picture back out as it reads the image. Photo scanners generally offer the same scan quality as a sheetfed scanner, and they run on any PC that can accept another IDE device. Unless you're sure that your scanning needs will be limited to film prints, consider a flatbed scanner (which is far more versatile).

✔ **Handheld scanner:** In olden times, when flatbed scanners were too expensive for most computer owners, handheld scanners were the cheap alternative. To use one, you run the scanner across the material you want to scan. A handheld scanner can read a strip only about four inches across, so if your source graphic is larger than that, you need to scan the entire picture in multiple strips and then "paste" the strips together using a graphics editing program. This *almost* sounds like fun, but in real life, most people I know with handheld scanners have *never* been able to successfully merge strips together. Plus, if you're not careful and deliberate about moving the scanner across the picture, you end up distorting the scan and have to start over. Figure 14-3 shows a handheld scanner.

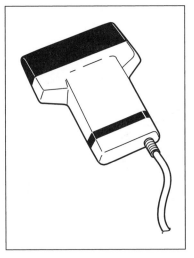

Figure 14-3:
A typical
handheld
scanner —
do not buy
this object.

Because of their low resolution and all the hassle (and the fact that flatbed scanners are so much more affordable today), handheld scanners have practically disappeared from the market. Unless you can scavenge one, I strongly recommend that you give handheld scanners a wide berth.

Diving into color depth

Most scanners advertise either 24-, 30-, or 36-bit color, which is a measure of how many colors the scanner can record in the electronic version of an image. Color depth is important because you want the electronic image to include the full range of colors found in the original. For example, if you're creating a Web site featuring famous paintings, you would probably rather offer images with 16.7 million colors (which is about the maximum the human eye can discern) than 16 colors (which would produce masterpieces that resemble paint-by-number pictures).

Any scanner you're considering should be capable of a minimum of 24-bit color. If a scanner is advertised as *true color*, it's probably a 24-bit model. A 30-bit scanner can record images in as many as 11 billion colors, and a 36-bit scanner can deliver more than 68.7 billion colors.

This same 24-bit color figure comes up again when computer folks discuss their video adapters. In the world of video adapters, 24-bit color is equivalent to the 16.7 million colors that can be displayed on an SVGA monitor by a video adapter card with at least 2MB of video RAM. (You can find more about video adapter cards in Chapter 6.)

Please pass the image

Another feature you should shop for in a color scanner is single-pass scanning. A *single-pass* scanner makes only one scanning "trip" across the source material and captures the entire image at one time. On the other hand, a cheaper *triple-pass* scanner must make three trips to scan the same image. If the scanner must make three passes, you introduce three disadvantages:

> ✔ There's more chance for a slight movement in the original material, which can cause distortion in the final image — any movement of the scanner (even a tiny bump) can affect the image. Of course, closing the cover on your scanner helps, but if you're scanning books or something that's not completely flat, it's hard to keep your material perfectly motionless. (For this reason, never scan material on a Ferris wheel or any other moving surface.)

✔ A triple-pass scanner typically takes three times as long to scan an image.

✔ A triple-pass scanner must store three separate images and combine them by using software, which usually means that your computer will need more memory and more hard drive space to store the final image. You need a minimum of 32MB of RAM to scan a full page at 24-bit color on a triple-pass scanner, and you need anywhere from 20MB to 40MB of hard drive space to store the completed image (depending on the number of colors and the detail of the image).

For these reasons, pick up a single-pass scanner if possible. They're usually a little more expensive, but it's money well spent. Generally, single-pass scanners offer better resolution, they last longer, and you spend less time waiting.

Resolving the right resolution

Many people tend to base their purchase of a scanner solely on the advertised resolution (usually in *dpi,* which is short for *dots per inch*) — the higher the resolution, the better the quality of your scanned image. Most scanners have these standard *raw* (or *optical*) resolutions:

✔ **300 x 300:** Appropriate for the kids and their school projects

✔ **300 x 600:** A better choice for scanning line art

✔ **600 x 600:** Good for scanning snapshots and photographs from books or magazines

✔ **600 x 1,200:** The standard resolution for a good-quality scanner

✔ **1,200 x 2,400:** Suitable for graphics artists who need high-resolution detail at a higher price

It's true that the higher the raw resolution, the better the scanner; however, some manufacturers also advertise the *interpolated resolution* for a particular model. What's the difference between raw and interpolated resolution?

The answer is in the software: The *raw resolution* value is the actual optical resolution at which the scanner reads an image. On the other hand, the *interpolated resolution* (the value of which is always higher) is calculated by the software provided with the scanner. In fact, the interpolated value adds extra dots to the scanned image *without* reading them from the original material.

Technoids would tell you that the interpolation step uses an *algorithm* (or a mathematical formula) to improve the quality of the image. In layman's terms, that's the equivalent of the imaging software inserting new dots by using an intelligent guess — but it's *still* a guess.

When you're shopping, judge the scanners by their optical resolution (and forget about the interpolated value). If you don't see the "raw" or "optical" resolution in the advertisement, check with the manufacturer to get that crucial bit of information first — before you buy.

Scanners and . . . Mark Twain?

Buying a *TWAIN-compatible* scanner is a good idea. (For once, a computer acronym that stands for absolutely nothing . . . *TWAIN* is just a name created by the people who developed the standard, and it actually stands for *t*echnology *w*ithout *a*n *i*nteresting *n*ame. At last, a group of technotypes with a sense of humor!) TWAIN is a standard which ensures that your scanner will work with the image-capture software and other graphics applications on your system. If both the hardware and the software are TWAIN compatible, it doesn't matter who manufactured either piece. (Pretty refreshing, eh?)

Figure 14-4 illustrates my favorite TWAIN-compatible image-editing software, Paint Shop Pro, in action as it acquires an image from a scanner. I heartily recommend Paint Shop Pro. You can download the shareware version of this great program from www.jasc.com.

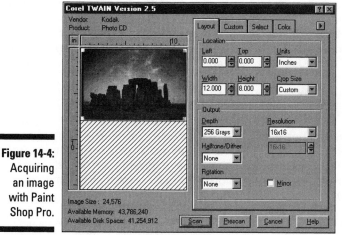

Figure 14-4:
Acquiring an image with Paint Shop Pro.

Because TWAIN-compatibility makes such good sense, just about every scanner made today supports TWAIN — although it never hurts to make sure before you buy.

Most scanners come bundled with various software programs, which should include the image-acquisition software you need for scanning. You may also receive other software, such as an image-editing program, a desktop publishing application, or an OCR program (which stands for *optical character recognition*). OCR software can "read" the contents of a printed page you've scanned and enter the text from the page right into your word processor — just as though you had typed the text yourself. Although OCR technology isn't perfect, and you may need to correct some errors, you don't have to manually retype the entire contents of a page into your word processor.

Digital Camera Details

Until the arrival of digital cameras, getting original photographs into your computer as images was a laborious chore. You had to take the exposed film to your friendly photo lab to get the pictures developed, and then you sat down at your expensive flatbed scanner and slowly digitized each of the finished prints into your computer.

If you need a large number of original digital images and you want to avoid the drudgery of scanning them, look no further than the *digital camera.* Like scanner technology, the digital camera has actually been around for some time, but until recently the typical digital camera has been so expensive that you needed a bodyguard to carry one. Prices on digital cameras have now dropped to less than $200 on some models, although the higher-priced models with more features still hover around $500 to 800 (or more). Popular brands include Casio, Canon, Kodak, and Olympus.

You may be wondering where a digital camera stores the pictures and how you "develop" them. The images you take are stored in a form of memory called flash RAM. *Flash RAM* is much like your computer's RAM, but it has the neat ability to store information *after* you turn the camera off. More-expensive digital cameras have more flash RAM onboard, so they can store more pictures. (Not every digital camera uses flash RAM. Some use removable cartridges, others have tiny hard drives, and one model of digital camera even uses standard 1.44MB floppies.)

Loading the pictures from a digital camera into your PC couldn't be easier: You simply connect a cable between the camera and your PC's serial port (some cameras use a USB port, SCSI port, or parallel port), run the camera's software, and the pictures download right from the camera into your computer.

Figure 14-5 shows an image taken with a typical digital camera (and displayed in Paint Shop Pro). The picture was taken with a Casio digital camera, which stores a maximum of 96 24-bit images. Ignore the strange guy with the vacuum cleaner; I couldn't crop him out of the picture.

Figure 14-5:
A very strange person photographed with a digital camera.

Most digital cameras look very similar to their film-based cousins (including accessories like a flash and that useless wrist strap). Digital cameras are typically just as easy to use as the simple *point-and-shoot* 35mm film cameras available in any drugstore. Here's a list of features that can help you spot a better digital camera while you're shopping:

✔ **LCD viewfinder:** Now *this* is a feature I really like! An LCD viewfinder can help you see what your picture will look like before you take it. Most digital cameras that offer this feature also let you review your picture immediately *after* you take it (which means that you can judge the results immediately and retake the shot if necessary). "Woops, little Sparky wasn't smiling in that one, was he? We'll just take it again from the top."

✔ **Photo management:** This feature gives you the ability to review and delete your pictures from the camera itself. For example, if you're out in the field taking shots of houses for your real estate company and you suddenly run out of RAM for new pictures, you can easily flip through your images and delete those you don't want. Deleting the unwanted images frees up additional RAM, and you're back in business. Some older digital cameras require you to hook your camera up to your computer to delete shots, or you have to delete all your pictures at once.

✔ **Removable flash RAM:** Although more-expensive cameras have more flash RAM elbow room, the ultimate is a *removable flash RAM card* system. If you have one of these cameras, you can simply buy another flash RAM card and swap the cards for more storage whenever you need it. The card you remove stores the images you've already taken until you can get them loaded onto your computer. The Iomega Clik! removable cartridge drive is especially designed for cameras with flash RAM: It enables you to download as much as 40 megabytes of images from your flash RAM card (without requiring a computer), so you can free up space for additional pictures.

✔ **Higher resolutions:** Just like a scanner, a digital camera has a resolution rating. In fact, many digital cameras can take pictures at more than one resolution. Cameras that can capture 24-bit (true color) resolutions greater than 1152x864 are generally more expensive, and those with lower resolutions now sell for less than $150. It's important to remember that the higher the resolution for an image, the more space the image takes in RAM. Therefore, cameras with multiple resolutions give you a choice. (You can have either a smaller number of higher-resolution pictures or a larger number of lower-resolution pictures.)

Important point approaching: Unless you spend a fair chunk of change on a digital camera (read that as $500 or more), you're not going to get anywhere near the fine detail of a 35mm film camera. If you need to save money but you still want high-resolution images higher than 1152x864, you may decide to stick with the tried-and-true method of scanning film prints. In general, a higher-resolution flatbed scanner is still much less expensive than a higher-resolution digital camera. (If you plan on scanning lots of photographs, check out the photo scanner information in the section "Recognizing scanners in the wild," earlier in this chapter.)

✔ **Compression:** Some digital cameras can compress your images so that they take less space in memory. These images are similar to the highly compressed JPEG-format images common on the Web. Although you lose some detail when you use compression, it's usually not noticeable. These cameras can pack many more images into their memory, so your "roll" of digital film may carry twice (or even three times) the number of pictures. A camera with variable compression may enable you to turn compression off, too.

✔ **Zoom:** More-expensive digital cameras have the same zoom feature found on standard film cameras. Zoom enables you to magnify your subject for more detail.

✔ **Special effects:** Some cameras now offer on-board special effects, just like the familiar special effects on a typical video camcorder. Typical effects include automatic color palettes — which give your images a special look, like sepia-tone or pastel — and negative imaging, in which the image looks like a photograph negative.

Digital Video Capture: Its Time Has Come

PCs now have the ability to *capture* digital video — you can display synchronized video and audio on your computer (or save it on your hard drive for playback later). You can record and store video from any source, including a videocamera or your VCR. You can use digital video in numerous practical ways on your computer, including videoconferencing, video clips for the Web, business presentations, and even multimedia programming for games.

Until recently, video capture and replay on a personal computer really was a losing proposition — 386- and 486-based computers simply didn't have the horsepower to properly display full-screen digital video. With the arrival of advanced video cards, DVD-ROM drives and the raw power of today's Pentium III series of CPUs, however, things have definitely changed for the better. At the time of this writing, Pentium III chips are the best choice for digital video — full-screen digital video now looks as good as a television broadcast.

You can use two general methods to capture video clips and still photos on your personal computer:

- **Computer videocamera:** Although these cameras have nowhere near the depth of field or the features of a standard videocamera that uses magnetic tape, they're perfect for videoconferencing, capturing simple video clips, or taking still images of you and the kids. These cameras usually look like a little ball or a small box sporting a camera lens; they sit on top of your monitor and connect to your parallel port (or the USB port because it transfers data at a much faster 12MB per second).

- **Video capture device:** Video capture devices attach to your computer in many ways — most are internal adapter cards, others are USB or FireWire-based, and a few use an external parallel port interface. After you install a capture device, you can plug a VCR, laser disc player, or videocamera into it as the source. Like a computer videocamera, you can capture continuous video clips or just snap still images.

With a video capture device, you can also take all those home movies you've taped on bulky videocassettes and transfer them to recordable CDs (see Chapter 8 for more about CD recorders).

The two most popular formats for digital video these days are *AVI* (the Microsoft standard supported within Windows 98 and Windows NT) and *MOV* (the Apple QuickTime format, which originated on the Macintosh but is now available also for the PC). Another popular format you encounter often on the Web is the *MPEG* standard, which is highly compressed and more suitable than AVI or MOV files for downloading.

I should also mention *MPEG-2,* the next generation of the MPEG format. MPEG-2 is used on DVD discs to provide satellite-quality digital video, and Windows 98 includes support for playing DVD discs. (For more about DVD video, check out the DVD discussion in Chapter 8.)

Keep in mind that even compressed digital video can take up a tremendous chunk of hard drive territory — don't be surprised to see 10 seconds of high-quality, high-resolution video occupying 10MB of hard drive space. However, you can adjust a number of settings to reduce the size of a video clip after you've recorded it:

✔ **The color depth:** Of course, video looks best in 24-bit true color, but you can reduce it to 256 colors and reduce the size of the file.

✔ **The frame rate:** A *frame* is an individual image, like the single images that make up a roll of movie film. Although a greater number of frames makes for a smoother video, you can reduce the *frame rate* to shrink the size of the video file.

✔ **The size of the video:** Traditionally, reducing the on-screen size of a video clip has been the solution most people take when working with digital video (which is why video clips have typically been three inches square for many years now). The smaller the on-screen size of the video, the smaller the size of the file.

With the recent improvements in hardware speed and video quality, a ton of commercial and shareware video-editing programs are on the market today. For example, a shareware video-editing package named Personal AVI Editor, from FlickerFree Multimedia Products (www.flickerfree.com), enables you to add digital effects and WAV-format digital sound to your AVI video clips. Video capture hardware typically comes with bundled software, which may include a video-editing program (like Personal AVI Editor) and a multimedia studio (such as Macromedia Director).

One Word: Printers, Printers, Printers!

If you ask computer owners what one peripheral gives them the most value and fun for their money, most would probably say either a modem or a printer. The printed page is still useful in today's world (at least for now), and the latest inkjet and laser printers can produce everything from T-shirts to transparencies, from greeting cards to stickers, CD-ROM labels, glossy photos, banners, and paper airplanes. Calendars, business cards, coloring books — you can see just how useful a printer can be, especially if you have kids.

In this section, I discuss what's available in a printer these days for less than $500 and how you can pick the right model for your needs.

Will that be laser or inkjet?

Three breeds of computer printer are out there:

✔ **Laser:** A laser printer uses heat to bond a fine powder (called *toner*) to the paper to form characters and images. Although laser printers used to be very expensive, the technology has dropped in price. Many low-end models are now available for less than $400.

✔ **Inkjet:** An inkjet printer shoots ink onto the paper. Inkjet printers (also known as *bubblejet printers*) are the most popular personal printers around these days. Inkjets can produce images ranging from standard black text to quality photographs. In fact, inkjet technology is used in high-resolution *photo printers* and in *multifunction printers* (which combine a fax, copier, and printer in one unit).

✔ **Dot matrix:** A dot matrix printer creates characters by pushing tiny pins through an ink ribbon (rather like an old-fashioned typewriter). The days when dot matrix was king are behind us. These printers are noisy and prone to jam, and they don't print graphics very well. Plus, they print only in black. However, you can still find dot matrix technology in limited use whenever the job demands forms with multiple carbon copies, because inkjet and laser printers can't print carbon copies.

The lazy person's guide to copyrights

Just because you can capture a video clip from a VCR or scan an image from a magazine doesn't mean that you can use it. It pays to be careful when you're choosing material for your documents or your Web site. Although I'm not a lawyer, I can provide you with a few pointers that may steer you clear of copyrighted material (original work that someone else has created). Keep these guidelines in mind:

✔ Beware the "hidden" copyright: Under current law, copyright is granted immediately upon creation of an original work, and copyrighted text or images may be protected by copyright regardless of whether a copyright notice appears with the material.

✔ Permission granted: You must obtain permission to copy any original copyrighted work, even if the author has previously granted you permission for other work. For example, just because you obtain permission to use one of a series of pictures on your Web page does *not* mean that you can use the entire series of images — you must obtain permission for each individual image.

✔ The source is unimportant: Most people think that images they receive from an Internet newsgroup or copy from a Web site can be copied, but it doesn't matter where you obtained the material. If it's copyrighted, sticking the text or image on a newsgroup does not make it *public domain* (intellectual property that's not protected by copyright because it "belongs to the community at large"). You still need permission from the author to use the copyrighted material.

✔ Alterations mean zip: Another common misconception is that "If I draw a mustache on this picture of Mr. Spock, it becomes my original work." Altering the original material does not "reset" or "clear" the copyright, and you still need permission.

✔ A change in media means nothing: If you scan a copyrighted image from an original on paper, the electronic image or document doesn't suddenly become your original work. (If it did, I would have claimed the works of Shakespeare, Edgar Allan Poe, and Mark Twain a long time ago.) You guessed it — the copyright still remains valid, and you need permission from the author to use the material.

✔ Consult your lawyer: Above all, if you're uncertain whether you can legally copy something, *ask your lawyer!*

You should look for a number of features if you're shopping for either an inkjet or a laser printer: Your new printer should be able to print legal- and letter-size paper, envelopes, labels, and transparencies. Of course, the bigger the paper capacity, the better. The printer you select for your system should handle at least 150 sheets of paper. Any printer you consider should also come with additional software, like a printing kit (with software and blank paper) for kids or a business printing kit, as well as the driver software that you need for your particular operating system. (See Appendix A for more about operating systems.)

Don't forget to buy a *bidirectional parallel printer cable* at the time you purchase your printer. Printer cables are typically not included with the printer.

Other features are specific to the type of printer, so it's time to examine the advantages of both inkjet and laser printers.

Advantages of inkjet printers

Inkjet printers offer these advantages:

- **Less expensive to buy:** Inkjet printers range from $100 on up, and the least expensive laser printers typically start at about $400. (I should note, however, that laser printers produce a better-looking black-and-white page for less money than a typical inkjet, and they can handle heavier printing loads — if you're looking for a heavy-duty monochrome printer with good quality for an office, a laser printer ends up costing much less in the long run when it comes to supplies.)

- **Cheaper ink:** Ink cartridges for an inkjet printer are much less expensive than a toner cartridge for a laser printer. You can also refill the black ink cartridge to save even more (you can also refill black laser toner cartridges, for that matter).

- **Cost-effective color printing:** Although laser printers also offer color, you can expect to pay at least $1,500 to $2,000 for a color laser printer (depending on the quality of the output). Most inkjet printers use a dual-cartridge system (both cartridges are loaded side-by-side). One ink cartridge contains black ink, and a separate color ink cartridge contains at least three colors of ink. Some inkjet printers also have optional cartridges that you can buy for printing true-color 24-bit images, which deliver really amazing results (they're very close to photo print quality). However, printing with these special cartridges also requires special paper.

Avoid buying a single-cartridge inkjet unless you have to limit yourself to $100 or less. These single-cartridge printers require you to manually swap the black cartridge with the color one during printing, or the cartridge prints a horrible "pseudo-black" by mixing the colors in a single color cartridge (which always looks purple to me).

If you crave color on a budget, stick with a more-expensive inkjet printer that has a higher resolution of 720 x 720 or 1,440 x 720 — you'll still spend less than $300.

✔ **Higher resolution:** A printer's resolution is measured in dots per inch (or *dpi*). Most inkjet printers can match the 600 x 600 dpi resolution of a laser printer, but many inkjet models under $300 can do even better, like 720 x 720 dpi. These printers are better choices for high-resolution graphics.

In general, inkjet printers are better suited to the home or to an office requiring quick color printing.

Advantages of laser printers

Thinking about a laser printer? Laser printers offer these advantages:

✔ **Faster printing:** Laser printers can hit anywhere from 8 to 16 pages per minute, which is faster than an inkjet's average of 6 to 7 pages per minute.

✔ **No smearing:** Because laser printers bond the toner to the paper, your documents are reasonably safe from water. The ink used to print pages on an inkjet printer smears if it gets wet.

✔ **True black:** Even a dual-cartridge inkjet printer can't deliver the true black of a laser printer, especially in graphics with large areas of black.

✔ **More pages per cartridge:** Although toner cartridges are more expensive than inkjet cartridges, they last much longer (you'll generally get about double the number of pages from a laser toner cartridge). Toner cartridges can also be refilled, saving you quite a bit of money over a new cartridge.

Laser printers are a better pick for offices of every size and any situation where the best-quality black print is required.

If you're looking for a comprehensive book that covers *all* the details of inkjet and laser printers — including evaluating, buying, installing, using, and troubleshooting a computer printer — I recommend another of my books, the *Hewlett-Packard Official Printer Handbook,* published by IDG Books Worldwide.

Installing a Scanner, Capture Device, or Printer with a Parallel Port Interface

The process of installing a scanner, external video capture box, or printer with a parallel port interface is the same. Follow these steps:

1. **Locate the 25-pin parallel port on the back of your computer case.**

   Figure 14-6 shows a standard parallel port.

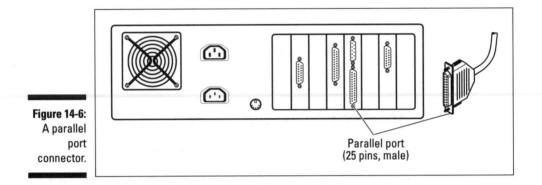

Figure 14-6:
A parallel
port
connector.

Parallel port
(25 pins, male)

2. **Align the connector on the end of your parallel cable with the parallel port and push it in firmly.**

   The angled edges on the connector are designed to make sure it goes on only the right way.

3. **If you like, you can tighten the connector by turning the knobs (or screws) on the connector clockwise.**

   If you feel the connector is in firmly, you can leave it as is.

4. **If you're installing a printer, connect the other end of your cable to the printer.**

5. **Connect the power cord from your printer to the wall socket, turn the peripheral on, and restart your PC.**

   If you're using Windows 98, your PC will automatically recognize the new device during the boot process. Depending on the age and type of peripheral, Windows may prompt you to insert the driver disk that came with the device, or — if the driver was included on the Windows CD-ROM — you may be prompted to load your Windows CD-ROM so that the computer can locate the driver.

Installing a Scanner, Capture Device, or Printer with a USB Connection

If you're using any of these devices with a USB connection under Windows 98 or Windows Me, follow these steps:

1. **If necessary, connect the USB cable to the device — some USB peripherals have their own cables permanently attached, and others accept standard USB cables. (It's always a good idea to check to see whether you need to buy a USB cable for your new device before you leave the store!)**

2. **Plug in the peripheral's power supply and turn it on.**

3. **After you've booted Windows normally, plug the USB connector on the cable into a USB port on your computer.**

4. **Windows should recognize that you've added a USB device, and you'll be prompted to load the manufacturer's CD-ROM that came with your device so that it can install the correct drivers (this happens only the first time you connect the peripheral). You may also be prompted to load your Windows CD-ROM.**

If you're adding a USB printer to your system, a new icon for your new printer should now appear in your Printers folder.

To remove your USB device from your system, simply disconnect the USB cable from the back of your PC. You can plug the peripheral back in at any time, without having to reboot your PC.

Chapter 15

Other Power-User Play Toys

● ●

In This Chapter

▶ Accessing the Internet through a satellite link

▶ Reading Macintosh floppy disks on your PC

▶ Controlling your games with your voice

▶ Protecting your privacy on the Internet

▶ Watching TV on your computer

▶ Storing your data on paper with PaperDisk

▶ Backing up your data on the Internet

▶ Feeling the feedback from your games

● ●

I'm the first to admit that I'm fascinated by gadgets and toys — most power users crave the smallest, newest, or fastest examples of computer technology, like the calculator watch that every technonerd wears all through high school. Although such technological marvels are rarely a requirement for your PC, power users crave these play toys anyway.

If you take a look at today's high-end computer gadgets, you find that most of these technological wonders are more than mere toys. They really do simplify your life by helping you keep track of data, speeding up the network and Internet connections you use every day, or reducing the size of your computer to the size of your checkbook (or even your business card).

In this chapter, I introduce you to some high-end hardware items, software programs, and services you can add to your PC. The power-user play toys I discuss in this chapter aren't completely necessary, although they can revolutionize the way you use your PC.

Please note that this chapter is an informative overview, so I don't tell you how to install the hardware and software discussed in this chapter.

Live, Via Satellite: The Internet!

You may be asking "Is there such a thing as an Internet connection that provides fast throughput without requiring me to install new telephone lines?" In fact, there is — a number of data communications companies are offering *satellite Internet links,* using the same type of hardware commonly used for satellite TV service.

By connecting your PC to the Internet via a *satellite connection,* you can download files, Web pages, graphics images, sound or movie files, or whatever your heart desires — at blazing speeds of as fast as 400 Kbps (the download speed advertised for the Turbo Internet Service, offered by Satellite Communication Services at `scs-ems.com/home.htm`).

Compare that speed with the puny 56 Kbps for a single modem analog connection, 112 Kbps for a *bonded* analog connection (using two telephone lines to increase the speed of a single connection), or 256 Kbps for a standard BRI ISDN line (512 Kbps with compression). You can see why the satellite system is no longer just a "neat gadget."

In Chapter 10, I discuss today's modem technology for Internet connections, and I mention that even today's 56 Kbps modems rarely reach their maximum speed because of the poor quality of analog telephone lines. Bonding the analog connection with two telephone lines gives you faster throughput, although you still need special hardware and the expense of two analog telephone lines.

In Chapter 13, the subject is ISDN, cable, and DSL — other methods for accessing the Internet at high speed — but the limiting factors are the hardware involved, the subscription rates, and the limited service area (especially if you live in a rural area with no access to these services).

How do you link your PC to the Internet via satellite? In fact, this connection has *two* main links:

> ✔ **The modem connection:** Even with a satellite system, you still need a regular modem and a regular ISP (Internet Service Provider): The data you send *to* the Internet needs to travel out over a standard analog dial-up connection. This data may include commands to display a Web page, search requests you submit to a search engine like Infoseek or Yahoo!, outgoing e-mail, or files you send from your computer. Because these commands typically take only a second or two to transmit, there's very little waiting on this part of the link. The data you're sending is routed to an Internet server, which acts on the commands and sends to the satellite the resulting data (whether it be a Web page, a file you wanted to download, or your incoming e-mail).

✔ **The satellite connection:** Data that you receive from the Internet is transmitted at up to 400 Kbps from the satellite to your receiving antenna on the ground. The data then travels over a coax connection between the ground antenna and a special card installed in your computer.

Figure 15-1 illustrates the elements in the PC/Internet link.

Because the satellite can't receive data from your PC (it just broadcasts data to you), sending (or *uploading*) a large file to another site on the Internet via FTP or e-mail takes just as long to send as it would on a standard Internet modem connection. All your outgoing information (your e-mail, files you send to a friend, as well as your commands to view Web pages) goes out through your modem and through a regular phone line.

If you consider how most people use the Internet, a satellite system (which gives you blazing reception speed) is a highly efficient way to browse the Web. For example, almost all my online time is spent waiting for my PC to *receive* a Web page, e-mail, FTP file, or the text of a newsgroup message. (The Web didn't earn the nickname The World Wide Wait for nothing!)

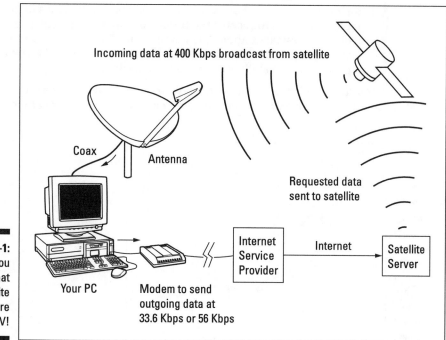

Figure 15-1:
And you thought that satellite dishes were only for TV!

Incoming data at 400 Kbps broadcast from satellite

Coax   Antenna

Requested data sent to satellite

Your PC

Modem to send outgoing data at 33.6 Kbps or 56 Kbps

Internet Service Provider

Internet

Satellite Server

What comes with an Internet satellite system?

Before you get too enthusiastic about an Internet satellite connection, let me outline what else is required to run a satellite system and what's involved to install it. (Too bad you can't just stick an antenna outside your window and start enjoying a superfast connection!)

Here's what you get with a typical satellite Internet system, and how it's installed:

- ✔ **Proprietary adapter card:** This specially designed card accepts the signal from the satellite dish and converts it to conventional data your PC can understand. Because the data is transmitted from the satellite to your antenna in an encrypted format for security, the adapter card also decrypts the signal. The adapter card also provides power to the antenna through the cable that links them together. This adapter card is installed like any other standard PC adapter card.

- ✔ **The satellite dish:** Figure 15-2 illustrates a standard 24-inch dish, which looks much like the dish used to receive satellite TV broadcasts. The dish can be mounted on your roof, a wall, or a pole. The satellite dish must be aligned to receive the broadcasts from a particular satellite, which usually takes about 30 minutes of trial-and-error experimentation (moving the dish back and forth) to get the best signal. (If you decide on a professional installation, this is done for you.)

- ✔ **LNB:** This black box mounts on your antenna; it receives the signal from the satellite and sends it along the cable to the adapter card in your PC.

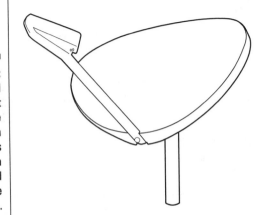

Figure 15-2:
A typical
Internet
satellite
antenna
(which looks
like a
standard
satellite
dish).

- ✔ **Coaxial cable:** Standard coaxial cable connects the LNB to the adapter card in your PC. Although this stuff is considered weather resistant, it should be protected from the elements whenever possible. If you bury your cable, I recommend that you route it through PVC pipe to your antenna.

- ✔ **Software:** Your PC requires special software to recognize the adapter card. This software is provided as a part of the package.

How expensive is a satellite Internet connection?

Prices for the basic satellite equipment range from around $700 to $1,200, depending on the source of your service. The basic package doesn't cover installation (which typically runs about $450). However, if you're comfortable installing an adapter card in your PC, mounting the antenna, and routing the cable, you shouldn't have any problems with the installation process; it typically takes only a day for two people to install the system.

The buck doesn't stop with installation charges. You still have to pay a basic rate for the connection (based on either a flat monthly fee or a fixed rate per megabyte downloaded) that starts at about $16 a month — unlike ISDN, DSL, or cable access, you're charged per megabyte, and that can *really* hurt PC owners who download large files. You also still need to maintain a standard dial-up Internet account with a local ISP so that you can *send* your e-mail data files and upload your Web browser commands.

Okay, it's neat, but. . . .

Does a satellite Internet connection make sense? Compared to ISDN, it's actually less of a hassle to install the antenna. And, if you want smoking download speed and the other types of broadband access I've discussed aren't available in your area, you can still make use of satellite technology.

However, the real determining factor is whether you *truly need* the raw speed delivered by this system. Most casual Internet Web surfers will be satisfied with a 56 Kbps connection, or perhaps even a bonded 112 Kbps connection. Only people with a need (and the money) for the fastest connection and are unable to connect using another type of broadband technology need to be interested in satellite technology; for example, Internet junkies living in the country who spend more than four or five hours a day on the Web, telecommuters, and those who receive large files via FTP regularly.

Reading a Pesky Macintosh Disk

Programs that read Macintosh floppy disks on a PC have been around for many years now, but a utility program named MacDrive 2000 (from Media4 Productions, at www.media4.com) is the first one that reads Mac disks transparently. After you've installed MacDrive 2000, you don't need to run a special program before you read a Mac disk — just stick that Mac disk in your PC running Windows 95 or Windows 98, Windows 2000, Windows NT, or Windows Me, and read those Mac files to your heart's content. Although most people might consider a program like MacDrive 2000 to be a useful tool, it also qualifies as a power-user play toy because it's so doggone *neat.*

In addition to reading Mac disks, you can actually format them on your PC — and you can also save and delete files from the Mac disk. (Older Mac-to-PC programs only enable you to read the Mac disk.) Again, the process is transparent to you — just use any Windows function or application to write files to the Mac disk, and your Macintosh can actually make sense of the result.

Conversing with Quake

I'll be the first to admit that I need another set of hands — at least another set — when playing the 3D games Unreal Tournament or Quake or flight simulators like Falcon or Gunship. Just because you're an ace typist doesn't make you better at fragging your buddies in a hot-and-heavy multiplayer game; you've got to control your weapon with your mouse, trackball, or joystick, but moving around, selecting weapons, and using special commands normally entails a quick leap toward the keyboard! It's easy to get confused when you can't take your eyes off your monitor without being blown to your component atoms.

Although you can solve the problem with a programmable joystick, it's an expensive solution — you have to create a button configuration by hand for each game, and you'll spend more than a few days teaching yourself all those button assignments. There is an alternative: If you're like me, you'd rather use your *voice* to control your character! With the Game Commander software from Mindmaker (www.gamecommander.com), you can program as many as 256 keystrokes that your computer will automatically "press" when you speak a single command. To change to the next weapon in Quake, for example, you'd say "Next" rather than reach for the bracket] key on your keyboard. Plus, voice commands in a game like Mechwarrior or Wing Commander seem much more realistic than pecking at your keyboard. With a little imagination, you really feel like you're talking to your ship's computer or your copilot! I've been using Game Commander for several months now, and the program has really helped to increase my scores.

It's also easy to configure Game Commander for new games using templates you can download for free from the Mindmaker Web site. These templates can be loaded within Game Commander to provide you with a complete ready-made set of spoken command assignments.

To use Game Commander under Windows, you need a full-duplex sound card (most sound cards made in the past two or three years are full duplex, but you can check the manual for your card to make sure) and a headset microphone (which is included with the standard boxed version of the program for $30).

Even People Like You and Me Need Internet Security

Stories abound on the Internet, TV, and the movies about the lack of Internet security. Although it's unlikely, it *is* possible for someone to intercept your electronic mail or discover personal information about you. You can take certain security measures, such as ordering products online only if your Web browser and the Web site can create a secure connection or using an encryption utility to encode the text within your e-mail messages. These procedures create a level of security for most Web surfers and casual Internet users.

However, large corporations make use of powerful firewall software to carry their Internet protection a step further. A *firewall* is a program that constantly monitors the company's Internet connection to prevent unauthorized access to the company's Web server (or, even worse, the company's network itself). Firewalls are typically very complicated beasts that cost hundreds (or even thousands) of dollars. A company without a firewall is a potential target for an attack by a computer hacker. Wouldn't it be nice if anyone could install a firewall, just to be safe?

If you're on the Internet for hours at a time visiting Web sites and downloading files, you're probably a combination of an Internet junkie and a power user (I would shake your hand if I could because I'm a member of the same club). McAfee Guard Dog is an inexpensive firewall you need for protecting your machine while you're online. Here's a quick list of the possible security violations that Guard Dog can monitor and prevent:

- ✔ Guard Dog alerts you to the use of Web cookies by a site and enables you to block them if you want. A *cookie* is a file that contains personal data about you, usually from a form you filled out online. Cookies are often stored automatically on your hard drive without your knowledge.

- ✔ A malicious program can use the e-mail application on your PC to transmit data without your knowledge. Guard Dog enables you to mark various types of files as *secure* so that they can't be sent with an e-mail application. You can also indicate which applications can open your e-mail files (or cut and paste data from them).

✔ Guard Dog monitors and controls which programs on your computer are allowed Internet access so that an unauthorized program written by a hacker can't automatically connect and transfer your personal information across the Internet without your knowledge.

✔ Guard Dog filters those irritating and bandwidth-hogging banner ads — you don't download them, so you surf the Web faster.

✔ Guard Dog takes care of a problem that has already plagued many Internet users — so-called *Trojan horse* Java applets and ActiveX controls that are run automatically by your Web browser. Although these hostile Trojan horse programs are very rare, they can destroy data or wreak havoc on your Windows system files. However, if you block all beneficial Java and ActiveX traffic, you can't enjoy many of the high-tech Web sites with animated graphics and interactive controls. Guard Dog solves the problem because any potentially hostile applet you receive is flagged before it runs.

Guard Dog runs under both Windows 95 and Windows 98. For more information on this program, visit the McAfee Web site, at www.mcafee.com.

Hey, I Can Get TV and FM Radio on My PC!

Do you love your PC? I mean, really, *really* love your PC? If so, you may have a comfortable reclining chair in case you fall asleep in front of the keyboard. Or you may have one of those little refrigerators to keep your source of caffeine and sugar close at hand. If you're considering a late-night burrito, I recommend that you keep the portable microwave a healthy distance away from both you and the computer.

The ultimate in PC *mouse potato* technology, however, is the FM stereo/TV tuner adapter card. Install one of these tuner cards and you can watch TV or listen to your favorite FM stereo station on your PC. These cards carry full-featured TV tuners and radio circuitry — but rather than use a separate TV tube or speakers, the display is shown on your monitor. Because the audio is routed with a cable from the TV card to your sound card, you hear the audio through your PC speaker system. Examples of a TV tuner adapter card include the TV/FM98 Stereo, from AVerMedia Technologies, Inc. (www.aver.com), and the DesktopTV, from 3dfx Interactive. (www.3dfx.com).

TIP

Bringing video to your PC

You can use TV tuner cards for more than just watching TV or listening to the radio on your PC. Most tuner cards also enable you to capture the incoming video or audio to your hard drive, making it a cheap source of multimedia material. If you want to watch or capture a movie, you can also plug your VCR into most tuner cards.

Capturing copyrighted video or audio and distributing it yourself is illegal. For more information about copyrights, see the sidebar "The lazy person's guide to copyrights, in Chapter 14.

Depending on the tuner card, you may also get bundled software that enables you to take individual still images from the incoming video. It's the perfect way to get a good image of Uncle Milton from that family-reunion video.

Most tuner cards provide an on-screen "remote control" that enables you to control the volume, change the channel or station, and choose the size of the TV display. If you're running another program on your PC, you can display the TV program as a picture-in-picture window or toggle it to full screen when it's time for that really important cartoon.

Store Digital Data the Old-Fashioned Way — On Paper

It's true: The entire idea behind the small office computer is to eliminate as much paper as possible. But what if I tell you that you can store a 1MB archived file on a standard 8½-x-11-inch piece of paper? Suddenly, paper doesn't sound so bad anymore.

That's exactly what PaperDisk, from Cobblestone Software, is designed to do. PaperDisk converts the contents of a digital file into special patterns called *datatiles,* which look somewhat like a cross between bar codes, Braille, and those punch cards that computer programmers fed into mainframes in the Dark Ages of computer history.

You can print out these datatiles whenever necessary, use them as a hard-copy archive, transfer them over a standard fax machine, or even take the low-tech approach and send the datatiles by snail mail. You can read the datatiles by scanning them on an ordinary digital scanner. The PaperDisk software on the PC reads the pattern, converts it back into an electronic file, and saves it on the local hard drive. Figure 15-3 shows a representative datatile created with PaperDisk.

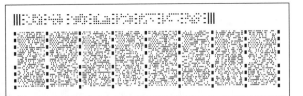

Figure 15-3:
A datatile,
ready for
faxing or
printing.

Most Internet e-mail programs support attachments, and you can certainly carry an electronic copy of a file on a floppy disk. So why go to all the trouble of creating a paper version of an electronic file? Here's a quick list of the reasons that PaperDisk is attractive to the power user:

✔ **Encryption:** PaperDisk includes an encryption feature. You can set a password that encrypts your file, making even fax transfers of a hardcopy document as secure as possible.

✔ **No Internet required:** If you need to send an electronic file to a remote site that doesn't have an Internet connection (or even a modem), PaperDisk makes faxing the file instead (or even mailing it) pretty easy.

✔ **Cut costs:** If you're constantly sending electronic files to other locations on floppy disks via Federal Express or UPS, you can fax the files instead. Or you can create multiple copies of an electronic file simply by printing multiple copies.

✔ **Version control:** Software developers know how hard it is to keep track of successive versions of a program under development. With PaperDisk, each version of the program can be stored indefinitely on paper or backed up off-site with no worries about lost data due to magnetic fields.

PaperDisk is a shareware program, which you can evaluate for 30 days. To download the shareware version, visit the company's Web site, at www.paperdisk.com. The program costs $29 to register.

Backing Up to the Web

Sure, backing up your PC's data is important. In fact, backing up your data is the only way to guard against hardware failures or the occasional "Uh-oh!" (or worse) indicating that you just accidentally erased an entire folder on your hard drive. Most computer owners back up using tape drives, and others use removable media, like Zip or Jaz drives. (Chapter 7 discusses each of these backup methods.) An unfortunate few probably still back up on floppies, but my advice to them is to enter the twentieth century, and soon.

Wait until you hear about the power user's dream backup method. No tapes to handle, and no time spent listening to your drive wind and rewind over and over again. Plus, you have the confidence of knowing that your data is stored safely off-site, ensuring that your data is secure even if your entire house or office is kidnapped by aliens. I'm talking about storing your PC's data on an Internet site with the software program named BACKUP (from Safeguard Interactive, at `www.sgii.com`).

Safeguard strongly advises not to use BACKUP with non-English versions of Windows 95, Windows 98, or Windows NT.

How does BACKUP work? All you need is Windows 95, Windows 98, or Windows NT, a copy of BACKUP, and at least a 28.8 Kbps connection to the Internet (of course, the faster, the better). BACKUP enables you to set up an automatic backup schedule, or you can perform a manual backup at any time.

At the scheduled time, the data you mark for backup is read from your hard drive, encrypted to a military-grade standard, and sent over the Internet to the Safeguard server. Safeguard stores your data with your password in encrypted form until you need it.

Safeguard Interactive charges $100 for a year's subscription or $10 on a monthly subscription plan. After you subscribe, you can store as many files as you like and back up and retrieve them as often as necessary.

Speaking of retrieval, your data can be retrieved and restored only to the PC where the backup originated, which introduces an additional layer of security.

Will You Move the Joystick, or Will It Move You?

The Microsoft SideWinder Force Feedback Pro may look like a fancy joystick, but it's also a bona fide power user's play toy. What sets this piece of hardware apart from the pack is its ability to provide actual tactile feedback. In other words, when something happens in the game, you can feel an authentic sense, force, or impact through the joystick. For example:

- ✔ If you're flying a light plane with a flight simulator, you feel the stick resist your movements as you begin a turn, and then relax gradually as the turn continues.
- ✔ If you're driving a tank, you feel the impact of each hit on your tank's armor, as well as the recoil of each shot you fire.

✔ If you're playing a first-person "shoot'em-up" (where you're immersed in a 3-D world), you feel your way around corners in the dark and recognize different wall textures.

✔ If you're bowling, you can tell whether your ball hit the lane too early or just right.

As a dyed-in-the-wool computer game fanatic, I can tell you that this kind of feedback really adds that extra touch of realism (along with the 19-inch monitor, wavetable sound card, and subwoofer I requested for Christmas). Much like a sound card with 3D support enhances the audio experience of a game, the Force Feedback Pro enhances physical sensations of your game-playing experience. After all, a game becomes much more realistic when your World War II fighter plane gets harder to control as you're dodging bullets with an enemy on your tail. The Force Feedback Pro reflects every hit on your plane as well as the force required to pull out of a power dive.

Like most of the more expensive joysticks on the market, you can program each button to perform a keyboard command. And the stick itself is especially designed for hours of hazardous flying through the enemy-filled skies of Planet SpeedBump without cramping your hand.

Before you tense your muscles to leap out of your chair and run to your local computer store for a Force Feedback Pro, don't overlook the downside:

✔ Compared to a standard joystick that costs $15 or $20, the SideWinder Force Feedback Pro costs a king's ransom, at about $110.

✔ The game you're playing must explicitly support the Force Feedback Pro to enable the tactile-feedback feature. So, for older games, the Force Feedback Pro becomes just another joystick.

Part V
The Part of Tens

The 5th Wave — By Rich Tennant

I HAVEN'T LOCATED THE PROBLEM YET.

In this part . . .

I provide you with worthwhile advice and tips (and even the occasional warning) concerning five different topics, ranging from the assembly process to speeding up your PC. Each chapter includes ten tips. Consider The Part of Tens as a quick dose of experience (without the hard knocks).

Chapter 16

Ten Reasons Not to Buy a Retail PC

*B*uying a PC from a retail computer store or a big mail-order company is easy: Out comes the credit card, the boxes arrive at your house, and installation is as simple as plugging in the keyboard, mouse, speakers, and monitor. Even the most experienced PC hardware junkie will have to admit that a novice can save time and potential headaches by buying a retail PC.

Therefore, you may be asking yourself, "Why don't I just travel the retail PC route like most people? Why go to the trouble of building my own computer?" In this chapter, I give you several doggone good reasons *why* you should assemble your own machine.

It Just Plain Costs Less to Build Your Own PC!

The first (and, for some people, the most important) reason for building a computer is to save as much money as possible over the cost of a retail PC. If you build your own computer, you're not paying for all the extra overhead tacked on to the original price of a computer (including a storefront, advertising, and a salesperson's paycheck). If you've been shopping for a PC, you already know that many retail PC packages don't include a monitor, so often the price you see isn't actually for a complete system. And yes, you can save a hundred dollars or more over the price of a complete PC offered by a big mail-order company. As I explain earlier in this book, it's simply a matter of searching for the right companies that sell computer components at rock-bottom prices. *Remember:* Using a Web site like www.pricewatch.com can bring you — in just a few seconds — the best prices available anywhere!

Even if you have to buy every single component from your computer case to your mouse pad, you're still likely to save a considerable amount of cash by assembling your own computer.

Recycle Used and Scavenged Hardware

If you have an older computer hanging around the house, does it make sense to throw it away, or sell it for a small fraction of what you paid for it several years ago? Why not recycle what you can out of that machine (for example, the case, keyboard, floppy drive, and monitor) and use those scavenged parts when you build your new PC? When you build your own PC, you can take advantage of used and scavenged hardware, and every part you avoid buying means even more money that stays in your pocket.

The constant urge among technotypes to upgrade means that you'll likely find sources of used hardware right in your own office or school, and those parts are often only a couple of years old! (My favorite example is "yesterday's" 3D video card that has a mere 8 megabytes of video RAM rather than the 16 or 32 megabytes that the hard-core gamers desire. If you're not interested in playing the latest games in high resolution, that 8 megabytes is a perfect choice for you.)

Avoid the Monster Myth

If you're shopping for a computer in a retail store, you're likely to be told that you should "buy more computer than you need right now." I call this the

Monster Myth: Buy a monster machine now, and you won't be sorry later. (Coincidentally, that more expensive and more powerful computer also earns the salesperson a higher commission — go figure.)

If you're going to be using your computer often and you know that you'll need more power and more features in the future, this line of reasoning is actually pretty good advice; you'll avoid upgrading your computer several times in the long run. However, the large percentage of new computer owners have little experience on a PC, and they're not really sure what they're going to do or how often they'll use their PC. Why spend all that money on a monster machine if you're not sure that you and your family will use it?

You may find yourself asking, "Do I really need all this stuff just to read my Internet e-mail and keep an address book?" The answer is "Definitely not." I know many computer owners who are still very satisfied with older, original first-generation Pentium PCs. Their machines run Windows 95, a browser, and an e-mail program, and that's all they need.

Too bad that most computer stores don't have a bare-bones PC you can choose — but if you assemble your own computer, you can start out with an economy-class Pentium II or Pentium III PC and add functionality later as you gain experience. In fact, you can customize your computer to your exact specifications and avoid buying unnecessary hardware. (One big retail chain now lets you build a "custom" PC, but its prices are sky-high compared to a machine you assemble yourself.) Some mail-order catalogs and Web stores are starting to get the idea too, and they're offering fairly low-cost machines . . . but you usually don't get to customize these inexpensive PCs very much, and don't forget to check whether they're using brand-name components before you think about buying one!)

Encourage Freedom of Choice!

If you build your own computer, it's much easier to select special components that don't fit the cookie-cutter mold of retail PCs. For example, don't expect to find specialized pointing devices like trackballs on most retail PCs at your local computer store; if you want to use a trackball rather than a mouse, you'll have to buy one separately if you buy a retail PC (and then you're stuck with a mouse you don't need). That may not seem like much of a hassle, but consider other specialized components, like a 3D spatial wavetable sound card, a gamer's 3D video card with 32MB of video RAM, or a SCSI adapter card; buying one of these adapter cards, removing the case, and substituting the adapter card you *really* wanted in the first place becomes a big deal.

When you design and assemble your own computer, you buy precisely what you need, including any specialized hardware or peripherals. The "perfect computer" you were considering at the computer store didn't have an internal Zip drive and a CD recorder, although you can certainly build a computer that does have these extras! If you're considering buying a PC from a direct vendor like Dell or Gateway and you need special hardware, the vendor can usually supply it — although you'll pay more for the vendor's version of the part than you would have paid for the part through a mail-order catalog. Having a custom PC is nice, but unless you build it yourself, you'll *always* pay more.

What Do You Learn When You Buy a Retail PC?

The answer: Not much. Sure, you get a crash course in removing Styrofoam and plugging in cables, but most owners of a retail PC are still afraid to remove the case from their computer. If you buy a retail PC, you'll be left in the dark when the time comes to upgrade your system to extend its useful life or replace a broken component.

On the other hand, if you build your own computer, you *know* what makes it tick — you'll suddenly blossom into a bona fide technowizard! With your assembly experience and your knowledge of PC hardware, you'll be better prepared to fix problems and upgrade hardware and peripherals whenever necessary. The technicians at your local PC repair shop will wonder what happened to you; perhaps you should visit them from time to time just to swap hard drive specifications.

"Ship My Computer Cross-Country? Forget It!"

When you buy a retail PC from a store (or even from one of the big-name mail-order companies), you'll probably be presented with a technical support number and assurances that your computer will be promptly repaired if it breaks. You'll find that the word *prompt* has many meanings, like waiting several minutes (or even an hour) to speak to a technical support representative, finding out that you'll be without your PC and the data you need for several weeks, or making an appointment with a service representative to eventually drop by your house and bring a replacement part. Oh, and don't forget that this coverage usually lasts for only a year, unless you paid big bucks for the extended service contract when you bought your PC.

When you build your own PC, you can buy parts locally — and, if a part breaks, you don't have to pick up the telephone and start waiting. You'll never find yourself repacking your computer to send it halfway across the country; instead, you can bring the faulty component back to the store for an immediate replacement.

Bundled Software Costs Extra

Retail PC salespeople like to crow about the cool software that comes included with their computers. You usually get a "productivity suite" (which includes a word processor, some sort of database application, and a spreadsheet program), a few Internet applications, and free hours on an online service. If you're lucky, you may also get a CD-ROM game or two with your computer. Generally, these programs are stripped-down versions of larger packages (for example, although you may get Microsoft Works, most retail PCs sold in stores don't include Microsoft Office 2000 unless you pay more for it).

Unfortunately, this bundled software isn't free at all: You pay for it along with your hardware, the documentation is usually sparse, it's rarely exactly what you need, and you usually can't subtract it from the total price of your computer. Often, you won't even receive the original disks or CD-ROM, so you can't reinstall the software. In fact, many new computer owners end up uninstalling the bundled software to make room for the programs they really want to run. If you build your own PC, you can select your own full versions of your favorite applications later and save additional money.

Avoid the Computer Sales Experience

Although used-car salespeople seem to rank the lowest on the social totem pole, computer salespeople aren't that much better. Many salespeople I've encountered in retail computer stores either consider the customer practically an idiot or have very little idea of exactly what they're selling (making them the perfect target for a few well-placed technoquestions — nothing's funnier than an embarrassed salesperson without a clue who treated you like a computer novice just a few seconds before)! Others try to pass off a computer that's been returned as near the quality of a brand-new machine. (Look closely for the word *refurbished* the next time you shop for a computer, and you may see this technique in action.)

By building your own PC, you can circumvent your computer retail store and all the techniques that salespeople use to try to talk you into a specific computer — and you end up with a better computer that *perfectly* suits your needs.

Select the Brands You Prefer

Are you looking for specific brand-name components in your computer, like a Maxtor hard drive or a genuine Sound Blaster Live! wavetable sound card from Creative Labs? If you buy a retail PC, you end up with whatever hardware the manufacturer deems satisfactory (and you'd be surprised by how many big-name manufacturers of retail PCs use no-name parts). Granted, it's easier to buy the exact monitor, scanner, or printer you want — these components can be purchased separately; as for the parts inside the case, however, often the only way you can determine what you're getting is to open the computer's case on the sales floor.

Even if you're buying a computer from a direct vendor that offers customized PCs, it's unlikely that you'll be able to ask for a specific brand for most of the components used to assemble your computer. Typically, these vendors do use brand-name parts, but only those brands and models the vendor prefers; if you need a different model, you're no better off than you would be buying a computer in a chain store.

When you build your own computer, *you* select the parts required to build it, including any specific brand-name preferences.

Get the Full Warranty for Each Part

If you've found a retail PC at the price you want that does include many of the brand-name parts you're looking for, you're not necessarily receiving the full manufacturer's warranty on each of those components. Instead, the brand-name components on many retail computers are covered by the computer company's warranty (typically a year for both parts and labor). If that name-brand hard drive breaks after two years in a retail PC, you may not be able to return it to the manufacturer for service or replacement (even though the drive has a three-year warranty if you buy it separately).

If you buy your own components and build your own PC, you're assured that each component is covered for the full length of the manufacturer's warranty.

Chapter 17

Ten Tools and Tasks for a Power User's PC

*T*o me, a *power user* is a person who is perfectly at home at the computer keyboard. For example, a power user knows those keyboard shortcuts that can speed up a favorite Windows program; experienced power users also know tips and tricks that can help make their computers run faster (such as defragmenting a hard drive), and they know how to diagnose problems with their computers. Power users are more efficient and more experienced with computers, and this ability makes them more productive at work and at home.

You can become a power user even if your computer isn't the fastest or most powerful PC on your block. Most people would say that it certainly helps to start with the best computer possible, and that's true in general: Speed and capacity never hurt. However, I've sat down in front of many a top-of-the-line retail computer system and noticed many features that could be added or improved.

In this chapter, I name ten computer hardware and software extras that help make your life easier behind the keyboard — they're not necessarily expensive, although each one of them does add convenience, comfort, or efficiency to your computer. By my definition, if you're comfortable, confident, and productive with your computer — no matter how fast it is — *you're* a power user!

Forget Your Mouse

The mouse is now the most popular computer pointing device — but many power users favor other pointing devices. Power users dislike mice because they take up too much space on the desktop, they trail their cord "tails" behind them at all times, and they get filthy after a few months of constant use. Mice are also terribly inefficient creatures because they require movements of your forearm (which often makes it necessary to pick up your mouse and relocate it in another area of your desk just to move the cursor all the way across the screen).

I heartily recommend that you select another pointing device rather than a mouse! These devices can include a touchpad, trackball, drawing tablet, or fingertip mouse. My favorite is the trackball, which offers precise control with movements of your thumb or fingers rather than your forearm. A trackball doesn't move across the surface of your desk, so it needs cleaning far less often, and it requires only a fraction of the desktop real estate necessary for a standard corded mouse. (For more information on these pointing devices, see Chapter 5.)

Guard That Power Supply!

It never fails. The moment you've finished the last chapter of your Great American Novel — you know, the one you've been working on for the past 20 years — someone on your block decides to juice up a new electric car, and every transformer within three miles goes up in smoke. You get hit with a power failure, and the crowning chapter of your novel is suddenly headed to that home for unfinished classics in the sky.

What can you do? Unfortunately, the answer is a big "nothing." If you've saved your work often, you can at least back up to the last revision, although the loss of power may have resulted in lost clusters on your computer's hard drive. In the worst-case scenario, you may have been recording a CD-ROM on your computer; if the recording process is interrupted by a power failure, you've just created a dandy coaster for your cold drinks (and wasted a blank CD-ROM in the process).

However, you can prevent such a catastrophe by adding a UPS (uninterruptible power supply) to your computer system. A *UPS* is essentially a giant battery that automatically provides power in a split second in case of a power blackout or brownout. A typical UPS provides your computer with another priceless 15 minutes or so of operation before it's fully exhausted, which should give you ample time to save your work and shut down your system normally (or finish recording that CD-ROM). Believe me, it's a weird feeling to see your computer monitor alive and well with every other light and appliance in your home as dead as a doornail — after you've finished saving your work, gather the family around for a computer game or two!

The UPS is constantly recharged from your wall socket, so it's always ready. Most of these power supplies also filter AC line noise (small variations in line voltage caused by some appliances, like vacuum cleaners and televisions) and provide some measure of protection against lightning strikes.

Back Up, Back Up, Back Up

Even if your computer is connected to an uninterruptible power supply, you can still lose data; for example, hard drives fail, and human error can result in deleted files. There's only one way to truly secure your computer from loss: *Back up your data to tape or removable media, and do it on a regular basis!*

As a consultant, I've seen individuals, small businesses, and even one or two larger companies that have been hammered by the loss of sensitive or irreplaceable data because of hardware failure — and that data could have been backed up to a tape cartridge in just a few minutes. If you have important data that would take time or money to replace if you lost it, learn the power user's secret weapon: Back up your data!

How often should you back up? It all depends on how often you significantly change your data. At minimum, I back up my work in progress every week, and many companies run automated backups of their entire network every night. If time is tight, back up only your user data (such as documents, graphics, and spreadsheet files). If I'm really in a hurry, I'll even create a second copy of an important document on a floppy disk, just in case disaster strikes. However, if you have the time, I recommend that you back up your entire system (including all your operating system files and application programs); this way, you avoid the hassle of reconfiguring Windows or OS/2 and reloading your programs on a new hard drive before you're back to normal.

Check Chapter 7 for more information on tape backups and how you can install one in your computer.

Back up your data! (Did I stress that enough?)

Diagnostics Software to the Rescue

It's a good bet that most power users have at least one diagnostics program; power users understand that hardware and system problems can lead to a slower computer, lockups, or even lost data. Unfortunately, these problems usually aren't obvious, so you need a program capable of both locating potential glitches and eliminating them (or at least identifying them and providing a possible solution or two). Some operating systems come with a simple disk-scanning utility — for example, SCANDISK.EXE under MS-DOS 6.22 or ScanDisk under Windows 98 and Windows 2000 — but these programs don't check for hardware problems, and they don't offer the range of features provided by commercial diagnostics software.

Probably the oldest and best-known diagnostics package for the PC is Norton Utilities, from Symantec; this suite of programs has been around since the days when DOS was king, and the Utilities have saved my neck more than once! The Utilities package includes one of the best disk defragmenters available, a system information and benchmark program, a Windows 98 optimizing and troubleshooting program, and a comprehensive "disk doctor" that checks for just about every conceivable file error. I run the disk doctor religiously at least once a day, so I know that the files on my hard drives are in good shape. You can download an evaluation version of Norton Utilities for Windows 98 from the Symantec Web site, at www.symantec.com.

Another well-known diagnostics program for the PC, First Aid 2000, from McAfee (www.mcafee.com), even offers automatic updates — you can download new information about the latest applications available for your PC so that your diagnostics software is never out of date.

Stick Your Keyboard in a Drawer!

If you're going to remain comfortable at your computer, you need to consider ergonomics: Your keyboard should be at the proper height for comfortable typing, your wrists should be supported to avoid carpal tunnel syndrome, and your monitor should be close to your natural eye level to avoid cramping your neck.

One of my first additions to my desktop computer was a *keyboard drawer;* it's a metal case that holds a sliding drawer for your keyboard (as well as a place to store a pencil and paper clips). Your computer sits on top of the metal case, and you simply pull the drawer out and begin typing. The drawer keeps the keyboard at the proper height and saves desktop space you would otherwise need for your keyboard. When you're done at the PC, slide the keyboard back into the case.

If your computer's tower case sits on the floor (with only your monitor and pointing device on your desk), I recommend a keyboard drawer that attaches to the bottom of your computer desk; if you're shopping for a computer desk, it's worth it to spend a bit more for a keyboard drawer.

Stop the Spread of Viruses

If you believe what you hear in the media, computer viruses are hovering outside your Internet connection 24 hours a day, just waiting to bite your computer like a rabid silicon dog. Even with the latest wave of e-mail and macro viruses, viruses are nowhere near as common as people think. However, it never hurts to be prepared, especially if you receive lots of e-mail or try out lots of demo and shareware software on your PC. Every computer power user worthy of the title runs a virus-scanning program at least once a week or runs an antivirus program constantly in the background.

The best-known virus scanning software for the PC is McAfee VirusScan. If you buy VirusScan, you can download the regular virus updates from McAfee at www.mcafee.com; these data files enable the program to recognize all the new viruses that have been identified since the last update. Symantec offers a similar scanning program named Norton AntiVirus, and you can download the trial versions for Windows 98, Windows NT, and MS-DOS at www.symantec.com.

Most virus-scanning programs identify viruses present in your computer's RAM, on your hard drive's boot sector, and within files stored on your drive. Some scanners can actually attempt to remove the virus from the program or data file, and other programs simply advise that you delete the infected file to guarantee that the virus is eradicated.

Be sure to update your virus signatures every week.

Organize Your Software

Floppy disks, backup tape cartridges, CD-ROMs, and Zip disks — where do you put all this stuff? It's easy to throw everything into a shoe box, but can you find a particular floppy or CD-ROM when you need it?

A power user keeps software organized and within easy reach. For CD-ROMs, I suggest an audio CD rack that stands on the floor or mounts on the wall. You should keep floppy disks and Zip disks in a disk case (preferably with dividers that can help keep your games separate from that spreadsheet work you brought home from the office); if you need a little extra security, look for a disk case with a lock. You can also store backup tape cartridges in a special tape case. (Although tape cases are a little harder to find, you should be able to buy one at your local office supply store.)

Use the Power of Your Voice

Does the idea of controlling your computer with your voice seem like science fiction? How would you like to dictate your next report or memo to your computer — without typing a single character of the text? Thanks to programs like NaturallySpeaking from Dragon Systems and ViaVoice from IBM, you can dictate text without adding artificial pauses between words; these programs understand your normal speaking voice, and they can handle more than 100 words a minute (which beats touch typing). Although this technology has come a long way, you still have to "train" the computer to recognize your speech patterns like older voice-recognition programs did, and voice dictation on a computer is still nowhere near 100 percent accurate. Unfortunately, using voice-recognition software doesn't get you out of proofreading your text.

What happens when you use a word your computer doesn't recognize, like a technical term or a phrase from a foreign language? It takes only a second to add a word to the computer's "dictionary," and after you save the updated dictionary to the hard drive, your computer recognizes and types the new word in future sessions.

At a minimum, your PC needs a 16-bit sound card and a microphone to use a voice-recognition program — however, the most advanced voice-recognition software runs much better with a sound card that uses a PCI bus, and the more system RAM you have, the better.

Everyone Needs a Good Image Editor

"A picture is worth a thousand words." That old adage is the foundation of today's World Wide Web as well as graphical operating systems like Windows. Power users add graphics to their documents, use images as backgrounds for their operating system or their Web pages, build animated GIFs (short for *Graphic Interchange Format*, one of the popular image formats on the Web), and demand high-resolution digital cameras for taking pictures of everything from the family dog to Stonehenge.

Because images are so important to today's computer power user, it's no accident that graphics editors like Paint Shop Pro, from JASC (www.jasc.com); Photoshop, from Adobe; and PhotoImpact, from Ulead Systems are popular applications of this type. With an image editor, you can alter the size and shape of an image, crop it to enhance a particular element, and rotate it as you please. It's easy to add text, or "paste" another image on top of an original. You can even edit the individual dots (or pixels) inside an image or draw on an image with a virtual paintbrush or spray can.

Keep It Clean!

What power user wants to sit at a dirty keyboard? After you've spent time and money building your own computer, it makes sense to clean the case, monitor screen, keyboard, floppy drive, and pointing device from time to time. Dust and grime can interfere with the proper operation of parts like your mouse or trackball — and if you don't clean the heads on your floppy drive and tape backup, they start losing data!

Here are a few tips for keeping your hardware squeaky clean:

- ✔ I recommend using a sponge with mild soap and water to clean the outside of your computer case; others have told me that they use one of the anti-static surface cleaners you can find at an office supply store.

- ✔ For your monitor, use a lens-cleaning solution and a soft lens-polishing cloth (both of which you'll find at your local computer store, eyeglass shop, or camera store).

- ✔ For your keyboard, nothing is better than a can of compressed air; it's great at cleaning hard-to-reach crevices. I've also used a cotton swab to clean the ridges on my keyboard.

- ✔ For your floppy drive and tape backup drive, visit your local computer store and pick up the appropriate head cleaner. These cleaning systems typically use some sort of cloth pad, which you soak in alcohol and then load into the drive.

- ✔ To clean your mouse or trackball, remove the retaining ring around the ball — usually you twist it in the direction indicated on the bottom of the mouse — and clean the contact points and rollers inside the mouse with a cotton swab soaked in alcohol.

Chapter 18

Ten Important Assembly Tips

In This Chapter

▶ Reading the instructions

▶ Creating the proper work area

▶ Keeping track of small computer parts

▶ Making sure that you have everything you need

▶ Calling for help if you need it

▶ Using a magnetized screwdriver

▶ Starting your own parts box

▶ Avoiding the urge to rush through assembly

▶ Leaving your PC uncovered until testing is complete

▶ Checking cables to make sure that they're connected

Assembling your own computer is really a simple job if you're handy with a screwdriver — but, like just about every other human endeavor, you gain experience each time you do it. In this chapter, I present a list of tips and tricks I've learned over the years that can help speed up the entire assembly process, help prevent accidents and mistakes, and generally make the assembly process more enjoyable.

Read the Instructions First! (Rule Number One)

I know, I know — nothing is more boring than reading the instructions for installing a hard drive or a CD-ROM; even technonerds dislike reading hardware and software documentation. However, every second you spend reading about and familiarizing yourself with the installation process for a computer component will save you hours of frustration when you're knee-deep in your computer, trying to get that new part to work. It doesn't matter whether you read the instructions 15 minutes before you start installation or three days ahead of time, just *read them completely* first. Trust me on this one — even the folks at NASA read instructions.

Build the Perfect Workspace

Your kitchen table may be the most convenient place to assemble your computer, but is it the best workspace? Your work area must be large and sturdy enough to hold your computer's chassis and parts and your tools. A well-equipped workspace also has these features:

- ✔ **Access to at least two or three power plugs:** During testing, you have to at least provide power to your computer and the monitor, but it never hurts to have a spare in case you need to add and test an external device, like a CD-ROM or tape backup unit.

- ✔ **An adjustable lighting source:** If you can't see it, you can't tighten it! I use an adjustable extension lamp that stays where I need it (the "gooseneck" variety can be positioned perfectly).

- ✔ **A smooth surface that won't scratch or mar your computer case:** The paint on a computer case is easily scratched; it pays to cover your workspace with a few sheets of newspaper to keep your case looking new. Unlike a tablecloth, that newspaper won't build up static electricity.

Keep Track of UTOs (Unidentified Tiny Objects)

Why do some pieces of computer hardware have to be so doggone small? I'm talking about screws, jumpers, terminators, and other assorted tiny objects you need to keep track of while you're assembling your computer.

Here's how you can make the perfect receptacle for these diminutive troublemakers: Glue a small magnet into the center of an old ashtray or ceramic bowl with a broad base, and keep this "parts basket" handy and near to you while you're assembling your computer. (Or, if you like, fasten it to your work table.)

The magnet will hold small screws, slot covers, and the like — and you won't be constantly digging in your pockets for small parts.

Make Sure That You Have Everything You Need

Before you start the installation of a new component, make sure that you have all the cables, screws, and connectors required for finishing the job. When you open your new part, check that the box contains everything it should; if you're scavenging a part from an older PC, you should also take any screws, cables, or wires you don't already have in your computer.

Similarly, it always pays to identify the requirements for a new part before you add it; for example, if you're going to install a new internal CD-ROM drive, does your power supply still have an unused power cable and connector of the right size? If not, you'll need a Y power cable adapter, which transforms a single power cable into two cables and connectors. If you're buying an external modem, do you have an RS-232 modem cable with the right gender connectors handy, or will you have to buy one? If you're buying an internal component, does your computer chassis still have an open bay of the right height?

A little preparation goes a long way toward avoiding simple frustrations (for example, suddenly realizing that you don't have the required batteries for your new multimedia speakers) — and big headaches (like discovering that you don't have a spare 16-bit adapter card slot for your new internal modem).

Yell for Help If Necessary

Some of the assembly steps you encounter in building your own PC may make you nervous — for example, installing a CPU or a memory module — whereas others may require additional configuration, like fine-tuning your computer for use with a new CD recorder or adding network drivers for a new network card on a PC running MS-DOS. Always keep in mind that several sources of assistance are available and that there's no reason to be embarrassed about asking for help.

If you can't find the answers you're looking for in the documentation that accompanied the new part, try these resources:

✔ Most hardware manufacturers offer technical support over the telephone, and many manufacturers also provide FAQs (lists of Frequently Asked Questions) about their products on their Web sites.

✔ A friend, family member, or fellow member of a computer club with experience in computer hardware can come in very handy. (Don't forget to pick up the check the next time you have lunch together.)

✔ Most computer repair shops are happy to answer a few questions for free; if you find yourself completely unable to install a particular component, it's likely, of course, that you can pay one of the store's techs to install the part for you.

✔ If you're willing to wait for the answer, you can usually find help on the relevant Internet newsgroup — for example, the good folks that frequent `alt.comp.hardware.homebuilt` and `alt.comp.hardware.pc-homebuilt` are always happy to answer questions.

Use a Magnetic Screwdriver

The carpenter has a trusty hammer, the woodsman is skilled with an ax — but the computer technician's tool of choice is a trusty magnetized screwdriver. Look for a reversible model that has both standard and Phillips tips. If you have your magnetized screwdriver by your side, you won't panic when you inevitably drop a screw deep within the chassis of your new computer; just poke around in the general area and let magnetism do the rest for you.

No need to worry about wreaking magnetic havoc on floppy disks or backup tapes; the magnetic field from a screwdriver isn't powerful enough to damage disks or tapes unless you park your screwdriver on top of them for at least a weekend. Therefore, when not in use, keep your screwdriver in a drawer or on the wall. Some true technonerds even keep their screwdrivers in a belt holder — thankfully, a screwdriver or all-purpose "multifunction"-style tool slung on your belt has replaced the old-fashioned pocket protector as the status symbol of the technowizard.

Start Your Own Parts Box

The last time you installed a computer component, did you find yourself with an extra unneeded screw, adapter card slot cover, cable, or connector? If so, *don't* throw those extras away. Instead, grab an empty cardboard box and throw all your unneeded computer parts in there (except for circuit boards and larger components, which should be stored separately in static-free plastic bags). Voilà! You've created your own parts box. The next time you suddenly find yourself one screw short or you need an extra jumper block and the manufacturer didn't give you one, check your parts box before you take off to Radio Shack; you may just save yourself both time and money by using a part from the box. The more you work with computer hardware, the more this box will grow; soon, you'll have a comprehensive treasure chest of small computer parts.

As you upgrade parts of your computer, you can always keep the older components as backup hardware in case of failure; as a general rule, however, I try to sell older components (or donate them to my local school or church if I can't sell them). Unlike the small parts in your parts box, older components you've "outgrown" end up taking too much room in your closet or garage.

Take Your Time: The Zen of Assembly

You may be excited about building your own computer, but rushing through an assembly step can lead to frustrating mistakes, such as mismatched cables and upside-down components. Follow the step-by-step instructions in this book and the documentation that comes with your hardware, and don't move to the next step until you've completely finished every task in the current step.

If you're working on a particularly delicate assembly step (like adding a CPU or a memory module to your motherboard) and it's not going well, step back and take a deep breath or two — then verify that you're trying to do the right thing. A friend of mine has a big sign above his workbench that reads "This isn't a race!" (That's good advice for any craftsperson.)

No one is timing you, so move at your own speed.

Don't Cover Up Too Quickly

I would never use a computer on a day-to-day basis without its case; the components would get far too dirty too quickly, and there would always be a danger of spilling liquids on exposed components or touching a circuit board while the computer is on.

However, everything changes when you're installing a new internal part in your computer: Keep the case off until you're certain that the new component is working properly. Nothing is more irritating than attaching the case on a computer and then finding that you forgot to connect the power cable to your new CD-ROM or hard drive. Before I learned this important rule, I would sometimes remove the case on my PC three or four times until everything finally worked. As long as you keep liquids away from your computer and don't touch any internal components while it's on, you're in no danger: Save time and trouble by leaving the case off until you're sure that your computer is working.

The Cable Rule: Check and Double Check

I've spoken to many computer technicians and hardware technowizards, and every one of them agrees: The number-one error that crops up while installing a new part in your computer is mismatched or disconnected cabling. Problems can even crop up with the cables that are supposed to be foolproof. Although internal power cables are designed to fit only one way, you have to remember to connect them in the first place. (This oversight is typically the cause of the classic line "Hey, it doesn't act like it's getting power at all!" That's because it isn't.)

On the other hand, most internal IDE and SCSI cables can be connected upside down, so remember the Pin 1 rule: Pin 1 of the male connector on the component should always align with the marked wire on the cable (which is the cable manufacturer's way of identifying which wire on the cable is Wire 1).

Although it may take a few seconds extra when you install a new part, I recommend that you check each cable connection — including cables leading to other parts — before you test the new component. It's very easy to accidentally unplug an existing connection while you're routing wires and moving things around inside your computer's chassis. If you install a new part and another part suddenly refuses to work properly, there's a good chance that you accidentally unplugged something.

Chapter 19

Ten Ways to Speed Up Your PC

● ●

In This Chapter

▶ Defragmenting your hard drive

▶ Using SCSI hardware

▶ Adding more RAM

▶ Upgrading your processor

▶ Using 256-color plain backgrounds

▶ Investing in a faster CD-ROM

▶ Removing resident programs

▶ Using a Windows accelerated AGP video card

▶ Running your PC under a native file system

▶ Using Turbo mode

● ●

*I*f computer owners have one universal desire, it's more speed. In this chapter, I outline several tricks you can use to improve the overall performance of your computer. Some of these tips cost money (like adding RAM or selecting faster hardware), and others won't cost you a cent. Go, Speed Racer, go!

Defragment Your Hard Drive

Over weeks and months of use, computers running Windows 98, Windows Me, or Windows NT — in other words, any operating system that still uses a variant of the original DOS file system — will slow down because of hard drive fragmentation.

First, a quick explanation: When you delete a file from your hard drive, that area of your hard drive can then accept data from another file; if the file to be saved is larger than this open area, however, DOS must *split* the file into fragments. When your computer needs to load a file, these fragments are automatically reassembled into the complete file; however, the more fragmented the files are on your hard drive, the longer this step takes and the slower your PC becomes.

How can you defragment your hard drive? If you're running MS-DOS 6.22, type **DEFRAG** at the DOS command prompt; if you're running or Windows 98, click the Start button, and then choose Programs⇨Accessories⇨System Tools⇨Disk Defragmenter.

My defragmenting program of choice for Windows 98 is the SpeedDisk program included with the Norton Utilities package.

Get SCSI (Speed Demons Love SCSI)

If you're interested in the fastest possible throughput from your hard drive, CD-ROM drive, scanner, and removable cartridge drives, like Zip or Jaz, your computer cries out for a SCSI adapter card. Because both IDE and SCSI devices can be mixed on the same computer, you can add a SCSI adapter card to your computer even after you've built it. If you've done your homework and you're looking for a power-user PC, however, it pays to build your computer around a SCSI device chain from the beginning. Chapter 11 provides the inside story on SCSI and what it can do for you.

Install More RAM

Any 32-bit operating system always benefits from more system RAM (that includes all breeds of Windows and Windows NT, OS/2, and Unix), and with RAM prices free-falling over the past few years, most PC owners can afford to bulk up to 128 or even 256 megabytes. If a program and its data don't fit in RAM, your operating system must save and read that data to and from a temporary file on your hard drive; this process, called *swapping,* can slow everything down to a crawl while your PC juggles data back and forth.

With 128 megabytes of memory or more, your operating system will have more elbow room, and it will have to swap less data to disk — which means that you can open more applications at one time and your entire computer will run faster overall.

Crank Up the CPU Steam

Now that you're familiar with processors and motherboards, you can consider an upgrade to your existing CPU — if your motherboard can accept a faster CPU, of course. You reap the benefits while you're using processor-intensive applications like graphics programs, spreadsheets, and the latest games. The old CPU can be stored as a backup, sold to friends or family, or donated to a worthy school or church.

As a rule, I don't go through the trouble of upgrading a CPU in a single step —
in other words, you probably won't see a dramatic increase in performance
when you upgrade from a Pentium II running at 333 MHz to a Pentium II running at 350 MHz. On the other hand, if your motherboard can "jump" at least
two steps — from 333 MHz to 400 or 450 MHz, for example — you'll be
extending the life of your existing motherboard and you'll *really* notice the
difference!

Some Web sites will advise you to *overclock* your processor — in other
words, configure the motherboard settings so that the CPU runs faster than
its rated speed. I *do not* recommend overclocking, for several good reasons: It
shortens the life of the CPU, and you have to use one (or sometimes two)
fans on the chip to keep it cool. Also, only older CPUs can be overclocked, so
you'd actually be better off buying a motherboard and a slower Pentium III
than attempting to overclock a Pentium II. Finally, overclocking is not an easy
task, and it doesn't work as often as it does work. To add it all up, overclocking just isn't worth the effort!

Keep Your Backgrounds Plain

Graphical operating systems such as Windows 98, Windows NT, and OS/2 can
be dressed up with 16-million-color photographs as backgrounds, animated
icons, and other exotic eye candy. If you want your PC to run faster under
one of these operating systems, however, select a simple, single-color background and run your computer in 256-color mode. Why? Your PC must use
extra RAM to display true-color images or animated icons. Some full-screen
background pictures I've seen are nearly two megabytes in size (they're
meant for resolutions of 1152 x 864 and higher, and they're 16-million-color
bitmaps)! If you use a high-resolution, full-screen bitmap with 16 million
colors as your background, your computer will slow down when it's loading
the background image (or redrawing it after you've closed a window).

Install a Fast CD-ROM

Paying for a higher "X factor" is worth the money when you're shopping for
your CD-ROM; this X factor is a method of describing the speed of the drive's
throughput as a multiple of the original single-speed drive, which delivered
150 Kbps.

The higher the X factor of your CD-ROM, the faster the drive can deliver data
to your computer. You especially notice a faster CD-ROM whenever you're
installing a new program from a CD or playing a game and the CD-ROM is
reading digital video. For complete details on adding a CD-ROM drive to your
PC, visit Chapter 8.

Remove Resident Programs

If you're running Windows, DOS, or OS/2, your computer may be harboring hidden programs that are sucking power and resources from your applications. No, I'm not talking about viruses; these programs, called *resident* programs, have been around since the very early days of DOS. A resident program is loaded automatically when you boot your computer, and the program continues to work "in the background" while you run the applications you want. Unlike a virus, a resident program is usually doing something you want, like checking the status of your disk drive, polling your Internet service provider for your e-mail, or displaying stock quotes.

Unfortunately, if you load down your computer with too many resident programs, your PC has to devote too much processor time and RAM to maintaining them, and your applications will slow down accordingly. To make sure that this slowdown doesn't happen, don't load more than two or three resident tasks, and avoid installing programs that automatically start each time you boot your PC unless you really need them to.

Under Windows 98, you can recognize most resident programs by their icons in the system tray, which occupies the far right side of the status bar opposite from the Start button. To determine what each of these icons does, you can usually left- or right-click the icon to display a menu (and most resident tasks have a menu item you can select to shut them down).

Under OS/2, Unix, or Windows NT, display your list of applications that are running and look for resident programs that may have been loaded during the boot process.

Under DOS, use the DOS editor to display your AUTOEXEC.BAT file, where resident programs are loaded during the boot process, and look for statements that may load resident programs. You can safely disable these statements by inserting the word *REM* (followed by a space) in front of the statement, like this:

```
REM C:\MONITOR\CLOCK.EXE
```

and then saving the new file. If you need to enable the statement again, just use the DOS editor to delete the word *REM* and the space and then save the file again.

Accelerate Windows with Your Video Card

If you're scavenging parts from an older computer for use with a new Pentium III-class PC you're building, buy a brand-new AGP 3D video card rather than use an older 16-bit ISA video card. Why? Because most video adapter cards sold a few years ago don't provide hardware acceleration support or 3D support for Windows 98, Windows Me, and Windows NT. A modern Windows 3D accelerated card speeds up your entire PC because it takes over most video-related tasks from your computer's CPU (which can then turn its attention to other, more important CPU stuff). The speed increase is most apparent when you're playing games designed for Windows 98 and when you're opening and closing several application windows on your PC; the heavier the graphical "load" on your PC, the more you benefit from an accelerated video card. (If your motherboard doesn't have an AGP slot, use a PCI video card instead — it's a little slower than an AGP card, but still light years faster than a 16-bit ISA video card!)

Use a Native File System

Traditionally, PC data storage has been formatted under the *DOS file system,* which is essentially a road map your computer uses to store files on your hard drive and retrieve them. Although the DOS file system has been used for many, many years, it really isn't the most efficient design, and it doesn't directly support neat features like long filenames.

If you've decided to use Windows NT, OS/2, or Unix, you'll find that you have at least one alternative format for storing and retrieving files: Each of these operating systems has a *native file system* that improves on the DOS file system. In every case, your operating system can save and load data faster from its native file system, which was designed for use in a 32-bit multitasking environment.

When you install Windows NT, OS/2, or Unix, you're given the chance to reformat your hard drive for native file system support, and I recommend that you use the native file system. If you still need DOS partitions on your computer — for example, if you've decided to run multiple operating systems — they should be formatted separately, and you should use a multiple-boot utility, like System Commander, from V Communications.

Don't Forget that Turbo Button!

Does your PC have a Turbo button? (Most computer cases manufactured today no longer carry this switch — and even if your case has this switch, it may not be connected.) If your PC does have a Turbo button, you may boot your computer one day and find that everything suddenly seems to run slower, as though the CPU has been dipped in concrete. If so, your first suspect should be that doggone Turbo button; if your PC isn't running in Turbo mode, it's actually forced to run slower. Try punching the Turbo button and see whether your PC speeds up dramatically; if so, grab a piece of tape and a marking pen and cover the button with a barrier that reads Hands Off! (In fact, the owners of some computers I've built have requested that I disconnect the Turbo Switch wire from the motherboard, which usually defaults to normal Turbo mode.)

Chapter 20

Ten Things to Avoid Like the Plague

● ●

In This Chapter

▶ Avoiding refurbished hardware

▶ Saying No to the Pentium chip

▶ Averting disaster from lost data on floppies

▶ Turning off unnecessary passwords

▶ Making sure that you don't violate a copyright

▶ Keeping small children away from the keyboard

▶ Giving pirated software a wide berth

▶ Leaving monitors and power supplies closed

▶ Avoiding a long-term lease on a computer

▶ Watching version numbers when buying software

● ●

*I*n this chapter, I name a number of computer-related things that can lead to lost data, hardware headaches, legal hassles, and even physical injury — in other words, things you should avoid at all costs! Some things on this list should be avoided while you're building your PC, and others are dangerous practices some people engage in with their computer after it's up and running. I recommend that you keep the following three sayings in mind; they seem to cover most situations in this chapter:

✔ If it seems too good to be true, it probably *is*.

✔ Let the buyer beware.

✔ Warning labels are there for a reason.

(That last one is mine, but it ought to be just as famous as the others.)

It's "Refurbished" for a Reason

The word *refurbished* seems to be appearing more and more often in computer hardware magazines, computer stores on the Web, and catalogs for discount computers. Refurbished hardware is hardware that was returned for some reason to the manufacturer (usually because it was defective), and the company fixes the defect and then resells the hardware to another distributor.

By law, refurbished computers and hardware components must be identified as refurbished in any advertising. The distributor usually trumpets the features offered on the computer, the fact that you get a warranty, and perhaps even that the merchandise is "like new." Usually, you do save a significant amount on refurbished hardware, so the prices these companies advertise will indeed catch your eye.

However, I recommend that you give refurbished components a wide berth and buy only new parts (or scavenge working parts from an existing computer). Personally, I would *never* purchase a refurbished computer or refurbished part, and here are the reasons why:

✔ You have no idea why the item was returned (but you can usually safely assume that it wasn't working properly).

✔ You have no way of knowing how it was treated by its former owner.

✔ The manufacturer's warranty is typically less than 90 days (which is usually a much shorter length of time than the warranty on a new item).

✔ Many refurbished parts are not completely retested before they are shipped back to the store.

✔ The sale is usually final, so if it breaks, you're stuck with it.

If you do decide to buy a refurbished item, I *strongly* recommend that you find out all you can about it before you spend your money!

Looking for an Antique? Buy a Pentium CPU

Many stores and mail-order companies that sell computer hardware are still selling CPU chips and motherboards based on the original first-generation Pentium design. The original Pentium was a grand chip, and many of us technotypes with several computers in the house can point to at least one — but the days of the Pentium are past us now. If you're building a new computer to run any operating system other than DOS or Windows 3.1, take my advice and buy a Pentium II or Pentium III CPU and motherboard.

Although the original Pentium PC can indeed run Windows 98, the older architecture simply isn't fast enough or advanced enough to offer anywhere near the performance of a Pentium II or Pentium III computer. Sure, these older components are much cheaper now, and you can save a considerable amount of money; it's likely, however, that you'll start looking for an upgrade CPU quite soon, and a Pentium-socketed motherboard doesn't accept a Pentium II or Pentium III CPU (both of which use Slot 1 motherboards).

If you're building a computer from the ground up, buy the fastest Pentium II or Pentium III processor you can afford; you'll thank yourself for many months to come!

Never Depend on Floppies

Floppy disks and important data just don't mix. Floppies are very susceptible to magnetic fields (never store them on top of a speaker or your PC's case), they have a low *shelf life* (the amount of time you can reliably store a floppy disk and then retrieve data from it), the exchange of floppies can spread viruses, they're easily mixed up or mislaid (even if you label them), and occasionally one computer just plain can't read floppy disks formatted on another computer. In my years as a computer technician, I've felt the pain of folks who had lost valuable data by trusting in those familiar floppies.

Don't get me wrong: Floppies are fine for carrying a program or two in your pocket or sending a program through the mail — as long as you have a backup copy of that data on your hard drive. From time to time, I even save a document on a floppy as a simple backup for a day or so — but I don't expect with absolute certainty to be able to read that document after six months.

If you need to store your data away from your computer or send it to someone else, *please* consider something more reliable, like a Zip or Jaz drive, or back up that information to DAT tape. The best solution, however, is a favorite of mine: A CD recorder can archive information for more than ten years at 650MB on each disc, and CD-ROMs are a much more permanent data-retrieval system than any magnetic method. (I discuss CD recorders in Chapter 8, and Chapter 7 contains more information about Zip and Jaz drives.)

Help Stamp Out Unnecessary Passwords!

Password protection is appropriate for sensitive files stored in an office network environment or connecting with your Internet Service Provider; however, unnecessary passwords you've assigned to Zip disks, backup tapes, screen savers, archived files in .ZIP format, and even BIOS passwords that don't allow your PC to boot are nothing but trouble for your typical home computer owner. If you have no reason to be overly cautious about your computer and its data, for heaven's sake, *don't assign passwords you don't need!*

Why do I despise unnecessary passwords? I've received countless calls from friends, family members, and consulting clients who can't retrieve data from a disk or an archive file (or log on to their own computer) because they've either forgotten the password or typed it incorrectly. In effect, you're locked out from accessing your own data — and, in the worst-case scenario, all you can do is reformat that backup tape or that Zip disk and bid that data goodbye. (And I can tell you that your memories of lost data will last a long, long time.)

Honor Thy Friend's Copyright

Computers and the Internet are the best tools ever invented by mankind for accessing and sharing information across the entire globe — and this dynamic duo also makes it extremely easy to cut and paste your way to plagiarism and copyright violations. If an image or document is not your original work, you *must* be careful (and that includes quoting — even simple phrases).

For a quick rundown on the basics of copyrights, jump to the Chapter 14 sidebar "The lazy person's guide to copyrights."

Your PC Is Not a Kindergarten

If you're a parent, you probably want your children computer-literate by the time they graduate from elementary school — and it's true, the earlier your children are exposed to a computer, the more comfortable they will be with a computer later in life.

However, I recommend that you keep very small children away from your computer until they're older; a good minimum age is about four years old. An active toddler can do a surprising amount of damage to a typical PC: jamming floppies into drives the wrong way, spilling juice or milk on the keyboard or the case, yanking on wires and cords, slapping the monitor (I've even seen a CD-ROM drive with peanut butter inside). To a 1- or 2-year-old, your PC is just another interesting toy with lights, and that child won't be learning anything useful about the computer for a while. Keep your computer safe until the kids are ready.

Don't Jump on the Pirate Ship

Programs illegally copied or distributed are referred to as *pirated* software, and you can download commercial software — like games, applications, and utilities — from a large network of Web sites and Internet newsgroups.

Pirating software just isn't worth it; you don't get a manual or technical support, and you may very well be getting more than you bargained for if you download that pirated copy of Photoshop or Quake III. Why? Besides being illegal, pirated software is an invitation for disaster; many renegade computer programmers use pirated software to distribute viruses and Trojan horse programs. (Although a *Trojan horse* program is described as a useful application and may even look like one while it's running, it destroys data on your computer).

Support the authors of shareware and the companies that produce the best commercial software: Buy their products, and don't pirate them!

Keep Out of Monitors and Power Supplies

Most of the components used in your computer are sealed — for example, your computer's hard drive — and even if you could open them, you'd never be able to repair them. Building a computer is a task of *assembly,* and you should never have to disassemble anything — besides, of course, removing components you're scavenging from an older computer.

However, two of these components deserve an even wider berth: your computer's power supply and your computer monitor. *Never attempt to open the case on either of these parts* because they can be repaired only by computer technicians or sent back to the factory, and they can be quite dangerous if plugged in while uncovered.

Don't Lease a PC for the Long Haul

Some mail-order companies and larger computer chain stores allow you to lease a computer for a monthly fee. If you need a computer for only a couple of months, leasing is fine — however, leasing a computer for more than six months is not a very good idea. PCs depreciate in value so quickly and advance in technology so fast that your leased computer will be significantly less powerful and worth less within just a year or two.

By building your own computer, you end up with the most power for the money, and you can continue to upgrade your PC to stretch its useful life over many years.

Keep Track of Version Numbers

If you're a novice at buying computer software for your new PC, pay close attention to the version numbers of the software you're buying. Often, you see expensive applications being sold for far less than the "going rate" in one catalog or on one Web site — for example, an integrated office suite of applications may be advertised at $500 at one store, but only $250 at another. Usually, the store selling the software for much less is actually selling an older version (for example, the more expensive office suite may be Version 7.0, and the cheaper version may be Version 6.0). The version number is usually listed in the advertisement, but can be stuck down at the bottom.

If you're unsure about the latest version number of a particular program, call the store and ask or connect to the manufacturer's Web site to determine the latest version.

Part VI
Appendixes

The 5th Wave   By Rich Tennant

"HOLD ON, THAT'S NOT A PROGRAM ERROR, IT'S
JUST A BOOGER ON THE SCREEN."

In this part . . .

You can find two helpful appendixes: a comparison of the popular operating systems now available for the PC and a glossary of all those awful computer acronyms, part names, and terms you don't want to memorize.

Appendix A

Choosing Your Operating System

● ●

*M*ost computer owners run whatever operating system came with their computer or whatever's the hot topic in this month's *CompuSmarts* magazine — whether it's right for them or not. Running under the wrong operating system is as bad as using the wrong workbench to build a piece of furniture: You'll probably get the job done eventually, but it will take much longer than it should and your finished work won't look as good.

How do you determine which operating system is right for you? In this appendix, I show you the good points and bad points of each major operating system used on PCs today: Is it fast enough? Stable enough? Does it support the applications you want? Most important, does it make life on the computer easier for you?

Become Your Own Consultant!

You may be asking yourself "Why don't I just run what everyone else runs?" It's true — today's common PC operating system of choice is Windows 98, and it does a great job for 70 percent or so of all the PCs around the world. But what if your needs fit in the other 30 percent? That's why you need to become your own consultant to choose an operating system. Heck, if you want to make things as authentic as possible, you can even charge yourself a tremendous amount of money. (Just don't try claiming it on your taxes.)

Consider these points when you're choosing an operating system:

- ✔ Are you looking for the fastest operating system? If so, score one point for the more popular 32-bit operating systems on your list: Windows 98, Windows Me, Windows NT, Windows 2000, and Linux. These platforms load programs and data faster because they improve on many of the shortcomings of older operating systems, provide native file systems (more on this later), and were designed for faster CPUs, like your Pentium II or Pentium III. DOS, the antique of the crowd, is naturally significantly slower.

- ✔ Do you want a *graphical user interface?* In terms mere technomortals can understand, do you want to use a mouse and icons to run programs or drag and drop a file on your printer? If so, you should lean toward any version of Windows, OS/2, and Linux (with a graphical shell). However, don't automatically assume that a graphical user interface is faster and easier for everything you do on a computer. Those of us who have been working with computers for many years often find the DOS command line better for many tasks — for example, you can open a DOS box from within Windows 95 to move files from one directory to another.

✔ Is stability a factor? Does your application need to keep running day after day, solid as a rock? If so, consider Windows NT, Windows 2000, and Linux/Unix, which are the most stable platforms; they're least likely to lock up (or, as computer types like to say, *crash*). OS/2 arrives third, DOS follows in fourth place, and the remaining Windows platforms unfortunately hit the finish line in last place.

✔ Will your new computer be running an older DOS program as its primary application? If so, consider leaving DOS as your operating system and don't upgrade (especially if the program will be controlling any special hardware, such as a light pen, cash drawer, or digital sensor). Although all versions of Windows and OS/2 enable you to access DOS through a special window, none of these newer platforms is as completely compatible as the real McCoy! This is the reason that many small businesses are still running PCs with DOS: The application they're running was written in the early 1990s, and because the computer is used for only that one application, there's no need for an upgrade to another operating system. (That's if the program recognizes that you've crossed into Y2K, of course — thank goodness *that* whole thing is behind us!)

Programs that were written years ago and are bugfree and dependable are called *legacy applications* — for instance, a movie rental shop might be using a checkout program and database written for DOS a few years ago. Sometimes it's better to follow the old programmer's adage: "If it ain't broke, don't mess with it!"

✔ Do you want your operating system to automatically configure new hardware whenever possible? If so, Windows 98, Windows Me, and Windows 2000 easily win the race, and Windows NT has most of this functionality. OS/2 comes in a distant third, and DOS and Linux/Unix don't finish at all; they offer no automatic configuration of any kind.

✔ Are you looking for the operating system offering the most applications and software? In that case, the definite winners are Windows 98 and Windows Me, which can run programs written for Windows 3.1 as well as most DOS programs. Windows NT can run most Windows 95 software, but it has more compatibility problems with DOS and Windows 3.1 applications. OS/2 can run OS/2 applications, Windows 3.1 programs, and DOS programs. At the end of the line are DOS and Linux/Unix, which can run only applications written especially for them (both Linux and Unix can run emulators for other operating systems, though).

✔ Will your new computer be used as a Web server, an intranet machine, or an Internet firewall? The platforms to watch are Linux, Unix, Windows 2000, and Windows NT. These operating systems include the low-level security features needed for an Internet server; in fact, the Internet was built on a backbone of Unix computers, and most machines carrying the Internet's digital traffic still use Linux or Unix. (This explains why Internet old-timers know all those cryptic Archie, Gopher, and FTP commands by heart!) If you prefer a graphical Internet platform, Windows 2000 has a special server version, and Microsoft offers a number of Windows NT- and Windows 2000-specific Internet applications for the network administrator.

✔ Will your new computer need to run on an office network? Give the nod to all versions of Windows and OS/2; all these platforms have built-in networking capabilities with automatic configuration. Linux/Unix and DOS can also network, although they require more work — and DOS needs additional software to run a network as well.

"But, Wait — I Collect Operating Systems!"

Many computer owners don't fit into one of those nice, neat slots that indicate precisely which operating system is the right one. I should know — I'm one myself. Because you can run only one operating system on a PC, does that mean you need more than one computer? Perhaps more than one of *everything*? (Hey, this could cost you a million dollars by the time you're through!)

Back up a second there. You *can* actually run more than one operating system on a single computer. Windows NT, Windows 2000, Linux, and OS/2 have a basic *multiboot* configuration built-in; in plain English, that means you can select from multiple operating systems when you turn on your PC. For example, you can select whether you want to run Windows 98 or Windows NT. This is the way to go if you sometimes need to run a particular OS/2 application, but you'd rather run Windows NT most of the time.

There's an even better way to take care of a multiboot computer, though: The classy way to choose an operating system at startup is with a commercial multiboot utility, like System Commander 2000, from V Communications (www.systemcommander.com). These programs keep track of all the different files you need for maintaining each operating system; you can even set up your hard drive with individual partitions for each platform. If you boot into one particular platform more than the others, you can set up a default operating system that loads automatically after a certain number of seconds have elapsed. You can add or delete operating systems at any time, and the better multiboot programs are easy to use.

If you've decided to run a multiboot configuration, make sure that you have more than enough hard drive real estate to comfortably hold all the operating systems you'll use (as well as the applications and assorted other junk that normally fills up a hard drive). For example, if you want to run a computer with both Windows 98 and Linux or Unix, you need a minimum of 5 or 6 gigabytes for an average installation.

DOS: The Old Workhorse Lives On

Name: DOS
Aliases: PC-DOS, MS-DOS, Pokey, Dinosaur
Learning curve: Novice to intermediate
Architecture: 16-bit, character-based, limited graphics

Sure, the guy at the computer store says "DOS is dead." Don't forget that DOS was around for many, *many* years before Windows arrived on the scene, and a mind-boggling number of freeware, shareware, and commercial programs have been written for DOS. Those applications still do the job — they just don't look as pretty, and they don't have the icon-encrusted, drag-and-drop visual controls of a Windows program. Figure A-1 illustrates a common DOS application. Okay, I'll admit it: That's a great old DOS game I still play called DND.

```
Welcome to DND

For those who would'st tread within,
know ye well the best of your kin,
for fearsome battles have they fought,
to win a place among this lot.


Type 'L' for list of options
DND>List options

Options are:
C    Create a character
F    Find experience needed for a level
H    Go to help lesson
K    Kill off a character
L    List options
N    Re-read the notice file
P    Print all characters
Q    Exit
R    Run a character
S    Visit the store
DND>
```

Figure A-1:
DOS may be old, but it ain't dead yet, pardner.

DOS has many other advantages: As I mention earlier in this chapter, many computer techie types who have been around for years find it faster to type commands than select them from a menu. DOS doesn't take up acres of hard drive territory, so you don't lose 350MB of space on your drive just to hold the operating system. Because it's not a multitasking system, DOS is inherently more stable than Windows or OS/2 — however, you can run only a single program at one time, so don't expect to handle your finances while you're e-mailing Uncle Milton.

Finally, DOS really isn't all that hard to learn, especially if you keep a reference book handy. (How about *DOS For Dummies,* written by Dan Gookin and published by IDG Books Worldwide, Inc.?)

DOS summary: At this time, the only major continuing development of DOS software is for specialized hardware like point-of-sale terminals and scientific devices, and even that is fading away. However, DOS will be around for many years, and it will probably continue as the "least common denominator" operating system for the PC for the foreseeable future.

Has someone given you a copy of DOS labeled *PC-DOS?* That's the IBM version of DOS, but it's probably an older version; it doesn't have many of the newer commands, and it isn't as efficient. If you want your computer to run the fastest under DOS, make sure that you install the latest version (and, as far as anyone knows, the last version): MS-DOS 6.22.

OS/2: The Original 32-Bit Wonder

Name: OS/2
Aliases: Warp, the Best, the Lost Cause
Learning curve: Novice to intermediate
Architecture: 32-bit graphical user interface

OS/2 inspires weird feelings of love and hate in different people. It was the first 32-bit operating system generally available for the PC, and it was mutually developed by Microsoft and IBM as the next-generation replacement for DOS — and then those two megacorporations had their legendary tiff, and Microsoft dropped further development of OS/2 in favor of Windows.

Well, you can guess who won the marketing battle between OS/2 and Windows, and OS/2 has taken a back seat ever since. IBM continues to improve it, and OS/2 has a significant number of diehard fans who maintain that it's the best thing since the invention of socks. OS/2 does indeed have a different "look and feel" from Windows, but it uses most of the same windows, icons, and visual controls. Diehard fans of OS/2 have been known to band together all over the world, decrying the rest of the "Windows planet" as backward Philistines. The critics of OS/2 claim that it's dying a slow, painful death — but then again, the considerable pull of IBM in the business world practically guarantees that many businesses will use OS/2 on their workstation PCs as part of a True Big Blue system package.

If you like to run multiple DOS applications, you should know that OS/2 is considered a better multitasking system than Windows 98 when it comes to juggling DOS programs. OS/2 also supports Windows 3.*x* programs transparently, which means that Windows 3.0 and 3.1 programs can't tell that they're running under OS/2. (However, OS/2 does not run programs specifically written for Windows 95 or Windows 98.)

Although experts differ in opinion, most technoids feel that OS/2 is slightly more stable than Windows 98, but not as stable as Windows NT, Windows 2000, or Linux/Unix when it comes to multitasking. It's also an easy operating system for beginners, with plenty of online help close at hand. Figure A-2 illustrates a snapshot from an OS/2 session.

OS/2 summary: As with DOS, most people in the computer world think OS/2 a dead end. Regardless, OS/2 heretics around the globe will continue to run the "wrong" operating system for as long as IBM supports it.

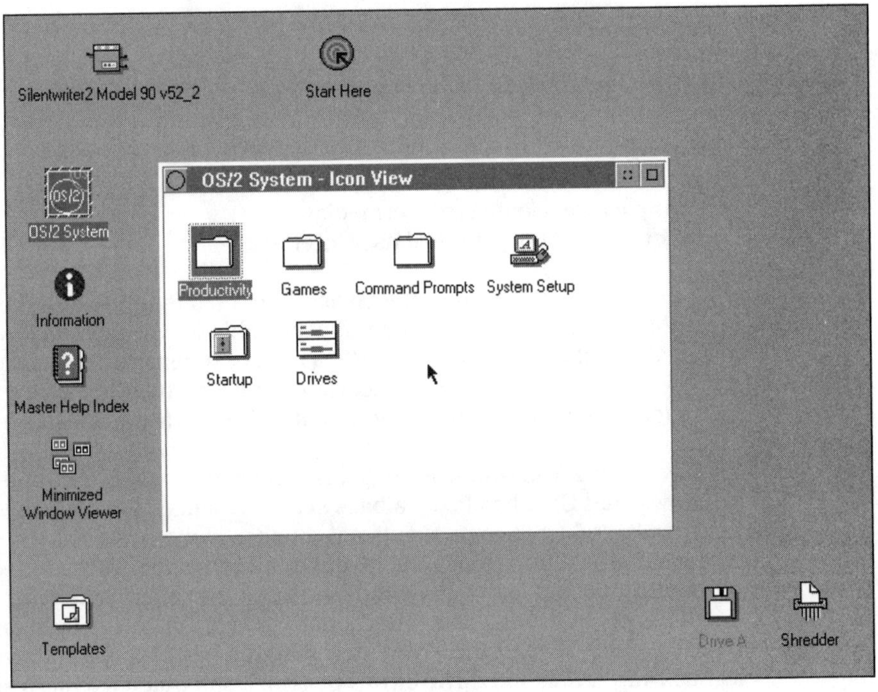

Figure A-2:
OS/2 offers a slightly different take on a graphical operating system.

Windows 95: Thanks for the Memories

Name: Windows 95
Aliases: Win95, WinDoze, the Mac lookalike
Learning curve: Novice to intermediate
Architecture: 16-bit/32-bit graphical user interface

Windows 95 has finally passed the crown to its offspring, Windows 98 and
Windows Me, so I don't go into great detail here. Suffice it to say that
Windows 95 doesn't have the driver support for today's hardware (majorly
important), it doesn't have the robust Internet and multimedia support of
Windows 98 and Windows Me (majorly important), and it doesn't have many
minor perks that have been added to Windows 98 and Windows Me (minorly
important).

However, if you've been given a copy of Windows 95, you can upgrade to 98
or Windows Me in the future, and virtually all Windows software still runs on
Windows 95. In other words, it makes a good start (and yes, it does take up
significantly less room on your hard drive than newer versions of Windows).

If you do decide to run Windows 95, remember that the first versions of the
operating system didn't support USB. If you have USB hardware, you need
the updated version of Windows 95 (called OSR2 or Windows 95 B by most
tech-types), which includes USB support.

Windows 95 summary: Although I can't believe it, it's finally time to wave
goodbye to Windows 95. Thanks, old friend.

Windows 98: The King of the Hill

Name: Windows 98
Aliases: Win98, WinDoze: The Next Generation
Learning curve: Novice to intermediate
Architecture: 16-bit/32-bit graphical user interface

There's no doubt about it: Windows 98 is now installed on more PCs than any
other operating system. Why mess with success? Like Windows 95 before it,
Windows 98 is universally supported, it runs 32-bit software, and it can still
run older 16-bit applications, so you have the largest base of programs to
choose from within the list of operating systems. So what improvements have
been added by the Microsoft crew to Windows 98 over Windows 95? The
major change is in the addition of Internet Explorer version 4 as both your

Web browser and your user interface, which makes using your computer more like surfing the Web. For example, you have to click only once on an icon within your desktop to run it, menus feature Forward and Back buttons, and you can add Web pages and Internet addresses to your Start menu on the Taskbar. Internet directories and search engines now appear on the Find menu on the taskbar. Your desktop background can even include HTML, ActiveX, and Java applets, practically making it a Web page itself. Figure A-3 is a typical Windows 98 screen shot.

If you're used to Windows 95 and you're stubborn, you can turn off certain parts of the new interface (or all of it, if you want to keep your Windows 95 functionality).

As somebody famous once said, however, "Beauty isn't just skin deep" — are there real changes behind the scenes in Windows 98? The answer is a big No, which is both good and bad news. On the good side, you don't encounter any compatibility problems when you run Windows 95 programs under Windows 98 — but Windows 98 isn't tremendously faster or more stable than Windows 95. When it comes to how programs run and the basic skills you need to use them, Windows 98 is almost identical to its older relative.

Windows 98 is easy to learn for the novice. As in OS/2, online help is plentiful and easy to access.

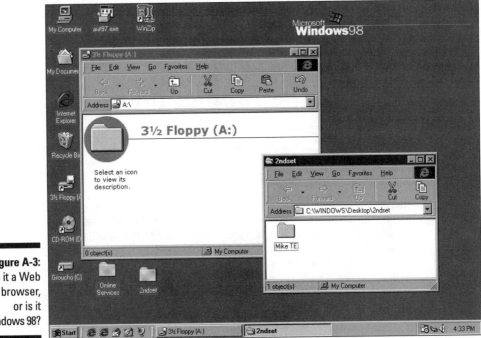

Figure A-3:
Is it a Web browser, or is it Windows 98?

Conveniences abound within Windows 98. For example, the automatic hardware detection it provides makes adding a new modem, printer, or scanner to your system much easier. Plug the new device in, or install it within your computer's case, reboot, and Windows 98 will likely recognize the device automatically. Windows 98 is especially fond of Plug and Play devices, and in some cases it can even configure a proper DMA or IRQ value for a sound card (see Chapter 9 for more information) or select a proper COM port for an internal modem. (Chapter 10 provides all the details.)

Windows 98 also includes built-in support for TCP/IP — the communications protocol used to connect to the Web and the Internet — as well as excellent all-around support for LAN connections (for more about networking, see Chapter 12). Game players will enjoy DirectX, the graphics engine that enables Windows games to use all the fancy features of your 3D video card. (Chapter 6 tells you all about video cards.) If you're interested in multimedia, Windows 98 includes support for digital video (in AVI format) and digital audio (in WAV format).

You also get a number of utilities and tools that help you keep your computer running in top shape, including a disk defragmenter, a scanning program that can check your computer's hard drive for errors, a scheduler that can automatically launch programs whenever you specify, and a backup program that helps you back up the data on your computer from time to time.

The downside? Although Windows 98 can run most of the same 32-bit applications as Windows NT and Windows 2000, it doesn't have their server-level security features — there have been a number of well-publicized loopholes in Windows 98 security — and Windows 98 is considered less stable and a little easier to crash than Windows NT and Windows 2000.

If you're a power user, you may be interested in a number of smaller tweaks that Microsoft has made to Windows 98 — tweaks that may float your boat. For example, Windows 98 includes USB support, you can run multiple monitors with different displays now, the entire computer takes less time to shut down, and you have built-in support for ISDN communications, bonded analog modem connections, and DVD drives. You can also enjoy the addition of FAT32 (an improved hard drive structure that allows for larger partitions and more efficient data transfer).

Just like its older brother, Windows 98 is a drive hog: Expect it to gobble up at least 250MB of your hard drive for a full installation, and that figure is bound to rise exponentially as you add programs and features. Whatever happened to the days when you could comfortably fit everything on a 40MB drive? (Oh, I remember — see the section entitled "DOS: The Old Workhorse Lives On," earlier in this appendix.)

Windows 98 summary: Windows 98 has taken the place of Windows 95 as it is bundled with new computers, and it's a great operating system for novices.

Windows Me: The Windows of Tomorrow

Name: Windows Me (short for Millennium Edition)
Aliases: Me, WinDoze WhyME?, Microsoft Bob II
Learning curve: Novice to intermediate
Architecture: 16-bit/32-bit graphical user interface

Windows Me — sounds faintly disturbing, doesn't it? At the time this chapter was written, the final copies of Windows Me were starting to roll off the assembly lines, although 98 still reigned supreme. What does Windows Me have to offer? Here's a list of the highlights you can expect:

- ✔ To start, Windows Me includes better support for digital video and audio: fancier media players, more supported formats, improved Internet search functions (you can finally locate that Brenda Lee song you wanted to hear), and better support for multimedia hardware, like DVD drives.

- ✔ Windows Me also makes scanning or importing photos from a digital camera easier than ever. You can now import pictures directly into your applications, including e-mail, your word processor, and printing software.

- ✔ It includes an improved version of DirectX, the high-performance gaming software, which provides even better and faster 3-D graphics and authentic surround sound. (Naturally, you need a sound card capable of surround sound to enjoy those laser rifles all around you.)

- ✔ You lose the option to boot directly to the MS-DOS prompt. If you're an old-timer like I am, that will sadden you somewhat ("get with it, Mark!"), but you can still open a DOS box in Windows Me.

- ✔ A new system restore feature automatically backs up your critical system files every 10 hours at a minimum, making it easier to restore your operating system if something really nasty happens.

So, do I recommend Windows Me? For most first-time computer owners, I'd have to say Yes! Like Windows 98 before it, Windows Me is an incremental update to the original Windows 95 — but I think that it's a good idea to upgrade if you use digital audio and video, if you work with your scanner or camera quite a bit, or if you're a heavy player of the latest games (see Figure A-4).

Windows Me summary: The next minor evolutionary step in the continuing development of Windows 95.

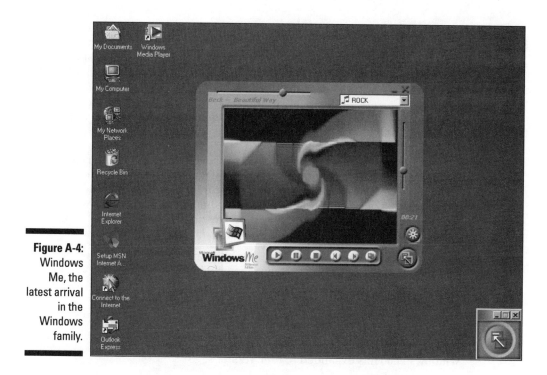

Figure A-4:
Windows
Me, the
latest arrival
in the
Windows
family.

Windows NT and Windows 2000: Microsoft's First String

Name: Windows NT, Windows 2000
Aliases: WinNT, Windows 2K, Neat, Windows with Teeth
Learning curve: Intermediate to advanced
Architecture: 32-bit graphical user interface

Windows NT is the preferred power user's platform for the PC, although it demands the best of everything to run at thoroughbred speed: A typical NT computer has a minimum of 64MB of RAM, the fastest possible processor, and as many gigabytes of hard drive space as you can pack into your case. The newest breed of Windows NT, Windows 2000, prefers at least 128MB. Because Windows 2000 is based on NT, my description of NT also holds true for the newer version (wherever things are improved or different, I point them out).

Windows NT and Windows 2000 support multiple CPUs with SMP (short for *symmetric multiprocessing,* if you hadn't guessed); in English, this means that you actually can put more than one Pentium Pro, Pentium II, or Pentium III processor to work in the same machine! (Of course, your motherboard has to support SMP.)

Windows NT comes in two flavors, both of them much more expensive than any other operating system in this chapter:

- ✔ **NT Server:** Because of its bulletproof security features, NT Server is a popular choice for an office network, intranet, or Internet Web server. Unlike with Windows 98, you can monitor and manage multiple individual logins on an NT Server system simultaneously — in other words, Windows NT comes with everything you need for setting up a small office network with computers running Windows 95 or Windows 98.

- ✔ **NT Workstation:** If you want the stability and power of Windows NT without the server functionality, you can buy the workstation version and save several hundred dollars. NT Workstation is still more stable and more secure than Windows 95, and it's the operating system of choice for computer drafting, 3D modeling and rendering, scientific applications, and programming.

Windows 2000 has expanded to four versions:

- ✔ **The Server Family:** Windows 2000 is available in three server flavors — Server, Advanced Server, and Datacenter Server. With its minimum of 256MB of memory required and its starting price of more than $1,000, I wouldn't recommend any of the three for a typical home PC. Windows 2000 Server, however, fits the bill for a small office, just like its ancestor, NT Server.

- ✔ **Professional:** Professional is more akin to Windows NT — it's relatively cheap at a little more than $300, and it works with between 64MB and 128MB of RAM, so it's better suited for the average Athlon or Pentium III system. I would recommend the Professional edition of Windows 2000 for power users who need security, robust network connectivity, and speed. Figure A-5 illustrates Windows 2000 Professional.

As you can tell, the claim to fame for Windows 2000 is its exceptional stability, even when programmers are testing buggy or beta programs. If you're multitasking a number of programs and one locks up or exits unexpectedly, other programs running under Windows NT and Windows 2000 continue running without a problem.

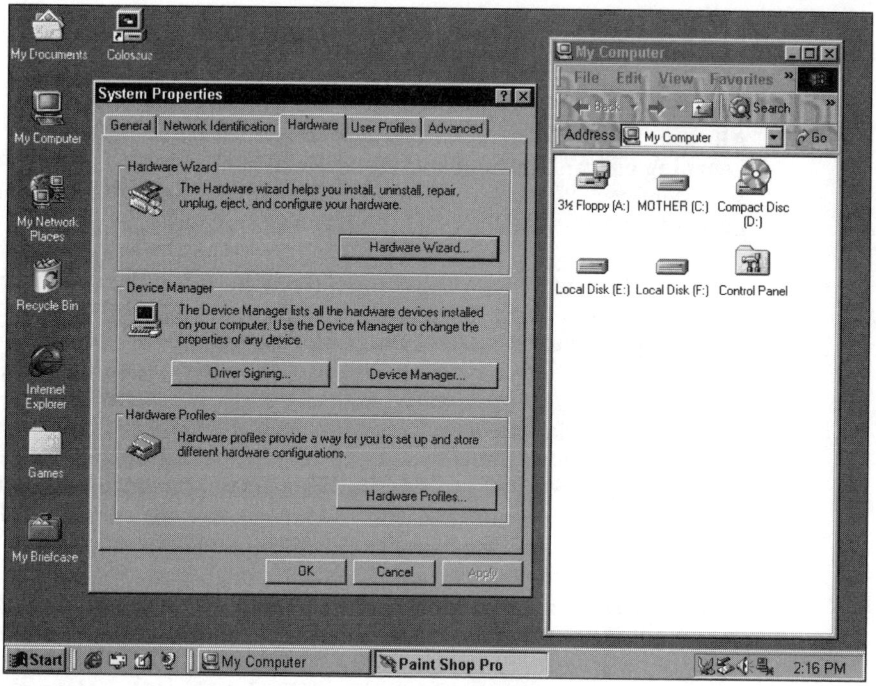

Figure A-5: The brave new power-user world of Windows 2000 Professional.

Moreover, Windows 2000 is significantly faster than Windows 98 (Microsoft claims that the program cruises along at speeds 30 percent faster than Windows 98 on PCs with 64MB of RAM or more), and it features better Internet connectivity and functionality than Windows NT.

Both Version 4.0 of Windows NT and Windows 2000 feature a user interface that's quite close to Windows 95, so if you're familiar with Windows 95, you can install NT without starting from scratch. However, NT doesn't have support for Plug and Play devices, and most of the automatic hardware detection featured in Windows 95 through Windows 2000 has been improved to include these features. Also, both Windows NT and Windows 2000 are nowhere near as compatible with 16-bit DOS applications as Windows 98; this shortcoming is especially true for DOS games, most of which simply don't run under Windows NT and Windows 2000. Consider these operating systems as strictly 32-bit.

Windows NT/Windows 2000 summary: If you can afford the high price, if your computer is powerful enough to keep up with the requirements of Windows NT or Windows 2000, and if you don't need to run many DOS applications, Windows NT is hard to beat.

Linux: It's Not Just for Technonerds!

Names: Linux
Aliases: "Freedom," "The Power Box," "Pain," "Torture"
Learning curve: Intermediate to Advanced
Architecture: 32- and 64-bit character-based interface (graphical shell available)

You can't discuss Linux without mentioning its roots: the commercial Unix operating system. Unix has a long history as an unbreakable and robust multitasking platform dating back long before a mouse was even imagined. In their pure form, both Linux and Unix are character-based like DOS, and their command language has inspired many a college computer student to change majors within minutes of first exposure. (However, both Linux and Unix can take advantage of graphical shells that can transform them into graphical operating systems.) Unix has airtight security features, and it's a highly efficient operating system that can even run on older 486 and slower Pentium computers with as little as 16MB of RAM.

Before the arrival of Windows NT, Unix machines were used as network servers, dial-up servers for modems, and other applications that required security, multitasking, and stability — and one of the primary uses of Unix over the past decade or so has been on the Internet. Many Internet functions familiar to researchers, scientists, and students today have their basis in Unix commands. Like Windows NT, Unix supports SMP (which I explain in the Windows NT section of this appendix), so you can put more than one CPU in your computer for extra processing power.

Now that you're more familiar with the history, let's talk about Linux. Why is it such a hot topic these days? A direct competitor with Windows NT and Windows 2000, Linux is basically a rewrite of Unix that has been created by programmers from around the world, working almost exclusively on the Internet to share code, specifications, and ideas. Linux is copyrighted, but it's free of charge for personal use (that's one of the reasons for its success right there)! It runs virtually all Unix software, and emulators that run most popular DOS and Windows programs are available for it. Linux can talk shop with most of the popular DOS, Windows, and Apple Macintosh networking protocols.

Linux is an Internet nut's dream. It provides built-in support for TCP/IP (the communications protocol used on the Internet), Ethernet networking (see Chapter 12 for networking details), ISDN communications (Chapter 13 discusses ISDN), and multiple modems, so it's no surprise that many Internet Service Providers and small businesses pick Linux to power their Internet and intranet servers. Linux handles FTP, Internet e-mail, the Web, and telnet with ease. Figure A-6 illustrates a typical Linux session; note, however, that this is "pure" Linux, without a graphical shell.

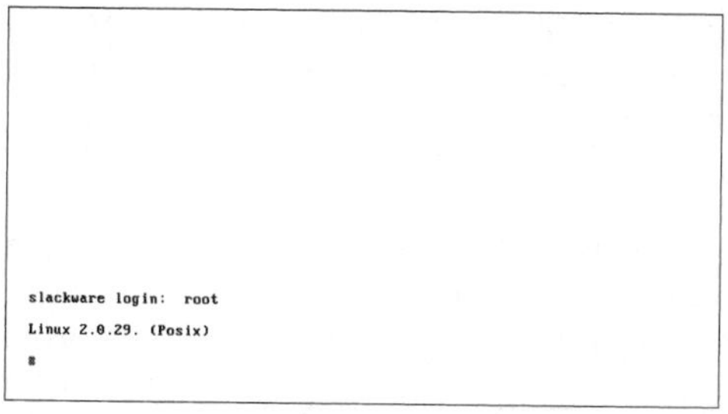

Figure A-6:
Without a
pretty GUI,
Linux is
character-
based
power.

```
slackware login: root
Linux 2.0.29. (Posix)
#
```

With a graphical shell, Linux suddenly blooms into a beautiful butterfly — figuratively, anyway — featuring a design very similar to Windows 98. Unlike with Windows 98, though, you can literally "pick your own interface" — a rapidly growing number of shells is available, each handling appearance and functionality differently (with variations both subtle and outrageous)! For example, your icons can rotate, your windows can "shimmer" in and out of existence, and menus can be rearranged at will. In my opinion, the most popular Linux GUI (short for *graphical user interface*), X, is practically as easy to use as Windows 98.

Linux has also proved popular because of its broad support and development among programmers. New hardware support is constantly added, and new technologies are often implemented within a few months. Linux is as well documented as Unix or Windows NT too, and programmers are constantly writing applications and utilities that run under Linux. In fact, the full source code package for the entire Linux operating system is available for the asking! (On the Web, you can download the source from the Linux Kernel Archives, at www.kernel.org.)

In the early years of its growth, Linux was also criticized for a lack of commercial programs — where were the applications and games that have built the Microsoft kingdom? Naturally, Linux can never enter the "mainstream" of the home computer world without these programs. And slowly, the times are a 'changin' — commercial-quality office applications like WordPerfect 8 and games like Quake are now on the Linux shelves at your local computer store (or even available free for the downloading)! Heck, I can remember when a store manager would have busted out laughing if you had even suggested a shelf dedicated to Linux.

Even with the appearance of mainstream applications, however, I can't say that Linux has reached the home market quite yet. Although new user-friendly commercial versions of Linux, like Red Hat and Caldera OpenLinux, now ship with simpler installation programs and automated setup and configuration utilities, the character-based behemoth that is Linux still hides underneath. If you're going to use the full power of Linux — for example, setting up the Apache Web server or an e-mail listserver or building your own network around Linux — then prepare to buy a shelf full of reference manuals. As a C programmer once told me, "It's not impossible to become a Linux guru, but you're going to lose weight!"

Unix and Linux summary: Linux is definitely not for the first-time computer novice, but if you've had experience with DOS, networking, or the character-based tools on the Internet, or if you've ever used Unix, it's certainly not impossible to figure out how to use it. Add to that factor the nonexistent price tag, the reduced system requirements, the arrival of new GUIs and commercial programs, the Windows NT-beating performance, and the constant development, and you can see why Linux is giving Windows NT and Windows 2000 stiff competition.

Before You Install Your Operating System

Because all these operating systems are installed differently, I can't give you one comprehensive set of instructions; however, here's a checklist of preparations that should make your installation run smoother, no matter which platform you choose:

- ✔ **Back up your hard drive:** If you've saved any data or created any documents that you'd hate to lose, back up your computer completely before installing your operating system.

- ✔ **Defragment your hard drive:** Many operating systems need to create large temporary disk files, and it's easier to create these huge files on a defragmented hard drive. Defragmenting optimizes all the files on a hard drive so that your computer can read them faster; if you're running MS-DOS 6.22, you can use the DEFRAG utility to defragment your drive. If you're running Windows 95 or Windows 98, click the Start button and choose Programs➪Accessories➪System Tools➪Disk Defragmenter.

- ✔ **Read the installation instructions:** Sure, your new operating system is designed to be installed by a kindergarten kid who's half asleep, but that doesn't excuse you from at least scanning the installation instructions.

- ✔ **Read the README file:** If something is important enough to include in a README file on the distribution disks (or CD-ROM), it may affect you during installation.

- ✔ **Keep your driver disks handy:** Although you've installed parts under DOS, you may need the specific drivers that came with your parts for your new operating system.

- ✔ **Don't forget a boot disk:** Make sure you have a bootable DOS disk handy just in case of dire emergency — the files on it should include FDISK.EXE and FORMAT.COM, and it should also load your CD-ROM drivers. Before you start a major installation, test this boot disk to make sure that it loads DOS and enables you to read your CD-ROM drive.

- ✔ **Impose on a friend:** Do you have a computer guru for a friend or a relative? Enlist an expert's help if you need it (especially if that person currently runs the same operating system you're installing).

- ✔ **Yell for the cavalry:** What do you do if something goes horribly wrong and you can't find anything about it in the installation guide? Don't panic! Keep the tech support number for the operating system close at hand; it should be located in the manual or the additional literature that accompanied your operating system.

Before calling for tech support: Have your serial number handy, and be prepared to answer questions about what type of computer you have and the parts you've installed. Be patient, too — tech support representatives for major software developers answer literally hundreds of calls per day, and you'll probably have to wait for at least five minutes before you speak to a human voice.

Appendix B

Glossary

access time: The amount of time a hard drive takes to read data. The faster the access time, the better.

adapter card: A circuit board that plugs into your motherboard to provide your computer with additional functionality; for example, a video adapter card plugs into your motherboard and enables your computer to display text and graphics on your monitor.

AGP: Acronym for Accelerated Graphics Port, a bus standard for video cards that offers graphics performance even better than "ancient" video cards using the PCI bus.

application: A task you perform on the computer; for example, an Internet application is a program that performs some useful function while your computer is connected to the Internet.

Athlon: The fastest processor from Advanced Micro Devices (more popularly called AMD). The Athlon runs significantly faster than a Pentium III of the same speed and offers the best performance for power-user applications and computer games.

AT-class: An older, standard set of dimensions for a PC's motherboard and case derived from the original IBM AT-class computer. If your PC will use an AT-class motherboard, you must also have an AT-class case. AT-class cases and hardware are rapidly disappearing as ATX-class cases and hardware become more and more popular.

ATX-class: The new standard set of dimensions and features for a PC's motherboard and case, with support for standard built-in ports on the motherboard and simpler connectors for power, case switches, and case lights. If you buy an ATX-class motherboard for your computer, you must also use an ATX-class case.

bank: A set of two sockets for RAM chips on your motherboard; most motherboards have at least two RAM banks. Each bank should typically be filled by two of the same type of RAM chips.

BBS: Acronym for *bulletin board system*, an automated online service you can call with your modem. These systems offer message bases, file downloading, and games. Most cities have several local bulletin-board systems, and most BBSs are free to use.

BIOS: Acronym for *basic input-output system*. Your PC's BIOS controls many low-level functions of your computer, like keeping track of your hard drive's characteristics and what type of monitor you're using. The BIOS resides on one or two computer chips on your motherboard.

bit: The smallest unit of information used by a computer; can have a value of either 1 or 0.

bonding: A technique for combining two ISDN data channels or two analog modem connections to double the throughput (as a single connection).

BPS: Acronym for *bits per second*, a common method of measuring the speed of a modem. Today's high-speed modems are usually measured in Kbps, or kilobytes per second, as in 33.6 Kbps.

BRI: Acronym for *basic rate interface*. A standard consumer configuration for an ISDN line, providing two data channels that can carry separate sessions or act as a combined session for faster throughput.

bus: A slot on your motherboard that accepts adapter cards. Bus slots on Pentium motherboards are generally either 16-bit ISA slots or 32-bit PCI slots.

byte: A group of eight bits that represents a single character of text stored in your computer's RAM.

cable modem: An external device that connects your computer to your cable TV company's coax cable. A cable modem is a requirement for connecting to the Internet through cable access. Although a cable modem really isn't anything like a traditional analog modem, it looks like one.

cache: A special bank of memory that holds data which is often used or which will be required in a few nanoseconds. Storing data in a cache speeds up the operation of your PC because the data doesn't have to be retrieved from RAM or your hard drive. Many components have a cache, including your CPU, your hard drive, your motherboard, and your CD recorder.

case: The metal enclosure that surrounds your computer and holds all its parts. The case, typically held on with screws or thumbwheels, may have a separate cover that you can remove to add or remove parts; other cases are one-piece and simply open up.

CD-R: (Also called a *CD recorder.*) A CD-ROM drive that also enables you to record your own CD-ROMs, which hold computer data, and audio CDs, which hold music. Discs made with a standard CD recorder can be read on any CD-ROM drive, but they can be recorded only once.

CD-ROM drive: An internal device that can read both CD-ROM discs (which store computer programs and files) and audio CDs (which store music). A typical CD-ROM disc can hold as much as 680 megabytes of data. CD-ROM drives cannot write to the disc; they can only read data.

CD-RW: A CD recorder that enables you to record and rerecord CDs and CD-ROMs repeatedly. Discs made with a CD-RW drive cannot be read on most standard CD-ROM drives.

Celeron: A less expensive version of the Pentium II CPU produced by Intel for the home market. Although a Celeron chip lacks the performance of a full Pentium II of the same speed, it's still a very popular processor for low-end PCs.

CGA: Acronym for *color graphics adapter,* the original IBM PC color standard. Programs with CGA support could display a stunning four colors at a time.

client-server: A network in which computers act as clients and retrieve information from a central server computer. Server computers can also hold common shared resources, such as modems or CD-ROM drives.

CMOS: Acronym for *complementary metal oxide semiconductor.* CMOS RAM stores configuration data about your PC's hardware, even after your PC is turned off.

coax: Standard Ethernet cable (also called *10Base-T*), commonly used on simple peer-to-peer networks.

color depth: A reference to the number of colors in an image; popular color depths are 16 colors, 256 colors, 64,000 colors, and 16 million colors.

COM port: A numeric designator for a serial port that uses standard hardware settings. Most PC serial ports can be set to one of four COM ports: COM1 through COM4.

Common Sense Assembly: The technique of preventing mistakes during the assembly of a computer by using your common sense. First postulated by the author of this book.

component: The technoid word for a piece of computer hardware; a computer part.

compression: The use of a mathematical formula to reduce the amount of disk space taken up by a file, a video clip, or an image. Some compression schemes can reproduce the original exactly; other compression schemes lose some detail from the original. Modems also use compression to reduce the time necessary to transfer a file.

CPU: Acronym for *central processing unit*, the chip that acts as your computer's brain; the CPU performs the commands provided by the programs you run.

DAT: Acronym for *digital audiotape*; a high-speed tape drive used to back up the data on your hard drive. DAT backup tapes, which can hold anywhere from 2 to 24 gigabytes of data on a single tape, are the most reliable backup drives on the market. Most companies with networks use DAT drives to safe-guard their data by backing up nightly — and you too should back up the data on your hard drive regularly.

digital camera: A camera that looks and operates much like a traditional film camera, except that its finished images are uploaded directly to a computer rather than processed into photographs. Digital cameras are more expensive than their film cousins.

DIMM: Acronym for *dual inline memory module*. A specific type of RAM chip usually used with Pentium II and Pentium III computers.

DIP switches: A bank of tiny, sliding (or rocker) switches that enable you to set different features on your motherboard, some components, and many adapter cards. Use the tip of a pen to slide or push the switches into their proper sequence.

DirectX: An extension to Windows 95 and Windows 98 that enables fast animation and graphics display within game and multimedia programs.

distinctive ring: A service from your telephone company that enables more than one telephone number to use the same physical telephone line.

DOS: Acronym for *disk operating system*. One of the oldest operating systems still in general use on PCs. This character-based operating system requires you to type commands to run programs.

dot pitch: The amount of space between pixels on a monitor; the smaller the dot pitch, the clearer and more detailed the display.

DPMS: Acronym for *display power management signaling*, a feature that enables your computer to power down your monitor after a specified period of inactivity. This feature helps save both energy and money.

drawing tablet: Looks like a larger version of a touchpad. Although the drawing tablet can be used as a pointing device, it is typically used by graphic artists for freehand drawing within graphics applications.

DSL: : Acronym for Digital Subscriber Line. A high-speed connection to the Internet offering top speeds, around 4 Mbps to 8 Mbps. Although DSL uses regular copper telephone line and is "always on," it's not available in many areas of the country.

DSL modem: An external device that connects your computer to a DSL line. The modem looks like a traditional analog telephone modem, but delivers data much faster.

DVD: Acronym for *digital video disc,* the replacement for the older CD-ROM disc. A single DVD disc can hold anywhere from 4.7GB to 17GB. DVD discs can hold both computer data and movies in MPEG format.

EDO: Acronym for *extended data output.* A standard type of RAM chip used on older Pentium-class computers that provided faster operation than older types of RAM.

EGA: Acronym for *enhanced graphics adapter.* Although the EGA standard's 16 colors and higher resolution improved greatly on the original CGA standard, EGA has been completely replaced by the VGA and SVGA standards.

EIDE: Acronym for *enhanced integrated drive electronics,* the standard hard drive and device interface technology now in use on PCs. An EIDE adapter card can handle as many as four EIDE devices, which can include additional hard drives, tape backup drives, and CD recorders.

Ethernet: A network topology in which data is broadcast across the network. Although Ethernet is generally less efficient than other network architectures, it's less complex and less expensive to maintain.

external: A type of peripheral or device that sits outside your computer's case and is connected by a cable — for example, an external modem.

fax modem: A type of modem that has all the functionality of a standard modem but can also exchange faxes with either another fax modem or a standard fax machine.

female: A cable connector with holes that accept the pins on a male connector.

fingertip mouse: A pointing device using a small button; to move objects on-screen, you push the button in the direction you want. Fingertip mice are common on laptop computers.

firewall: A program or device designed to protect network data from being retrieved by a computer hacker. Most Internet and Web sites use a firewall to provide security for company data.

FireWire: The popular name for the IEEE 1394 high-performance serial bus connection standard, developed by Apple. A FireWire connection is similar to a USB connection: Devices can be added or removed without rebooting the computer, and you can daisy-chain as many as 63 FireWire devices from a single port. Because of a FireWire port's high data-transfer rate of 100 megabits per second and its ability to control digital devices, it is especially well suited for connecting digital videocameras and external hard drives to your PC.

flash BIOS: An advanced BIOS chipset that can be updated with new features by running an upgrade program (usually available from the manufacturer of your motherboard).

flat-panel monitor: A monitor that uses liquid crystal display (LCD) technology rather than a traditional tube. LCD monitors have been used on laptop computers for years, and they're becoming more popular for full-size desktop computers. A flat panel is much thinner than a traditional tube monitor and uses less electricity.

floppy drive: Stored inside your computer, a floppy drive can save program and data files to floppy disks, which can be stored as backups or loaded on other PCs. Computers now use 3½-inch floppy disks that can store as much as 1.44 megabytes of data on a single disk.

game port: A port for connecting joysticks and game peripherals. Game ports can be installed separately, although most sound cards have a game port built-in.

gigabyte: A unit of data equal to 1,024 megabytes.

hacker: A computer user who attempts to access confidential information or steal data across the Internet or a network without authorization. Hacking is a criminal offense.

hard drive (or hard disk): A component that usually fits internally inside your case. Your hard drive acts as permanent storage for your programs and data, enabling you to save and delete files. Unlike the RAM in your computer, your hard drive does not lose data when you turn off your PC.

infrared port: An external lens that allows fast, wireless transfer of data between your PC and another computer equipped with a compatible infrared port.

inkjet: A method of printing in which ink is injected from a cartridge onto paper to create text and graphics on the page. Color inkjet printers are relatively inexpensive.

interface: A technoid term that refers to the method of connecting a peripheral to your computer. For example, printers use a parallel port interface; hard drives use either an EIDE interface or a SCSI interface. Some interface types refer to adapter cards, while others refer to ports and cables.

interlaced: An interlaced monitor is redrawn every other line, resulting in a noticeable flicker.

internal: A component you install inside your computer's case — for example, a hard drive or an internal modem.

ISA: Acronym for *industry standard architecture*. ISA bus slots accept 16-bit adapter cards to add functionality to your computer. ISA cards are typically slower than PCI adapter cards.

ISDN: Acronym for *integrated services digital network*. An ISDN line provides a true digital connection between two computers. ISDN connections to the Internet are much faster than standard analog modem connections, with speeds as fast as 512 Kbps.

Jaz drive: A removable cartridge hard drive; each cartridge can store either one or two gigabytes of computer data, which you can remove, take with you, and use on any other Jaz drive. A Jaz drive is as fast as a standard hard drive, but requires a SCSI interface.

joystick: An input device (for games) that's similar to the control stick used by an airplane pilot. Predictably, joysticks are usually used by game players who enjoy flight simulators.

jumper: A set of two or more pins that can be shorted with a tiny plastic-and-metal crossover. Jumpers are commonly found on motherboards, components like hard drives, and adapter cards.

keyboard port: Every PC has a keyboard port, where the cable from your keyboard connects to your computer. Keyboard ports come in two sizes: the older, larger port and a newer, smaller port. You can buy an adapter to make any keyboard fit either size of keyboard port.

kilobyte: A unit equal to 1,024 bytes.

LAN: Acronym for Local Area Network. *See* network.

laser: A printer technology in which a powder is bonded to paper to create text and graphics. Laser printers are fast and produce excellent print quality.

Linux: A 32-bit operating system similar to Unix, popular on the Internet for use with Web servers. Unlike Unix, Linux is freeware and its source code is available.

male: A cable connector with pins that fit into the holes on a female connector.

megabyte: A unit equal to 1,024KB.

megahertz: The frequency (or speed) of a CPU as measured in millions of cycles per second.

MIDI: Acronym for *musical instrument digital interface.* The MIDI hardware standard enables computers of all types to play the same music and enables interaction between the computer and the instrument. MIDI music files are common on the Internet.

MIDI port: Enables you to connect a MIDI-compatible musical instrument to your computer. Notes you play on the instrument can be recorded on your PC, or your PC can be set to "play" the instrument all by itself.

MMX: Acronym for *multimedia extensions,* an enhanced instruction set offered on many original Intel Pentium processors (and on all Pentium II and Pentium III CPUs) that speeds up the display of multimedia, digital video, and 3D graphics.

modem: A computer device that converts digital data from one computer into an analog signal that can be sent over a telephone line; on the opposite end, the analog signal is converted back to digital data. Modems are widely used to access the Internet, online services, and computer bulletin-board systems.

monitor: A separate component that looks something like a TV screen; your computer's monitor displays all the graphics generated by your PC.

motherboard: Your computer's main circuit board; it holds the CPU, RAM chips, and most of the circuitry. Adapter cards plug into your motherboard.

mouse: The standard computer pointing device. You hold the mouse in your hand and move it in the desired direction to create movement on your screen. A mouse also has buttons you can press to select items or run a program.

Mozart, Wolfgang Amadeus: My favorite classical composer, and a doggone good piano player to boot. He created the world's most beautiful music.

MP3: A very popular digital sound format used to download CD-quality music from the Internet. Your computer can play MP3 files through its speaker system, or you can record MP3 files to a CD-ROM and play them in any standard audio CD player.

MPEG: Acronym for *m*oving *p*ictures *e*xpert *g*roup. A popular digital video format and compression scheme often found on the Web. MPEG-format video is used on commercial DVD movie discs.

network: A system of computers connected to each other. Each computer can share data with other computers in the network, and all computers connected to the network can use resources like printers and modems.

newsgroups: International Internet message areas, each of which is usually dedicated to a special interest. Reading and posting questions in these newsgroups is a fun way of learning about a subject (as well as receiving tons of unwanted Internet e-mail, which is lovingly termed *spam*).

NT1: Acronym for *n*etwork *t*ermination *1*. A terminator for an ISDN line that provides power for the connection; every ISDN line must have a single device with NT1.

OCR: Acronym for *o*ptical *c*haracter *r*ecognition. OCR software can "read" the text from a fax or a document scanned by a digital scanner and "type" that text into your computer word-processing program.

Orb drive: A removable cartridge hard drive similar to the Jaz drive. An Orb cartridge can store 2.2 gigabytes of computer data. Orb drives are available for USB, parallel, SCSI, and IDE connections.

OS/2: A 32-bit graphical operating system that has proven a solid alternative to Windows 3.1, Windows 95, and Windows 98. Like Windows, OS/2 is quite user friendly and practically requires a pointing device.

parallel port: A standard connector found on every PC that enables you to add peripherals. Parallel ports are generally used to connect printers to PCs, although other devices, such as Zip drives and digital scanners, are available with parallel port connections.

PC card (or PCMCIA card): A device resembling a fat business card that plugs directly into most laptops. The card can provide many of the functions of a full-size adapter card, like a modem, a network interface card, a SCSI adapter, or even a hard drive. A PC card can also be used on a desktop computer equipped with a PC card slot.

PCI: Acronym for *p*eripheral *c*omponent *i*nterconnect. A PCI bus slot can hold a 32-bit adapter card to add functionality to your computer. PCI cards are faster than older ISA cards, so they're often filled by hard drive controller cards or SCSI adapter cards.

peer-to-peer: A type of network in which every computer is connected to every other computer and no server computer is required.

Pentium: The original Pentium CPU, the successor to the 486 series of processors. It's manufactured by Intel.

Pentium II: The descendant of the original Pentium CPU chip. As you would expect, the next-generation Pentium II ran much faster than the standard Pentium chip.

Pentium III: The latest and fastest processor in the Pentium CPU line from Intel, with a new instruction set designed to speed Internet applications. At the time this book was written, the Pentium III is the most popular CPU chip made for IBM-compatible personal computers.

Pentium Pro: An advanced CPU chip designed by Intel for use on network server computers and high-powered workstation PCs (typically used for computer-aided drafting and 3D artwork). It was considerably more expensive than the standard Pentium CPU. The Pentium Pro was replaced by the Pentium II and III Zeon chips.

Pentium Zeon: The fastest Intel CPU designed for network server computers and high-powered workstation PCs.

pixel: A single dot on your monitor. Text and graphics displayed by a computer on a monitor are made up of pixels.

Plug and Play: A term describing a type of adapter card that can automatically be configured by a motherboard (if it also supports Plug and Play). If your PC offers Plug and Play, the chances are greatly reduced that you have to manually configure the settings on a new adapter card.

port: A fancy name for a connector you plug something into — for example, your keyboard plugs into a keyboard port, and your external modem plugs into a serial port.

power supply: Your computer's power supply provides a number of separate power cables; each cable is connected to one of the various devices inside your computer that need electricity. A power supply also has a fan that helps to cool the interior of your computer. *Never attempt to open or repair a power supply!*

PRI: Acronym for *primary rate interface.* An ISDN line carrying 23 separate data channels. Although very expensive, a PRI configuration can provide ISDN service to an entire small office.

printer: An external device that can print text, graphics, and documents from your computer on paper. Most printers sold these days use either inkjet or laser technology.

PS/2 mouse port: Most Pentium-class motherboards feature a port reserved especially for your mouse or pointing device. This special port first appeared on the IBM PS/2 computer (hence the name).

RAM: Acronym for *r*andom *a*ccess *m*emory, the type of chip that acts as your computer's short-term memory. This memory chip holds programs and data until you turn off your computer.

refresh: The number of times per second that your video adapter card redraws the image on your PC's monitor. Higher refresh rates are easier on the eyes.

rendering: A technoid term for creating 3D objects and full 3D scenes on your computer. The classic films *Toy Story* and *A Bug's Life* feature rendered 3D characters.

resolution: The number of pixels on your screen measured as horizontal by vertical; for example, a resolution of 640 x 480 means that there are 640 pixels across your screen and 480 lines down the side of the screen.

RPM: Acronym for *r*evolutions *p*er *m*inute. The speed of the platters in a hard drive; the faster the RPM, the faster the drive can access your data.

scanner: A device that converts (or captures) text and graphics from a printed page into a digital image. Scanners are often used to "read" pictures from books and magazines; the digital version of the picture can be edited and used in documents or placed on a Web page.

SCSI: Acronym for *s*mall *c*omputer *s*ystems *i*nterface, a popular hard drive and device interface technology that is faster and supports more devices than EIDE, but costs more. Macintosh computers use the SCSI standard.

SCSI ID: A numeric identifier assigned to each device in a SCSI chain. Each device requires a unique SCSI ID for proper operation.

SCSI port: A connector built-in to most SCSI adapter cards that enables you to add external peripherals, such as CD recorders and scanners, to your SCSI device chain.

serial port: One of the standard connectors on every PC that transfers data to and from an external device. A serial port is generally used to connect an external modem to your computer.

SIMM: Acronym for *s*ingle *i*nline *m*emory *m*odule, a specific shape of RAM chip usually used with older 486 and original Pentium-class computers.

Slot 1: The motherboard slot designed to accept a Celeron, Pentium II, or Pentium III processor.

sound adapter card: An adapter card that enables your computer to play music and sound effects for games and other programs. Sound cards can also record audio from a microphone or stereo system.

star: A network topology in which data is routed through a central switch. Star networks are very fast and efficient (and much more expensive than a typical Ethernet network).

static electricity: The enemy of all computer circuitry, and especially computer chips. You should always touch the metal chassis of your computer to discharge any static electricity on your body before you install anything in your computer.

subwoofer: A separate speaker you can add to a standard two-speaker computer sound system. As with a standard stereo system, subwoofers add deep bass response and can bring realistic depth to sound effects.

SVGA: Acronym for *super video graphics array.* The most common graphics standard for PC video adapter cards and monitors now in use. The SVGA standard allows for more than 16 million colors (24-bit or true color).

SyncDRAM: Acronym for *synchronous dynamic RAM,* a type of RAM chip that offers faster performance than the standard EDO RAM chips used on most Pentium-series computers.

tape backup drive: A type of drive that enables you to back up your computer's files to removable magnetic cartridges, which is much more convenient than backing up the contents of a large hard drive to floppy disks.

terminator: A switch or small resistor pack found on every SCSI device. (Each end of a SCSI device chain must be terminated for everything to work properly.) A different type of terminator is also required at each end of an Ethernet peer-to-peer network.

token-ring: A network topology in which data is attached to a token and circulated among computers on the network.

topology: The structure or design of a network.

touchpad: A pointing device that reads the movement of your finger across the surface of the pad; this movement is translated to cursor movement on your screen.

trackball: A pointing device that resembles an upside-down mouse. You move the cursor by rolling the trackball with your finger or thumb and clicking buttons with your remaining fingers.

Travan: A popular and inexpensive tape drive used for backups. A typical Travan tape can hold anywhere from 800 megabytes to 8 gigabytes of compressed data. Although not as fast as a DAT backup drive, a Travan drive is a good choice for a home PC system.

Turbo mode: A feature available on older motherboards that enables you to switch your computer to a slower speed; although this option used to make it easier to run older software, Turbo mode is no longer very useful, and many new cases and motherboards don't support it.

twisted pair cable: (Also called *10Base2.*) A form of network cable that looks much like telephone cord, commonly used on Ethernet networks with a central hub.

UART chip: The main chip that handles communications within a serial port. High-speed modems that transfer data faster than 14.4 Kbps require a 16550-series UART chip.

Unix: A 32-bit, character-based operating system. Like DOS, Unix is controlled from a command line, but graphical "front ends" are available. The Unix commercial operating system is well known for security and speed, and Unix computers have run servers and support computers on the Internet for many years.

USB: Acronym for Universal Serial Bus, a standard connector that enables you to "daisy chain" a whopping 127 devices, with data transfers at as much as 12 megabits per second. USB connectors are becoming the standard of choice for all sorts of computer peripherals, from computer videocameras and scanners to joysticks and speakers.

VGA: Acronym for *video graphics array.* The IBM PC graphics standard that featured 256 colors. Replaced on most of today's computers by the SVGA standard.

video adapter card: An adapter card that plugs into your motherboard and enables your computer to display text and graphics on your monitor. Advanced adapter cards can speed up the display of Windows programs and 3D graphics.

VLB: Acronym for *VESA local bus,* an older bus architecture that improved on the speed of the 16-bit ISA bus. VLB adapter cards are hard to find these days because Pentium-class motherboards usually accept only AGP, PCI, and ISA adapter cards.

voice modem: A computer modem that can also act as an answering machine and voice mail system. Voice modems typically have a speakerphone option as well.

WAV: The Microsoft standard format for a digital sound file. WAV files are common across the Internet, and they can be recorded in CD-quality stereo.

wavetable: A feature available on advanced PC sound cards. A wavetable sound card produces more realistic instrument sounds (and therefore more realistic-sounding music).

Windows 98: The most popular 32-bit operating system for the PC. Windows is a multimedia, graphical operating system that relies heavily on a pointing device, like a mouse. Windows 95, the predecessor to Windows 98, has fewer features and lacks support for the latest hardware (on the other hand, it occupies less space on your hard drive than Windows 98).

Windows 2000: The latest "advanced" version of the Windows operating system from Microsoft. The direct descendant of Windows NT, it comes in a number of "flavors" designed to appeal to small businesses. Windows 2000 makes a great network server or Internet server, but, like NT, is much more expensive than Windows 98 or Windows Me.

Windows Me (or Millennium Edition): The latest "home" version of the Windows operating system from Microsoft. This incremental update to Windows 98 ships with most retail computers now on the market.

Windows NT: A faster, more secure, more stable, and much more expensive version of Windows 95. Windows NT comes in server and workstation flavors. NT is popular as the backbone of many office networks.

wireless mouse: A pointing device similar to the standard mouse, but without the cord that connects it to the computer. Wireless mice require batteries, but are a little more convenient without the cord.

ZIF socket: Acronym for *zero insertion force*, a socket that makes it easy to upgrade your computer's CPU in the future; the lever unlatches the CPU so that it can be easily removed from the socket, whereas the new CPU drops right in.

Zip drive: A type of drive that uses a removable cartridge about the size of a floppy disk, although each Zip disk stores anywhere from 100 to 250 megabytes of data and the data can be retrieved much faster from a Zip disk than from a floppy disk. Zip drives are available with both parallel port and SCSI interfaces.

Index

YOUR ONLINE RESOURCE

WWW.DUMMIES.COM

Discover Dummies Online!

The Dummies Web Site is your fun and friendly online resource for the latest information about *For Dummies* books and your favorite topics. The Web site is the place to communicate with us, exchange ideas with other *For Dummies* readers, chat with authors, and have fun!

Ten Fun and Useful Things You Can Do at www.dummies.com

1. Win free *For Dummies* books and more!

2. Register your book and be entered in a prize drawing.

3. Meet your favorite authors through the IDG Books Worldwide Author Chat Series.

4. Exchange helpful information with other *For Dummies* readers.

5. Discover other great *For Dummies* books you must have!

6. Purchase Dummieswear exclusively from our Web site.

7. Buy *For Dummies* books online.

8. Talk to us. Make comments, ask questions, get answers!

9. Download free software.

10. Find additional useful resources from authors.

Link directly to these ten fun and useful things at
http://www.dummies.com/10useful

WWW.DUMMIES.COM

SURF THE NET

For other technology titles from IDG Books Worldwide, go to
www.idgbooks.com

Not on the Web yet? It's easy to get started with *Dummies 101: The Internet For Windows 98* or *The Internet For Dummies* at local retailers everywhere.

IDG BOOKS WORLDWIDE

Find other *For Dummies* books on these topics:

Business • Career • Databases • Food & Beverage • Games • Gardening • Graphics • Hardware
Health & Fitness • Internet and the World Wide Web • Networking • Office Suites
Operating Systems • Personal Finance • Pets • Programming • Recreation • Sports
Spreadsheets • Teacher Resources • Test Prep • Word Processing

IDG BOOKS WORLDWIDE
BOOK REGISTRATION

We want to hear from you!

Register This Book and Win!

Visit **http://my2cents.dummies.com** to register this book and tell us how you liked it!

- ✔ Get entered in our monthly prize giveaway.

- ✔ Give us feedback about this book — tell us what you like best, what you like least, or maybe what you'd like to ask the author and us to change!

- ✔ Let us know any other *For Dummies* topics that interest you.

Your feedback helps us determine what books to publish, tells us what coverage to add as we revise our books, and lets us know whether we're meeting your needs as a *For Dummies* reader. You're our most valuable resource, and what you have to say is important to us!

Not on the Web yet? It's easy to get started with *Dummies 101: The Internet For Windows 98* or *The Internet For Dummies* at local retailers everywhere.

Or let us know what you think by sending us a letter at the following address:

For Dummies Book Registration
Dummies Press
10475 Crosspoint Blvd.
Indianapolis, IN 46256

...FOR DUMMIES™

**BESTSELLING
BOOK SERIES**